The President Is at Camp David

An early morning shot of part of the Camp David ground captures the mood of a gray day in the Catoctins. *Courtesy Dwight D. Eisenhower Library and the U.S. Navy.*

The President Is
at Camp David

W. Dale Nelson

Foreword by David Eisenhower

Syracuse University Press

First Edition 1995
95 96 97 98 99 00   6 5 4 3 2

The paper used in this publication meets the minimum requirements
of American National Standard for Information Sciences — Permanence
of Paper for Printed Library Materials, ANSI Z39.48-1984. ∞™

Library of Congress Cataloging-in-Publication Data
Nelson, W. Dale.
The president is at Camp David / W. Dale Nelson ; with a foreword
by David Eisenhower.
p.   cm.
Includes bibliographical references and index.
ISBN 0-8156-0318-5 (cl)
1. Camp David (Md.) — History.   2. Presidents — United States — Homes
and haunts.   I. Title.
F189.C26N45   1995
973.9'092'2 — dc20   94-37083

For
Joyce and Mark
and for
Eric, Kirsten, and Barbara

W. Dale Nelson spent forty years as a reporter and editor with the Associated Press in the Pacific Northwest and Washington, D.C., where he covered the White House as well as Congress and the Supreme Court. Mr. Nelson is also a poet whose work has been published in many magazines in the United States and Canada. He and his wife, Joyce Nelson, a painter, live on Antietam Creek in western Maryland.

Contents

Illustrations

Foreword

The President Is at Camp David is the first complete history of Camp #3, Shangri-La, NAVSUPPFAC, Thurmont, Maryland, or as it is better known today, Camp David. Dale Nelson puts together the facts, figures, and dates to tell the story of an important, yet still largely hidden aspect of the presidency. And truthfully, most of the information contained in this book is news to me. People often ask me what I know about Camp David. I have had to plead general ignorance of its history; I know only about the years in which we used it.

I remember that by 1969, camp personnel had assembled a small brochure summarizing the history of Camp David. As far as I know, the brochure was not updated. At the time, we hardly gave the story of Camp David a second thought. We went there to relax—Camp David was a getaway from "history," which inevitably bears on every waking moment, whether official or private, spent in the White House. We probably assumed that the camp would be closed or converted into something else by a future president. That may yet happen, but Camp David has been around long enough now to warrant the history that Dale Nelson has written.

My association with the camp goes back almost as far as I can remember. In the early days of my grandfather's administration, we and the camp personnel called it Shangri-La. The name seemed to fit the place. Like the fictional setting of James Hilton's *Lost Horizon,* the camp was locked away, remote, a place of "peace and contentment," an ideal setting for relaxation or concentration. The camp I first visited in the summer of 1954 must have been kept exactly the way FDR left it, and FDR had called the camp his Shangri-La.

As Dale Nelson shows, Granddad took office in 1953 determined to cut back drastically on presidential perks, which he thought had gotten too lavish. Shangri-La was to be closed, and it might have been but for Granddad's good friend, George Allen. As a Washington lawyer and politician, Allen had been an intimate friend of FDR and had been to Shangri-La with him. He insisted that Granddad visit the place and evaluate it before he took any rash action. Shortly after the 1953 inaugural, the Eisenhowers, "Min" Doud, Mamie's mother, and the Allens drove up and spent a wintry evening there. Allen knew that Granddad loved mountains, rustic settings, and privacy, and the camp provided all three.

The cabins were drafty and sparsely furnished. Deer freely wandered around the grounds, especially at first light. On my earliest visits, mornings were spent hiking through the hills or practicing chip shots to a green Granddad had installed. Midday was spent poolside deep in the forest. Evenings, there were often a dozen or more guests. Often, Granddad, an excellent cook, would spend the afternoon in the Aspen kitchen preparing the steaks for a cookout. After dinner, the grandchildren staged skits and sang songs on the porch behind the presidential cabin, then were packed off while the grown-ups watched movies.

Camp David, as Granddad eventually named it, was mostly a summer place. Even in summer, the nights were cool and the daytime temperatures were invigorating compared to Washington and Alexandria, Virginia. In winter, before helicopters, access up the winding Catoctin roads was difficult, so wintertime visits were less frequent. But I do remember making my first ski run ever on the hill behind Aspen.

After his heart attack in September 1955, Granddad began to use the camp more often. Improvements and renovations were made and the base establishment grew. In 1958, I spent the summer working as a farm hand on my Granddad's farm in Gettysburg and living in Thurmont with a Navy chief who was assigned to the camp. On evenings at the "base," we blended in with the NAVSUPPFAC personnel in the snack bar, the bowling alley, and the movie theater. The ambiance was indistinguishable from that of Army posts I lived on as a grade school kid. The vacant presidential cabins, several hundred yards away, seemed as remote and forbidding as general's quarters at Fort Benning or Fort Belvoir.

In time, the public learned of Camp David. By 1959, Granddad was routinely entertaining foreign visitors. The most notable was Soviet Premier Nikita Khrushchev, who visited America in September 1959, during an acute cold-war crisis over Berlin. The Eisenhower-Khrushchev meetings in Aspen kindled hopeful talk of a "spirit of Camp David." The spirit did not last, but awareness of Camp David did. The association of the camp with peacemaking was reinforced by President Carter in 1978, when he hosted the discussions there between Anwar Sadat of Egypt and Menachem Begin of Israel that led to the "Camp David Accords."

A president can call "Camp David" by whatever name he chooses, and as Granddad left office in January 1961, we assumed that President Kennedy would rename the place "Camp Caroline," let it revert to "Shangri-La," or close it. Perhaps public familiarity with the name "Camp David" caused the Kennedys to hesitate. Inertia was definitely a factor. The Kennedys had decided that they would not use the camp. Indeed, Kennedy had not even been to "Camp #3," as it was first known, when he met there with Granddad to discuss the Bay of Pigs disaster in late April 1961; by 1963, however, the Kennedys were visiting the camp frequently. President Johnson used the camp so rarely that he eventually invited Granddad to use it at any time and for any purpose he wished. The "Camp #3" era ended when President Nixon took office in January 1969.

Mr. Nixon, who had been a guest at Camp David several times, resolved early on that he would use it only as an occasional getaway. Otherwise, he would make it available to his staff and Cabinet. But a war was on and President Nixon found in late 1969, as FDR had in 1942, that he desperately needed a place where he could have privacy to think and relax. Improvements were ordered so that the camp could accommodate staff members and the president for extended periods of time.

Helicopters made frequent use of Camp David practical in the Nixon era. The habit carried over; Presidents Ford and Carter both used the camp often, although Carter, like Granddad, gave some thought to closing it. The Reagans are said to have used it more than anyone before or since and President Bush was frequently there, particularly at the height of the Desert Shield-Desert Storm crisis. The Clintons have used it less often.

I suspect that there is now a movement afoot to restore the seclusion and mystery of the camp that was characteristic of Shangri-La. Several years ago, my wife and I, our children, and several friends decided on a whim to make a detour into the Catoctins to see how the area had changed. We almost missed the camp entrance. The sign at the gate had been taken down and the fence and security towers were heavily camouflaged. Automobiles were so infrequent that we wondered whether traffic was being diverted and we had somehow slipped through. Indeed, as we pulled the car over to get turned around, we could see that we had excited the curiosity of Marine sentries who, we saw at second glance, were spaced along the entire perimeter. Apparently, the Navy was attempting to conceal the whereabouts of the camp and keep tourists away, something that had never been attempted even in the days when the camp was less publicized. It struck me as futile — at first.

Later, it occurred to me that restoring the privacy and seclusion of Camp David might not be so hard after all. First, access by road is fairly difficult and can be cut off without inconveniencing tourists and campers. Second, the public memory is fairly short. Curiosity could fade if presidents decide to use the camp less frequently — as the Clintons have decided to do — and gradually cut back on the practice of entertaining high profile visitors there. Indeed, the day may not be too far off when the camp will have reverted completely to its earlier role of hideaway and retreat. If so, then information like that in *The President Is at Camp David* might be impossible to come by. Dale Nelson has therefore written a story that is not only complete for an era, but timely and in the nick of time.

Why should a president have a retreat like Camp David? In theory, the American presidency is a democratic office charged primarily with tending to the welfare and happiness of the citizens who elect the president. But, for a long time, the president has been much more than that; since the 1930s, Americans have reluctantly but inevitably accepted responsibilities for world peace and progress, and the presidency has been the institution responsible for coordinating American action toward that end. So it is today, and so it became at some indefinable moment at about the time *Lost Horizon* was published in 1933.

Hilton's novel clearly foretells the catastrophe of World War II. It describes the mission of the mythical community of Shangri-La in undertaking to spare mankind's cultural treasures from the plague of barbarism about to descend. In the story, Hugh Conway, a British diplomat, is anointed by the High Lama of Shangri-La to assume charge of the community and its mission. Conway declines at first and leaves

Shangri-La, sensing that the task would be beyond him. The book ends just as Conway resolves to try after all and begins his arduous journey back.

It is not a stretch to conceive of FDR during 1941–42 as seeing parallels between Conway's mission and his own; that as president of the United States it was his duty to mobilize America to serve as a bastion against the assault of fascism and twentieth-century totalitarianism. Conceivably, like Conway, he felt that he would need a camp, a "paradise" where he could be fortified to face the decisions he knew were necessary to defend America and the future of civilization. The cold war challenged his successors in the same way.

Times have changed. In this post-cold war era, it is no longer so simple to predict how America's international role will evolve. Even with the end of the cold war, however, the president is being asked to make judgments and decisions that will profoundly influence the future contest between progress and darkness. As long as this holds true, the president will continue to need, and to look for, the solitude and uplift of a Shangri-La, whether it be at Camp David, at Hyannisport, or somewhere else.

Seen in this light, Dale Nelson's *The President Is at Camp David* is more than a description of a particular installation maintained for the convenience and pleasure of the president. It is the story of personal quests by particular American presidents at special and critical junctures in American history, of presidents who consciously or unconsciously emulated the fictional hero of *Lost Horizon*, of men who were called on to make a difference in the country that in the past fifty years has played the biggest role in deciding whether the world's future would be determined in the spirit of fear or of hope.

Berwyn, Pennsylvania   David Eisenhower
October 1994

Acknowledgments

I am indebted to my former colleague at the Associated Press, Michael Putzel, for suggesting that I write this book.

Along the way, many people have contributed to it. For giving of their time to be interviewed, I wish to thank Capt. Edward L. Beach, Howard Benedict, former President Jimmy Carter, Richard B. Cheney, Bob Clark, Clark Clifford, Frank Cormier, Mary Freeze, Gen. Andrew J. Goodpaster, Ted Graber, Bill Gulley, Stephen Hess, Charlie Huoy, Anna Perez, Kenneth Plummer Sr., David F. Powers, Ron Reagan, Comdr. William M. Rigdon, Lynda Robb, Chalmers Roberts, Dorothy Rosenman, James Rowley, Greg Schneiders, Mark Weinberg, and Conrad Wirth. A special debt of gratitude is owed the late Adm. Evan P. Aurand for extraordinary kindness during his final illness in making his recollections available.

I am grateful for the help provided by staff members during visits to the Franklin D. Roosevelt, Harry S. Truman, Dwight D. Eisenhower, John F. Kennedy, Lyndon Baines Johnson, Gerald R. Ford and Jimmy Carter presidential libraries, as well as the National Archives' Nixon Presidential Materials Project (both while it was in Alexandria, Virginia, and after it moved to College Park, Maryland) and the National Archives branch in Laguna Niguel, California. Archivists of the Ronald Reagan and George Bush presidential libraries responded helpfully to requests by mail and telephone.

I also wish to thank librarians at the Library of Congress, the Theodore C. McKeldin Library at the University of Maryland, the Department of the Interior Library, and the public libraries of Montgomery County and Washington County, Maryland, and of the District of Columbia.

James C. McKinney, then director of the White House Military Office, went out of his way to make it possible for me to visit Camp David. Some people provided information on the condition that they not be identified, so I reluctantly do not thank them by name. My wife, Joyce Nelson, helped with editorial suggestions, assistance with illustrations, and her invaluable presence.

The President Is at Camp David

Prologue

Franklin Delano Roosevelt was in an ebullient mood as he met reporters in the Oval Office on April 21, 1942. He had reason to be, and it was about time. In the four and a half months since the Japanese attack on Pearl Harbor, young watch officers in the White House Map Room had become accustomed to the sight of Roosevelt's long cigarette holder hanging loosely in his mouth as he studied the war maps in dejection.[1]

On this day, the cigarette holder was at its familiar rakish angle. After disaster upon disaster in the Pacific, Lt. Col. James H. Doolittle, a former stunt flier with a science degree from the Massachusetts Institute of Technology, had led an audacious air strike deep into Japan — fulfilling a hope FDR had nourished ever since Pearl Harbor plunged the United States into the war. The raid had little strategic significance, but was a major boost to American morale when news of it reached Washington.

Roosevelt, receiving the reports by telephone at his home in Hyde Park, New York, was warned that he should be prepared to field questions from reporters on where the bombers had been based. Over a cup of tea, New York Supreme Court Judge Samuel I. Rosenman, an informal adviser who later became counsel to the president, gave him the advice he would act upon. The question put to him, as the reporters crowded around his desk in the Oval Office, was simply, "How about the story about the bombing of Tokyo?"

Assuming his best squire-of-Hyde-Park manner, the beaming Roo-

1

sevelt told them that "some sweet young thing" among his dinner guests the previous night had asked him if he could tell her where they came from, and he had answered, "Yes, I think the time has come now to tell you. They came from our secret base at Shangri-La." The reporters recognized the allusion to the Tibetan lamasery that was a refuge from the ravages of war and age in James Hilton's 1933 novel, *Lost Horizon.*

Clearly, the president was speaking with tongue in cheek. Jimmy Doolittle and his men, roaring off at full throttle from the rolling and pitching carrier *Hornet* as waves sloshed over the flight deck 668 miles from Japan, were a far cry from the Shangri-La of which Hilton wrote, "Its forsaken courts and pale pavilions shimmered in repose from which all the fret of existence had ebbed away." The answer was, as Rosenman had told him, "a polite way of saying that you do not intend to tell the enemy or anybody else where the planes really came from."[2]

The reporters did not know that, on the very next day, Roosevelt would be driven sixty miles north into the Catoctin Mountains of Maryland to choose a site for a presidential weekend retreat from the "fret of existence" of the wartime capital.[3] Within a little more than half a century, eleven presidents would take advantage of that site, some almost compulsively, others scarcely at all. The secluded cluster of cabins in the woods became the American equivalent of Chequers, the stately country home of British prime ministers, or of the elegant dachas maintained by Kremlin rulers in the Moscow suburbs.

"A president needs a place of that kind to get away," elder statesman Clark Clifford said after years of watching presidents come and go. "If every weekend you had to stay in the White House, after a while you would have men in white coats walking around."

But relaxation was not the only purpose the camp served. FDR and Winston Churchill huddled there over the groundwork of the Normandy invasion. Dwight Eisenhower and Nikita Khrushchev went there to seek a new spirit in United States–Soviet relations, marking a first brief thaw in the cold war. John F. Kennedy invited Eisenhower to the Catoctin retreat to seek his predecessor's counsel after the debacle at the Bay of Pigs.

Lyndon Johnson, too, took his troubles with him when he went there, holding meeting after meeting with his advisers on the war in Vietnam. The secluded setting suited the introverted Richard Nixon, but even in the solitude of the camp's leafy trails he was unable to escape the woes of Watergate.

Its seclusion was part of its charm, whether for a relaxed weekend or a tense international conference. It was largely off limits to the press, visitors were few, and security was rigid. Because of its informal atmosphere and isolation from reporters, Jimmy Carter found it the ideal place to bring Anwar Sadat and Menachem Begin together to seek accord. Nancy Reagan was delighted that she could renovate the cabins without the publicity that dogged her borrowed designer gowns or her efforts to upgrade the White House china.

In Roosevelt's day it was a rustic hideout with little hot water and with brush growing to the windowsills. Harry Truman had the brush cleared and Eisenhower built a putting green in the clearing; Nixon added a heated swimming pool. The camp was a two-hour drive from the White House for Roosevelt and a twenty-minute flight after Eisenhower introduced helicopters.

Presidents and their families persisted in calling it rustic. Others called its trappings luxurious, even princely. It was not to everyone's taste. Truman visited seldom and his daughter, Margaret, found it cold and gloomy. Begin likened it to a glorified concentration camp.

It was called Hi-Catoctin. It was called Camp #3. It would be called the Naval Support Facility, or NAVSUPPFAC, Thurmont MD 21788. It would be called Camp David. The Secret Service would call it Cactus.

Roosevelt called it Shangri-La.

1

The Shangri-La of Franklin D. Roosevelt

From the early days of the American republic, presidents sought summertime relief from the swampy, humid site George Washington had chosen as the nation's capital. Thomas Jefferson journeyed to Monticello in the Virginia hills; Ulysses S. Grant favored Long Branch on the New Jersey shore; Calvin Coolidge stayed at a commercial hotel in Custer State Park in South Dakota.

The methodical Herbert Hoover set one hundred miles as the maximum distance from the capital and stipulated a mosquito-free site with trout streams, woodlands, and a mountain view. Finding what he wanted, he bought approximately 164 acres of land in the Shenandoah Valley of Virginia and named it Rapidan. Before leaving office, Hoover signed the land over to the National Park Service as a retreat for future presidents.[1] Roosevelt, whose asthma was aggravated by the damp bottomland of the Shenandoah, visited the camp only once. Richard Nixon, no outdoorsman, had a helicopter pad built at nearby Big Meadow, but never used it, and Jimmy Carter, a fisherman, used it only once. In the 1980s, the camp was being used from time to time by members of Congress and presidential aides. In 1992, the Interior Department closed it to all but official business.

For his own summer relief, Roosevelt spent weekends relaxing at sea on the presidential yacht *Potomac* or visiting his home in Hyde Park. In the two months after Pearl Harbor, however, German U-boats sank 132 ships in the Western Atlantic, sometimes coming close enough to see the glow of New York's skyline.[2] Yachting was out. The Secret

4

Service objected to the president using the little 350-ton *Potomac* even on inland waters because it had no protection against air attack. Roosevelt was unwilling to remove a fighting ship from sea duty to serve as an escort.[3] As for the trip to Hyde Park, it used scarce fuel and took the president an overnight journey away from the capital.

There was talk of making the official residence of the chief of naval operations on the grounds of the Naval Observatory a home-away-from-home for the president, but it came to nothing. By the 1970s, when the handsome Victorian building became the vice president's official residence, the observatory's Massachusetts Avenue site was near the downtown of a much-expanded capital. In 1942, it was on the outskirts, but not out far enough. It was also only 270 feet above sea level, just 220 feet higher than the White House.[4]

The White House family quarters had been air-conditioned in 1933, but Roosevelt's doctor, Ross McIntire, still believed a cool mountain retreat would be good for the presidential sinuses.[5] Following Hoover's lead, FDR asked Newton B. Drury, director of the National Park Service, to survey sites within a hundred-mile radius. Drury called Conrad Wirth, his chief aide for recreation and land planning, to his office and told him the president was looking for a place at an elevation of about fifteen hundred to two thousand feet.[6]

Roosevelt initially wanted Sugarloaf Mountain, a 1,282-foot peak thirty-two miles north of Washington, but, he later told reporters, "It belongs to a 'dirty rat.' He's going to give it to the government some day, but he didn't want the president going there."[7] The owner, Gordon Strong, a Chicago banker and an heir to the Atchison, Topeka, and Santa Fe Railway fortune, had acquired the property parcel by parcel in the 1920s after seeing it as he was bicycling. Confronted with Roosevelt's request by Harold Ickes, Strong told the secretary of the interior, "A handful of people will benefit from it if you do that, thousands can enjoy it if I keep it."[8] The mountain was later developed as a free, privately operated environmental preserve by the Stronghold Foundation.[9]

The Park Service submitted a report suggesting three sites. One was Comer's Deadening, at thirty-three hundred feet, near Skyland in Shenandoah National Park, about three hours' drive from the White House. One was undeveloped Camp Site #4 in the Catoctin Recreational Demonstration Area, one of about fifty areas established throughout the country under a New Deal law to provide summer camp experiences for poor children. It was seventeen hundred feet high and within a two-hour drive. The Park Service estimated it would cost $150,000 and take two to three months to build a camp at either of these sites.

The third suggested location was Camp #3, also known as Camp Hi-Catoctin, about half a mile uphill from Site #4, at eighteen hundred feet. A camp had already been built on the site, with three units of six four-cot cabins, a swimming pool, craft shop, playing field, camp office, central showers, and recreation hall. Originally planned as a boys' camp, it had been converted for use by families. The Park Service estimated it could be adapted to the president's needs by June for $18,650. More important, it was five to ten degrees cooler in the summer than Washington.[10]

Roosevelt quickly eliminated the Shenandoah site, finding it "practically impossible to get to."[11] The Catoctin Mountains, however, were an area he knew and liked. As assistant secretary of the Navy during World War I, he had enjoyed the countryside around Braddock Heights, fifteen miles to the south of the camp sites and just west of Frederick.[12]

The first presidential motorcade to what would become Camp David left the White House at 2:00 P.M. on April 22, traveled a winding route northward, and passed through downtown Frederick, where the president was recognized, at 3:45 P.M. At Camp #3, according to William G. Renner, a camp workman, Roosevelt was helped from his car and exclaimed, "This is a Shangri-La!"

At 5:55 P.M. the caravan passed through Frederick again, stopping for a red light and continuing south, getting the president back to the White House some time after the 6 P.M. arrival that Mike Reilly, head of the White House Secret Service detail, had estimated. The White House refused to answer questions about where FDR had been. The next day, Drury said he was quite sure Roosevelt wanted Camp #3.[13]

FDR swiftly put his stamp on the place, choosing the recreational lodge of the camp's Unit B as the nucleus of a weekend White House. Mike Williams, the former railroad land appraiser who oversaw construction of the camps, had chosen the site for its view of the Monocacy Valley. The lodge consisted of one room seventeen feet six inches by twenty-eight feet, with an open porch and roofed-over kitchen.[14] On April 30, when Wirth and an aide accompanied him to the site, the president drew a sketch calling for enlarging and screening the porch and adding a paved terrace, a bedroom corridor, four bedrooms, two baths, and an indoor kitchen and pantry. The outlines of what would be "The Bear's Den" for Roosevelt and "Aspen Lodge" for Eisenhower and his successors had been set. The president also pointed out diseased and misshapen trees he wanted cut in order to improve the view southeastward from the lodge over the broad valley.[15] He wanted the dogwood trees and shrubs in the foreground to remain, "just as God made them."[16]

In notes he penciled in on the Park Service's cost estimate sheet, FDR ordered the craft shop altered to provide sleeping quarters for six male servants. ("Phillipinos [*sic*] and valet," he called them; the building would be known as "Little Luzon.")[17] "S.S. to sleep in tents (excess)," the president jotted down. In fact, quarters for the Secret Service agents were found first at the Cozy Motel in Thurmont; then in cabins near the Bear's Den; and finally in old Civilian Conservation Corps barracks that FDR rechristened "221B Baker Street" after Sherlock Holmes' address, but that the agents called "The Long House."[18] There was even a rustic dog house, just outside the main lodge, for the president's Scotch terrier, Fala.[19]

The crippling effects of polio, which kept the president confined to a wheelchair, had to be taken into account. "FDR was terribly afraid that he might be caught helpless in a fire," said William Rigdon, an assistant naval aide,[20] so a section of wall was hinged at floor level and had counterweights placed inside it to enable it to be lowered by pressure to form an inclined bridge from the floor to the ground.[21] Plans were also made to remove Roosevelt to a nearby slit trench in the event of an air raid.[22]

Security quickly became a problem. Power to the pumphouse went out on May 28. After a five-day search for the cause, a piece of four thousand-volt wire with one end apparently severed by a bullet was discovered. Laboratory examination showed traces of lead on the wire. When Secret Service agent William D. Cawley visited the nearby Catoctin Mountain Army Camp, an officer told him soldiers had been practicing firing, but not toward the pumphouse. "There are many natives from children up capable of hitting the wire with a rifle with little difficulty," Cawley reported. The case was closed.

Reilly visited the site with Wirth on May 14 and ordered construction of a nine-foot-high fence with eighteen strands of barbed wire and an overhang. Army Engineers detailed a forty-man crew to do the job, placing sentry boxes and floodlights at regular intervals along the fence. Using wood from nearby abandoned farms, the engineers built a rustic gate at the entrance. A warning device that would sound an alarm if a wire was cut was also installed. With Roosevelt's approval, officials decided to station Marines to guard the perimeter of the camp. Reilly thought twenty guards should be on duty whenever the president was in residence. This was later increased to one hundred.[23]

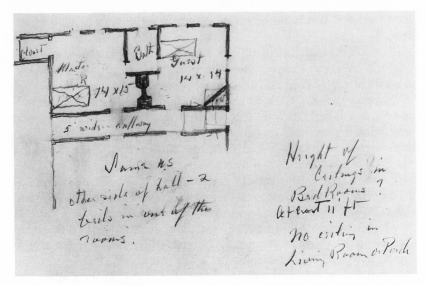

1. Roosevelt's sketch and notes for design of the presidential lodge.
Courtesy Franklin Roosevelt Library.

With WPA workers, Marines, and soldiers sharing the work, the camp was virtually completed by July 1.[24] Roosevelt inspected it on July 5 and made the first entry in a blue-bound nautical logbook that was to provide a record of the camp's role in the three eventful years ahead. Heading the first of the heavy cream-colored pages, "U.S.S. Shangri La — Launched at Catoctin July 5, 1942," he signed it and had his guests sign below him.[25] Aside from some problems with Secret Service radio transmissions, the trip went off without difficulty, as would so many in the future. The party was back at 1600 Pennsylvania Avenue by nightfall.[26]

Meanwhile the camp's woodland surroundings were increasingly on a war footing. As early as June 1941, six months before Pearl Harbor, British sailors were quartered at nearby Camp Greentop for rest and relaxation while their ship was in drydock in Baltimore. A year later, facilities of the camp for children with disabilities were moved to French Creek, Pennsylvania, for the duration of the war to make way for the men of Wild Bill Donovan's Office of Strategic Services, the forerunner of the Central Intelligence Agency. Among those who went through two weeks of basic training there was James Jesus Angleton,

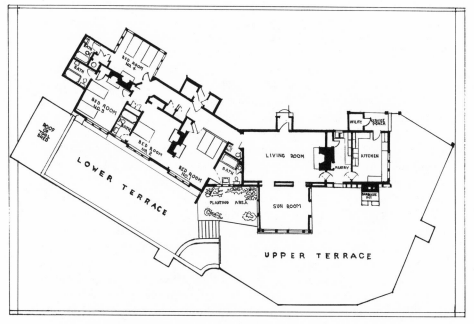

2. By 1959, the presidential lodge had a living-dining room, a sun room, and four bedrooms. *Source: Department of the Navy, Bureau of Yards and Docks.*

the Ivy League intellectual who would become the CIA's chief of counterintelligence in the Cold War.[27]

Roosevelt's first overnight stay at the camp—the "1st trial run" as he called it in the logbook—was July 18–20. With him were Donovan and Supreme Court Justice James F. Byrnes. Donovan took Byrnes and his wife next door to the OSS camp, where a former Shanghai police chief was putting the spies-in-training through paces that included being thrown off balance and then shooting a papier-mâché figure of Japanese Premier Hideki Tojo in the head. It struck Byrnes as "circus stuff" and he took the ex-chief back to Shangri-La to regale Roosevelt with trick weapons and stories.[28] The president was back the next weekend for what he called the "final trials."

On August 8, FDR logged the mythical vessel *Shangri-La* as "accepted" by the Navy. In the party that weekend were the trusted Sam Rosenman, who had given Roosevelt the advice that figured in the naming of the mountain camp, and his wife, Dorothy; Archibald MacLeish, the poet then serving as librarian of Congress, and his wife, Ada; Grace Tully, the president's fast-talking private secretary; and Margaret, or Daisy, Suckley, a distant cousin of the president.

The four White House automobiles drove north on Route 15, stopping for all traffic lights, and turned left into the mountains at the little town of Thurmont, passing a Marine guard posted at the bridge over Hunting Creek just outside town. It was pouring rain, so few people were out. Of the few who were, few recognized the cars' best known occupant. Since Pearl Harbor, the license plates of the vehicles had been changed from their traditional low numbers to avoid recognition. There was no police escort. About a mile up Maryland Route 77, the blacktop paving gave way to a dirt road through the deepening woods, with Wolf Rock and Chimney Rock towering to the right at the stone-walled headquarters of the recreation area, and the road grew steeper.

"We reached Shangri-La about four," Mrs. Rosenman wrote in her diary. "It was pouring too hard to sit on the lovely stone-floored screened-in porch which overlooks the valley which can be seen through an opening cut in the dense forest. The president was wheeled through the little house so he could show us to our rooms, and see where the pictures he had just sent up from Washington had been hung."

Roosevelt commended the stewards who had hung the naval prints and other pictures, but added in an aside to his guests, "I may make a few changes tomorrow." Over the weekend, the thirty-second president of the United States gave directions as his guests rehung the pictures.

"The president very gleefully told us that all of us in the guest rooms would have to share one bathroom," Mrs. Rosenman wrote. "I had had an account of this from Sam who had been here two weeks ago." One of the things Mrs. Rosenman's husband had told her was that the bathroom door did not close quite securely. Roosevelt used to warn guests of the fact, but the door was not repaired.

Dinner table conversation touched on the fate of six German saboteurs who had been executed that noon at the District of Columbia jail after a review of their cases by Rosenman. The saboteurs had come ashore from German submarines off Long Island and the Atlantic coast of Florida. The president worked on his stamp collection after dinner while the other guests played gin rummy with Miss Tully. She beat them all. At 10:00 P.M., everybody went to bed.

In the morning, the camp was again pelted by a hard rain. Roosevelt stayed in bed until noon, as he routinely did at Shangri-La, working with his appointments secretary, William Hassett. After rising, he con-

3. The presidential lodge in the Catoctins would later be named Aspen, but Franklin D. Roosevelt called it "The Bear's Den." *Left to right:* Presidential Counselor Samuel Rosenman (partly obscured), Ada Mac-Leish, Dorothy Rosenman, and Librarian of Congress Archibald Mac-Leish. *Courtesy Daisy Suckley Collection, Franklin Roosevelt Library.*

ferred with Rosenman and MacLeish over a draft of a message to Winston Churchill on the first anniversary of the Atlantic Charter, the statement of aims he and the British prime minister had issued at the end of a conference that took place off the coast of Newfoundland four months before the United States entered the war.

About 12:45 P.M., Roosevelt's naval aide, Capt. John McCrea, came up from Washington with war news he did not want to discuss over the telephone. When the president's guests rose to excuse themselves, FDR told them to remain, saying, "We have no secrets to talk about — but if we have, we'll talk in a low voice — we'll whisper." They did, in fact, whisper most of the time. Nevertheless the guests knew in a general way what Roosevelt and McCrea were talking about. The U.S. Marine 1st Division, in the first major U.S. offensive in the Pacific, had landed on Guadalcanal in the Solomon Islands two days before and seized an airfield the Japanese were building. As Mrs. Rosenman sat six feet away, not able to hear the hushed conversation, Roosevelt studied a map that McCrea had unrolled. During the night of August eighth, Japanese cruisers and destroyers, attempting to hold Guadalcanal, had sunk four allied heavy cruisers — three U.S. and one Australian — near Savo Island. One Japanese cruiser was sunk and one damaged.

"Things are not going so well in the Pacific," the president said after McCrea left. "There are heavy losses on both sides."

After a pause, Mrs. Rosenman, changing the subject, asked where the Nazi saboteurs were to be buried. FDR said he and McCrea had also discussed that, but had not made up their minds. In fact, two Army ambulances had taken the bodies of the six from the District of Columbia jail to Walter Reed Army Hospital the previous afternoon, arriving about a quarter of an hour after the president and his party rolled into Shangri-La. They were buried secretly in paupers' graves at Blue Plains in the District of Columbia.

Despite the grimness of the news, FDR found time to work on his stamps, bringing out the square wooden box in which he kept his magnifying glass, *Scott's Stamp Catalogue* and hinges, and the incoming envelopes the State Department sent over to him weekly. Later he read a mystery for a while, and again it was early to bed.

The next day Undersecretary of War Robert Patterson visited and the group discussed the Civil War. Two of its fiercest battles, Antietam and Gettysburg, were fought not far from where they sat. FDR and Patterson then met privately in the living room to discuss more immediate battles, while the others sat on the screened porch. Afterward Roosevelt and his guests went for a drive in the surrounding country. At 10:00 A.M. Tuesday, they left to return to Washington. It had been, said Sam Rosenman, "a typical Shangri-La weekend."[29] There were many such visits — more than twenty from the camp's completion through 1944.[30]

Both Elliott and James Roosevelt, in books about their parents, said that Eleanor Roosevelt never accompanied her husband to the mountain retreat.[31] Mrs. Roosevelt's own letters, however, reveal that she made several visits. In October 1942, just back from a trip to wartime England, she wrote her friend Lorena Hickok, "Quite sleepy and must go tomorrow to Shangri-La — but only for the night." She was there again with her daughter, Anna, on the weekend of May 14–17, 1943, and on May 22 she and Elliott Roosevelt's first wife, Betty Winsor, and son Bill, rode to Shangri-La along with FDR. Eleanor wrote that she "had time for a good walk" in the woods with Fala before she, Betty, and Bill returned that night to the White House.

On July 25 and 26, Mrs. Roosevelt was spending twenty-four hours at the camp, where "F. is writing a speech . . . pretty good," designed to deal primarily with efforts of the conservative minority in Congress to kill the New Deal's National Resources Planning Board. On November 6, 1943, Mrs. Roosevelt wrote to Anna that she was at the White House and "Pa's up at Shangri-La, trying to get a last rest" before embarking on the USS *Iowa* from Hampton Roads, Virginia, for meetings in Cairo with Churchill, Chiang Kai-Shek, and Josef Stalin. Roosevelt had told his wife she could not attend the meeting, as no women would be there. She was hurt when she found that both Madame Chiang and Churchill's daughter, Sarah, attended. Clearly Mrs. Roosevelt, whose relations with her husband had cooled after his affair with her social secretary, Lucy Mercer, years before, was not as regular a visitor to the camp as most of the first ladies who followed her.[32]

For others, an invitation to Shangri-La was a prized sign of presidential favor. Young Supreme Court Justice William O. Douglas may have exaggerated the frequency of his own visits when he wrote in his memoirs years later that he was invited "more often than not . . . as a companion for some other guest, my function being to stick with the guest while FDR worked." The log shows only one visit by Douglas, on Roosevelt's last Shangri-La weekend of 1943.

"I had rather a lonely time at Shangri-La because FDR was holed up doing homework on endless problems—he would read, then doze, then dictate, then read, then doze," said Douglas. "I was company-in-waiting, ready to mix his favorite cocktail or to join him in idle chit chat."

The president's favorite cocktail was the dry martini, and Douglas said he had learned the art of mixing one, holding the mixer up to the light as he added "just that touch of vermouth that gave a very slight yellowish tinge to the gin."[33]

It was not always cocktail hour, though. On July 25, 1943, on the French telephone[34] in the Bear's Den, Roosevelt received a call from his press secretary, Steve Early, at the White House. Rome radio was reporting that Italian dictator Benito Mussolini had resigned. A similar rumor had come during the May 14–17 weekend at Shangri-La, but had proven false. "May it be true this time," Roosevelt wrote in his log. And this time it was.

As dispatches came in to the Bear's Den, the president and his adviser Harry Hopkins sat under the wagon wheel chandelier[35] in the liv-

4. The president's hideaway, later to be extensively remodeled, was truly rustic in the era of Roosevelt, who is seen here playing solitaire on the screened-in porch. *Courtesy Daisy Suckley Collection, Franklin Roosevelt Library.*

ing room if it was wet weather, or beside the telescope tripod[36] on the screened porch if it was sunny, and wrote out messages to Army Chief of Staff George Marshall and to Winston Churchill, Stalin, and Chiang Kai-Shek. "Sometimes generals or admirals drove up from Washington on matters of pressing import, the veins on their temples distended with urgency, and I often thought that they must be annoyed by the calmness with which their Commander in Chief received them and their reports," wrote Robert E. Sherwood.[37]

Others were not always so calm. On August 30, 1942, Hopkins handed Grace Tully a cable from FDR to Churchill, in Hopkins' difficult handwriting, for her to type. The subject was the long-debated invasion of North Africa, code-named Torch. "It is my earnest desire to start the attack at the earliest possible moment," Roosevelt wrote. The president's secretary, daunted momentarily by the information in her hands, finished her typing and handed Hopkins both the original and the carbon. "This is all yours," she said. "You put it in your brief case. I want no part of it."

"Full Steam," Roosevelt wrote in his log.

Roosevelt was back at Shangri-La on November 7 when a call came from the War Department. The president had been preoccupied during the automobile trip from Washington, and his hands shook as he took the telephone. He listened intently for a few moments. Then, "Thank God. Thank God. That sounds grand. Congratulations. Casualties are comparatively light — much below your predictions. Thank God."

"We have landed in North Africa," he told his companions. "We are striking back."[38]

As the tide of the war continued to turn, Churchill arrived in the United States aboard the *Queen Mary* for the Trident strategy talks in Washington, and he and FDR took a break at Shangri-La on May 15. There was a disagreement in the White House driveway when Mrs. Roosevelt proposed that she sit in a jump seat, allowing Churchill to be seated by the president. "I would not have this, and the British empire went into action," the prime minister said. "After about three minutes' conflict of wills, I won, and Mrs. Roosevelt took her proper place by her husband's side."

Passing through Frederick, Churchill asked about a roadside sign in the shape of a giant peppermint stick advertising Barbara Frietchie candy, named for the semilegendary character of the Civil War about whom John Greenleaf Whittier wrote a famous poem. This moved Roosevelt to recite the only two lines of the poem that most people can remember: " 'Shoot, if you must, this old gray head, / But spare your country's flag,' " she said." They were all Roosevelt could remember also. The visiting Briton, however, although he claimed not to have looked at the poem in thirty years, started from the beginning, "Up from the meadows, rich with corn" and sailed on through Whittier's thirty rhymed couplets. "I got full marks from my highly select American audience, none of whom corrected my many misquotations," Churchill later said.

At Shangri-La, which he summed up as "in principle a log cabin, with all modern improvements," Churchill watched for perhaps half an hour as Roosevelt stuck stamps into his album "and so forgot the cares of State . . . but soon another car drove up to the door, and out stepped Gen. Bedell Smith, quick-winged from Eisenhower's headquarters, with a budget of serious questions on which decisions were urgently required. So sadly FDR left his stamp collection and addressed himself to his task. . . . By evening we were all tired out, and went to bed at ten."[39]

The two world leaders did get to spend some time relaxing over drinks and smokes on the veranda of the Bear's Den. Churchill went to the Cozy Restaurant in Thurmont, where he enjoyed a cold beer and gave a waitress some coins for the juke box.[40] They also were taken by back roads to Hunting Creek, a mountain stream that crossed the road to Shangri-La about two miles west of the camp entrance. The six-mile stretch of the stream between its source near Foxville and the Thurmont municipal dam had been heavily stocked with brook trout and set aside for fly fishing, although most local fishermen used bait. The fishing spot chosen by FDR and his guest was an old ore pit of the Catoctin Iron Furnace, a Thurmont industry dating to prerevolutionary days. As Rigdon and Secret Service Agent Jim Rowley stayed within earshot, the president and prime minister sat on the bank in portable canvas chairs.[41] In a July 1 "Dear Winston" letter, Roosevelt enclosed photographs of the fishing trip. The pictures, taken in the shade of the hickories along Hunting Creek, were dark and he apologized that they "did not turn out very well but at least it proves that you and I tried to catch a fish. Better luck next time."[42]

From the beginning FDR set the dress code that was to govern with few exceptions at Shangri-La and Camp David—casual clothes, no shirts and ties, no fuss. His favorite outfit was slacks and a woolen shirt.[43] As for food, it was markedly better than at the White House, where Mrs. Roosevelt's handpicked housekeeper, Henrietta Nesbitt, laid down the rule "plain foods, plainly prepared" and the president said the fare "would do justice to the Automat." At Shangri-La, with the Navy's chefs in charge, FDR had "a chance of sampling oyster crabs with whitebait or peach cobbler with thick cream" of the kind his mother used to serve.[44]

In addition to the president's personal party and the Secret Service men, there would often be as many as a hundred people in attendance during his visits, including secretaries, a doctor and medical assistant, cryptographers, radio and telephone operators, chauffeurs, a valet, and a movie projectionist. Most stayed in unheated cabins of rough lumber and washed in long outside metal troughs, often twenty-five chilly yards or so from where they slept. Few of the approximately twenty buildings had running water and almost none had hot water.[45]

"When we went up there in cold weather, we took a lot of newspapers and put them under the mattress to keep the cold out," Agent

5. FDR and Winston Churchill went fishing without success in nearby Hunting Creek, where Jimmy Carter would later have better luck. *Courtesy Franklin Roosevelt Library.*

Rowley recalled years later.[46] It was an area notorious for, in words used by an Army journalist, raining continually, "one day from the sky and two days off the trees."[47]

For the president, the accommodations were better: his wash basin raised for convenient use as he sat in his wheelchair, the mirror lowered so he could see to shave.

Most of the furniture for the camp came from the attic of the White House, left over from previous administrations. "The rugs had come from the same place and were in a bad state of repair," said Rosenman. The president's bedroom had a green carpet, a single plain iron bed, a dresser and chair painted a low-luster white, and a clothes locker. The three guest bedrooms were similarly furnished, with simple metal beds, dressers, and chairs. The president's room had a bedside box divided into sections marked "Secret Service, Valet, Secretary, and Pantry." There had been one fireplace in the building already, and Ickes had fireplaces added in each bedroom. "Although construction for winter use was not a requirement, it was deemed wise to acknowledge that summer nights at 1,800 feet altitude are often cool, and to make provision for a comfortable occupancy beyond the span of the summer months," he said.[48] On one wall, the president had hand-printed and hung a jocular sign aimed at his gin-playing secretary: "VISITORS WILL BEWARE OF GAMBLERS (ESPECIALLY FEMALE) ON THIS SHIP."[49]

For the most part, additions to the buildings were made of hardwoods logged and sawed in the area, as the buildings had been in the first place. Two cabins that interfered with the northeast view from the lodge were moved and combined with a cabin north of the lodge to house a twenty-four-hour telephone switchboard and shortwave radio equipment. It was nicknamed "One Moment, Please." Other cabins were named "Grace Tully Cottage" or "Reilly Cottage" for the aides who stayed in them. A separate fifty-position switchboard was installed for communications within the camp. The Army had to blast through solid rock to lay the telephone lines.

Between the gate and the lodge was a nine-foot-wide drive, approximately 1,050 feet in length and designed to "approximate the appearance of a meandering logging road." Near the lodge were planted azaleas, spicebush, dogwood, hazelnut, witch hazel, ninebark, blueberry, arrow wood, and hawthorn. Native ferns and wildflowers had seeded themselves. Next to the screened porch, workmen built a terrace around a large rock outcropping, using weathered stones of from three cubic feet to twenty-five cubic feet or more to form rock ledges for the walls. Slabs of local flagstone were laid, with grass joints, for the terrace pavement and a walkway. In front of the lodge, with the presidential seal over its main door, a small pool was stocked with trout. Beside it was a log seat for the president. The terrace had two tables with three wire and iron chairs of the type found in ice cream parlors at each. At the swimming pool, a Marine Corps tent on a platform served as a dressing room. "It all adds up to something that looks like a medium quality boys' camp without horses or canoes," said journalist Merriman Smith, who visited the 143-acre camp after the war.[50]

Secret Service agents had flown many times overhead and reported that the natural wood buildings were nearly invisible in the dense forest. They remained troubled, however, by the possibility that hostile forces might seek out and attack the presidential retreat. The week before the president's first visit of 1943, single-engine airplanes were seen flying over the camp. Earl F. Ward, chairman of the Interdepartmental Air Traffic Control Board, wrote to airport managers at Taneytown, Frederick, and Baltimore, Maryland, and Waynesboro, Pennsylvania, asking them to restrict pilots from flying over the Catoctin Government Reservation, giving the excuse, "Many government workers are using the reservation for rest periods." As a result, the reservation was added to a restricted list that already included the White House and Hyde Park.[51]

During an August 29, 1942, visit, Sherwood told guests that one of his friends had surprised him by saying she knew where FDR's hideaway was. When he pressed her, it turned out that she believed it was Hoover's place at Rapidan. Other rumors around Washington had the president retreating to a place of luxury and lavish living like Hitler's Berchtesgaden in the Bavarian Alps.[52]

A few trusted reporters were usually told in confidence when the president was leaving the White House, but were not always told where he was going. On October 15, 1943, however, United Press carried a story by Smith, its White House correspondent, describing the camp as part of the Catoctin Recreation Area and reporting that Churchill had visited there. The National Park Service confirmed for Smith that Roosevelt had used the camp several times but relayed requests for further information to the White House. Aides at the White House would not even tell the reporter when the land was purchased. When a Washington *Daily News* clipping of Smith's story was received at the Secret Service office in the Treasury Department, Reilly penciled in, "Exact location may be censored — but — any foreign agent could find the camp after reading."

The next day's Washington *Times-Herald* carried a similar story. On October 18, Reilly discussed the news stories with Byron Price, a veteran journalist on leave from his post as Washington bureau chief of the Associated Press to head the government's Office of Censorship. "It is Mr. Price's opinion that such articles do not come within the restriction of the Censorship Act inasmuch as they make no mention of any particular trip of the president," the disgruntled Reilly wrote that day.[53]

A neighbor whose family had lived in the Catoctin area for one hundred years wrote to Roosevelt that she believed "outsiders" who had recently moved into the neighborhood had spread word of the location. Among the old-timers, she said, even "Republican Thurmont had been . . . pleased and silent" regarding Shangri-La. Mrs. Roosevelt, apparently unaware of the desire for secrecy, added to the frustrations of the Secret Service by chatting, at one of her weekly sessions with newswomen, about a summer White House "up the river." On one 1943 weekend, FDR was driven by a circuitous route northward through Thurmont and then south toward the camp because of Secret Service fears that the area had been penetrated. Agents and Marines searched all night, but no intruders were found.[54]

Despite concerns about the president's safety, Shangri-La was not immune from the cost-cutting that set in with the war's approaching end. On March 23, 1944, Reilly submitted a report defending the need for a Marine detachment of 132 enlisted men and four officers. "I believe the detail cannot be decreased, as all posts are virtually essential," he wrote.[55] Nevertheless, on April 28, Secretary of the Treasury Henry Morgenthau released the Marines. A military police patrol from the Marine Barracks in Washington would be moved to the Catoctin hideaway as needed.[56]

Toward the end of 1943, the Secret Service proposed that a place be found where the president could have better security from air attacks. So in the spring of 1944, Roosevelt looked around for another retreat and considered taking the train to Miami and then flying to the U.S. Naval Base at Guantanamo Bay in Cuba. He decided against Guantanamo, he told reporters off the record, because "Cuba is absolutely lousy with anarchists, murderers, etcetera and a lot of prevaricators."

On the advice of the Secret Service, he accepted the invitation of financier and presidential confidante Bernard Baruch to vacation at Baruch's plantation, "Hobcaw Barony," near Georgetown, South Carolina. In off-the-record remarks at a news conference there on May 4, he lamented publicity about Shangri-La, singling out a story by Washington society writer Evelyn Gordon Peyton. "She goes ahead and spills the beans," he said. "I don't know whether that would make it impossible for me to go there again or not, but they are afraid that a certain bunch of crackpots will take some planes—wouldn't take more than two or three planes—they could use training planes—and fly over and unload some bombs on the place. It is pretty well guarded on the ground, but not from the air."[57]

The dangers to FDR were not all from the sky, though. As he ended a vacation that aides had hoped would restore his vigor, he was suffering from the deepening arteriosclerosis that would take his life a little more than a year later. Unable to work more than a four-hour day, often dozing off at his desk, he was requiring twelve hours of sleep a night even as he prepared for the rigors of a reelection campaign.[58] "My plans—my medical laboratory work not being finished—are to be here about three days a week and to spend the other four days a week at Hyde Park, Shangri-La or on the Potomac," he wrote to Hopkins from the White House on May 18.[59] He had begun that schedule the previous weekend, rolling to Shangri-La in a new bulletproof black Packard touring car for a Thursday-to-Sunday rest. While there he received the welcome news of an Allied offensive on the Italian front. He was back again May 27–30 and again June 24–26, both times with his daughter Anna and son Major John Roosevelt. On the latter visit, he noted in the log, "Cherbourg Falls June 25!"[60]

In July, the often-troublesome Free French leader, General Charles de Gaulle, was at the White House for consultations. Hassett noted that the talks appeared to be going smoothly but added, "The Boss has devoted so much time to his visitor that he will not be able to go to Shangri-La this week." The next day, however, De Gaulle was on his way back to Algiers without the recognition he sought for his group as the government of France, and Roosevelt was on the road into the Catoctins again. Despite the difficulties of dealing with de Gaulle, he made it to Shangri-La for a few hours once more, leaving the White House at 11:15 A.M. and returning at 10:15 P.M.[61] But it would be his last visit. The great days of the "Bear's Den" were over.

2

Harry Truman Comes to Shangri-La

Until Franklin D. Roosevelt died of a stroke in Warm Springs, Georgia, on April 12, 1945, and his personal belongings at Shangri-La were shipped to Hyde Park,[1] Harry S. Truman had never been to the president's mountaintop hideaway. The former Missouri senator, chosen as a compromise candidate for the vice presidency on the 1944 Democratic ticket, was not part of FDR's inner circle.

When the new president first visited the camp in the Catoctins in May 1946, more than a year after taking office, he was not impressed. "The general atmosphere of 'Shangri-La' at the end of the war was that of a place hastily slapped together in an emergency," wrote a local historian.[2] The president told naval aide Rigdon that he might like it better if the brush Roosevelt had allowed to luxuriate were cleared away. "I look out the window and there's nothing but trees," he said.[3]

"The outside growth was almost right up to your windows," Rigdon recalled years later. "In other words, you couldn't open your window at that stage of the game, and it was left that way for President Roosevelt's wishes. He wanted to be, I guess, guarded from too many eyes and particularly from any enemies that might be looking for the president's camp. But Truman practically made an edict that day that if things weren't changed that he would lose interest in Shangri-La in a hurry, that he couldn't see anything up there appealing to him." A crew of twenty-five to thirty men was assembled from the presidential yacht *Williamsburg,* successor to the *Potomac,* and set to work with axes, saws, and bulldozer. When they were through, the brush was cleared and a rise of land to the east of the president's lodge had been leveled. The view was improved and the way was open for what was to be Dwight Eisenhower's golfing green. "Once we got the place cleared out and the roads leading to the main house widened somewhat, it looked more like a suburban spot rather than a place hidden in the forest," said Rigdon.[4]

Truman went to the camp only nine times in nearly eight years as president. For nearly two years, from August 1947 until the end of July 1949, he did not visit it at all. His last trip was on August 21, 1950, nearly two and one-half years before he left office. Altogether, he spent twenty-seven days there.[5] Truman preferred to relax with poker companions on the *Williamsburg* or at Key West, Florida.

Bess Truman first visited the retreat on a rainy October day in 1945 and found it dull, although she came back from time to time with her husband or used the camp for informal women's lunches after Truman had the buildings steam-heated.[6] Daughter Margaret, for her part, wrote: "Deep in the woods, Shangri-La was damp and cold most of the time. I thought it was a terrible place and went there as little as possible."[7]

On his infrequent trips, Truman made active use of the camp. He went for long walks, swam occasionally in the frigid pool, and explored the countryside in a jeep, with Mrs. Truman pointing a precautionary finger at the speedometer. Rigdon, occupying the rear seat with a Secret Service agent, found that he needed to brush up on forestry. The Missourian in the White House "tried to compare everything as far as the shrubbery and the land itself with Missouri, and he would ask me what this was, point to a tree or bush and ask, 'What kind of a tree is this? We don't have any of these in Missouri.' "[8]

In fact, oaks predominated. Occasionally, there were patches of pine. Chestnut trees once covered about 50 percent of the mountains, but were destroyed as an important timber tree by the chestnut blight of 1912. The Catoctins are a spur of the Blue Ridge Mountains, part of the Appalachian Chain that stretches more than twelve hundred miles from the Gaspe Peninsula in Quebec to Alabama. At the time European settlers arrived in 1732, Maryland was neutral ground in Indian wars. No bands lived permanently in the Catoctins, although small tribes had hunted, fished, and farmed there. The first white settlers were German immigrants who pushed west from Philadelphia and turned southwest after reaching the Susquehanna River. By 1880, a census of the area in Northwestern Frederick County that would later embrace the site of Shangri-La showed 1,176 free residents.

The woods had other enemies besides the chestnut blight. For about one hundred years ending in 1890, patches were clear-cut every twenty-five to thirty-five years to provide charcoal for the Catoctin Iron Furnace. Cattle tramped the ground dry and hard, destroyed seed beds, and checked growth. Fires spread rapidly in the dry woods. By 1920, more than five million cubic feet of timber were being cut annually in Frederick County and the estimated annual growth was only 3,600,000 cubic feet. "Measures must be taken immediately to increase the growth," State Forester F. W. Besley warned in 1922.[9] Little was done, and the land suffered. In 1936, the federal government paid $155,000 for the property that became Catoctin Mountain Park and Camp David. The resettlement agency planned artificial lakes, campsites, weekend cabins, playgrounds and other facilities to demonstrate how rough topography and eroded soil could be put to better use. The property was called the Catoctin Recreational Demonstration Area.[10]

The New Deal's Works Progress Administration, or WPA, employed local woodsmen to erect three cabin camps, using horses to drag dead chestnut trees from the forest. More than two and one-half million feet of the blighted wood was used to build cabins. Young men of the Civilian Conservation Corps arrived in 1939, reforesting the area with red maples and pitch pines and transplanting native trees and shrubs to screen the open playing field where presidential helicopters would later land.

On November 14, 1936, the land was transferred to the National Park Service and Catoctin Mountain Park was created. Even before construction was finished, Camp Misty Mount was adopted by the Maryland League for Crippled Children as a summer camp for disabled youngsters. Because the steep terrain was difficult to negotiate with wheelchairs, the children were taken instead to the second camp after it was completed in 1938. The city youngsters, thrilled by the abundance of trees on top of the mountain, dubbed it Greentop. Except for an interruption during World War II, when the park was closed to the public, Greentop continued as a summer camp for disabled children into the 1990s. Camp #3, Hi-Catoctin, was completed in the winter of 1938–39 and used for three years as a family camp for federal employees before being taken over by FDR.[11]

As the war ended, there was confusion about the future of Shangri-La. Roosevelt evidently at first intended that it revert to the National Park Service, but may have changed his mind. Some government officials felt it should be maintained as a national shrine or monument. At any rate, Truman, in a letter to Maryland Governor Herbert R. O'Connor, wrote, "I have decided because of the historical events of national and international interest now associated with the Catoctin Recreation Area that this property should be retained by the National Park Service of the Department of the Interior. This action is in accord with the position expressed by the late President Roosevelt before his death."[12]

One of the original landowners of the Shangri-La site, ill and living in California, wrote to the president that she would like to buy back the old family homestead. Her letter was referred to the Interior Department, but the land remained part of the presidential retreat. Maryland claimed that the original plan had been to transfer the demonstration area to the Maryland State Forest and Park System, but Truman denied the claim. In 1952, he approved a compromise under which 4,446 acres, the portion south of Route 77, became Cunningham Falls State Park.[13]

Secretary Morgenthau had decided in 1944 to relieve the Marines of their Catoctin duties. The Marine Corps, however, does not take its orders from the secretary of the treasury; the Marines stayed at Greentop. The Maryland League for Crippled Children, unhappy with its Pennsylvania site, agitated for their removal. The children's buses would not need to pass the "Little White House" but could go by a back road, a spokesman said. Secretary of Agriculture Clinton Anderson sided with the league, citing reports that Greentop was being developed as a summer retreat for the Marine Corps commandant, Brig. Gen. Alexander A. Vandegrift. Secretary of the Interior Julius A. Krug denied this rumor, but conceded that improvements had been made to accommodate the commandant on inspection trips. The league was offered Camp #1, which it had used in 1937, but still found it too steep. In April 1947, the Marines were moved to Shangri-La, making Greentop available again to the disabled children. On August 3 of that year, Truman visited the handicapped youngsters. He was invited again next year, but did not make it, although the hundred or so children were given a visit to Shangri-La in his absence.[14]

Truman began the wondrous transformation that FDR's rude camp in the woods was to undergo in the years to come. Deciding the retreat should be kept open year round, he had the buildings winterized as well as having steam heat installed in the presidential lodge and some of the guest cabins.[15] On September 16, 1945, the first published photographs of the camp appeared, complete with laundry hanging from a clothesline between the presidential lodge and its flagpole. Reporter Frank Henry and photographer Frank Miller of the *Baltimore Sun* had flown over the site in a rented airplane and, two weeks later, reporters

6. In the Truman era a lone sailor and a rustic gate were the only security at the entrance to Shangri-La. *Courtesy Harry S. Truman Library.*

and photographers were allowed inside the grounds. With the lid off, news organizations sent reporters when the president went to Shangri-La. They were not allowed inside the camp, but stayed at the Cozy. Rigdon or presidential press secretary Charles D. Ross came and briefed them.[16]

With the passing of the war, security was relaxed. By the end of 1947, the one hundred Marines of wartime had given way to twenty-four sailors and four messmen under the command of a chief petty officer. At any one time, one seaman guarded the gate while another walked patrol. The sailors were frequently rotated back to their regular assignments on the *Williamsburg* so they could collect pay for sea duty. Still, there was enough security to irritate two Democratic Party officials of Frederick County, who showed up at the gate one July day in 1949 to pay their respects to the president and were told by a guard that they needed to get permission.[17]

Truman first visited the camp on Mother's Day in 1946 for lunch with his wife and her mother, Mrs. David Wallace. They traveled in a plain sedan with a District of Columbia license, with Secret Service

7. The rustic gate and sailor had been replaced by Marine guards and a heavily reinforced fence by Ronald Reagan's administration. *Courtesy Ronald Reagan Library.*

agents following a short distance behind. When the presidential party stopped at a red light in Frederick, the agents remained in their own vehicles rather than surrounding the car as they had come to do when Roosevelt rode through. "The fewer Secret Service he had, the better he liked it," said Rigdon.

One weekend, Truman had Ross alert the reporters at the Cozy that he was making a surprise trip to the Gettysburg battlefield. Once there, they got another surprise. The president dismissed the park ranger and conducted the journalists on a guided tour himself.[18]

The informal chief executive sometimes drove himself to the camp. In July 1946, Mrs. Truman wrote her daughter that they were spending "the most peaceful Fourth I have any recollection of" at Shangri-La. Truman had gone for one of his walks, which covered a mile and a half or more and took up to half an hour. Unlike FDR, whom Rigdon and Secret Service agents did not remember using the unheated pool, he planned to go for a swim afterward. But, said Bess, "Not for me! I've been reading or just sittin'." For the first time also, the men of the Secret Service were permitted to swim in the pool.[19]

In the evening, the Trumans would walk to the Navy mess for movies. Mrs. Truman said Margaret had missed a good one in *Anna and the King of Siam,* but the first lady chose to pass up the Marx Brothers in *A Night in Casablanca.* Margaret suspected that her mother identified herself with Margaret Dumont, the actress who played the dignified matron so constantly tormented by the brothers in earlier movies.

More often, the camp was used by Truman's aides. He made it available, as Roosevelt had not, to members of his staff when he and Mrs. Truman were not there, a practice to be followed intermittently by his successors. "It was in use a part of nearly every week," Rigdon said.[20] Passes were issued, signed at first by a young Naval Reserve officer, Capt. Clark M. Clifford. Clifford served briefly as the president's naval aide, although, in the opinion of regular Navy man Rigdon, "I'll swear he didn't know the front end of a ship from the rear of it." He was not the first to receive the assignment for reasons more political than nautical. His predecessor, Commodore James K. Vardaman Jr., was a banker from St. Louis. In Missouri society and politics, St. Louis was southern; Kansas City was western. Vardaman was St. Louis to the core, a founding member of the city's Grand Opera Guild. He was also one of the few St. Louis businessmen who supported Truman, the product of the crass Pendergast political machine of Kansas City, when he ran for the Senate in 1934. The debt was paid, and Vardaman came to Washington. He so irritated Secretary of the Navy James Forrestal that Truman shifted him to the Federal Reserve Board. When Truman's second term was marred by scandal over a Chicago perfume manufacturer who gave food freezers to officials, Vardaman donated the one that he received to Shangri-La.[21]

Persuaded that a regular Navy officer was needed for the aide's job, Truman named Adm. James K. Foskett, and Clifford went on to other duties, eventually becoming Lyndon B. Johnson's secretary of defense. Foskett, who had commanded the cruiser *Augusta* that took the president and his party from Norfolk, Virginia, to Europe for the postwar Potsdam Conference, made a significant change in the operation of Shangri-La. "Up until this time, the commanding officer of the president's yacht sent a detail of men up to the camp and was more or less in charge of the thing," Rigdon recalled. When the then skipper of the *Williamsburg,* Capt. J. H. Kevers, retired in the spring of 1946, Foskett made Rigdon officer in charge at Shangri-La. The new officer in charge wrote in his signature over Clifford's printed name in issuing passes.[22]

Before leaving the White House, Vardaman had outlined regulations for guests in a memorandum to the president, prohibiting "wild parties," excessive drinking, or gambling for high stakes. Conflicts over who was to use the camp were to be resolved on a basis of seniority, but once a junior staffer had made reservations he could not be "bumped" without his permission.[23]

Rigdon was not at the camp full time, but went up most weekends, usually stopping off at his Washington apartment to pick up his wife, Jane. "If there were no guests, Mrs. Rigdon and I actually put up in the president's house, just to test out and see how things were going," he said. Even though visitors to the camp were required to pay their own mess bills and other expenses, it was a fondly remembered life for a naval officer and his wife, with the president's stewards and cooks on hand to take care of their needs. "Mrs. Rigdon and I did much of our entertaining there," Rigdon said.[24]

One of the most frequent visitors was William Hassett, FDR's appointments secretary, who had offered to stay on in the Truman administration. A seventy-one-year-old Vermonter, Hassett often entertained Vermont friends, as well as officers from Bethesda Naval Medical Center and Walter Reed Army Hospital, officials of the Smithsonian Institution, and the radio commentator H. R. Baukhage.

While presumably falling within Vardaman's strictures, the parties were evidently lively. On August 8, 1949, Neil M. Judd of the Smithsonian wrote Hassett of his "delight in having been included among your boisterous, if scientific and journalistic, friends." Judd was included in a similar gathering the next year when the hard-drinking Hassett wrote to him, "The trip to Shangri-La kills two hours, but we will make it leisurely and allow for stops on the way for administration of first aid." Except for one wedding anniversary celebration for a Walter Reed colonel and his wife, the names on the guest lists were male. Hassett would dispatch a White House limousine to pick up his guests at the Smithsonian, the Bureau of Standards or the Cosmos Club on Massachusetts Avenue.

On March 3, 1950, Hassett gave a stag dinner of New England clam chowder and fried chicken for Vermont Governor Ernest W. Gibson. In a haunting echo of James Hilton's grand lama, who told the contemplative hero of *Lost Horizon* that "the airman bearing loads of death to the great cities will not pass our way," one guest wrote Hassett in thanks, "I had the distinct feeling that if the rest of the world had blown up that night, Shangri-La would have remained."[25]

Truman had not been present. The man from Missouri used the camp seldom and entertained no foreign visitors there, but made the first improvements to it and made the decision that it would remain a presidential retreat.

3

Dwight D. Eisenhower
Camp David Comes into Being

To William Rigdon, listening to the radio in his naval aide's office in the East Wing of the White House, the news came as "a travesty." Dwight D. Eisenhower, declaring that "'Shangri-La' was just a little fancy for a Kansas farm boy," had renamed the Catoctin retreat. It would now be called Camp David, after his father and five-year-old grandson.

"I figured that it was a downright markdown on what he thought of the place," said Rigdon, staying on temporarily in the Eisenhower White House.[1]

Markdown or not, it was easily accomplished. There was just one sign that identified the camp by the name Roosevelt had fancifully given it. Hanging on a chain from the peak of a shake roof surmounting two five-foot posts at the entrance, it said in Chinese red letters, "Shangri-La." Capt. Edward L. Beach, taking over from Rigdon as White House naval aide and officer in charge of the retreat, ordered it changed. A week or so later, as he drove through the gate, he saw that the old sign had simply been covered with a new backing with the words "Camp David" carved into it.[2] Roosevelt loyalists would object to the change for decades, but the deed was done.

Eisenhower was cool to such trappings of office as a presidential hideaway in the mountains, having campaigned on a platform of austerity. He ordered the presidential yacht *Williamsburg* laid up on standby

30

at the Washington Naval Gun Factory as "a symbol of unnecessary luxury." He gave up Truman's quarters at Key West and an aide was quoted as saying he did not plan to use Shangri-La. Sen. J. Glenn Beall of Maryland promptly urged that the Catoctin retreat be handed over to the state.[3] Local officials, innkeepers, and private citizens wrote suggesting alternate vacation retreats in Maine, Virginia, New Hampshire, Maryland, Tennessee, Ohio, California, Colorado, Florida, Wisconsin, Arizona, and Georgia. All were told the president had not made up his mind.

A presidential inspection trip to Roosevelt's Shangri-La was proposed for May 2, possibly with Beall as a member of the party, but Eisenhower was unresponsive and the idea was dropped. Attorney General Herbert Brownell and eight top Justice Department officials, including Assistant Attorney General Warren E. Burger, spent three days at the camp and sent the president a mock "Petition for Executive Clemency," saying the retreat had been condemned "without any examination of the facts or any firsthand experience, but merely upon the advice of counsellors."[4]

Ike did visit the retreat on May 12, and wrote his verdict to his boyhood friend, Everett E. Hazlitt. "I have kept only the little camp up in the Catoctins," he said.[5] When Mamie Eisenhower paid her first visit to the presidential lodge, late in the winter of 1953, she found it little changed from Roosevelt's day—paneled in rough wood and furnished with the big, heavy pieces he fancied. The new first lady found it cramped, dark, and uncomfortable. Accustomed to the comfortable life of the wife of a general officer in the Army, Mrs. Eisenhower announced that she would not go back to the Catoctin retreat unless it was modernized. "It would be nice if we only had the money to redecorate it," she said. There were no funds for the purpose in the White House budget, but an aide suggested the Navy might undertake the expense. "I think I'll just pass a hint along to the commander-in-chief," said the commander-in-chief's wife.[6]

Evan P. Aurand, a Naval aviator assigned to the White House, summoned a southern California interior decorator, Harold Grieve, whom he had known as a Naval Reserve captain during the war. Grieve, who had been president of the American Institute of Interior Decorators, dramatically altered the Bear's Den, tearing out low beaverboard ceilings to expose the beams and replacing the east wall almost entirely with glass to expand the view. FDR's wagon-wheel chandelier was removed. Grieve added a booth so that the movie projector didn't have to be set up in the living room, and a motorized screen that was with-

8. A sign with Chinese lettering stood outside the gate of the Roose-
velt-Truman retreat. *Courtesy Harry S. Truman Library and the Department of Defense.*

drawn into the ceiling when not in use. The oak paneling in the presidential bedroom was painted a very pale pink and the twin beds upholstered with a pattern of pale green leaves. On the wall above the
headboard, the first lady had three large floral prints hung. Sand-toned
tile with gray fixtures and light green curtains highlighted what had
been FDR's spartan bathroom.

A picnic and outdoor cooking area was built, and the outlying
cabins were repainted and refurnished. Mrs. Eisenhower ordered the
buildings renamed for native trees. Aurand thought Redwood would be
fine for the presidential lodge, but Eisenhower thought his wife would
prefer something associated with her home state, so it became Aspen,
the Colorado state tree. The staff simply called it "The Big House." The
conference lodge was called Laurel and other buildings Dogwood,
Hickory, Witch Hazel, Maple, and Sycamore.[7]

By July 1, 1953, Eisenhower was telling reporters, "I hope to be out
of town for the weekend, up in Camp David, and spend Saturday and

9. President Eisenhower ordered the name changed in honor of his grandson, here posing with the new sign. *Courtesy Dwight D. Eisenhower Library and the U.S. Navy.*

10. Eisenhower watches from the Aspen terrace as his grandchildren play in the snow. *Courtesy Dwight D. Eisenhower Library and the U.S. Navy.*

Sunday there, as I did last week — very quietly, doing nothing."[8] Doing nothing often included Eisenhower's hobby of oil painting.[9] Another of his hobbies, however, he could not indulge. Standing on the sloping lawn at Aspen with Ned Beach, he said, "Gee, wouldn't it be great if I could practice my golf swing out here?"

Beach had once built a small course for his own use in his backyard as a boy. "Let me try," he said. Beach's idea was "to create a place where the president could not play golf but he could play three holes and he could vary the directions that he played them from." It proved more than the naval aide's backyard experience had prepared him for. "You guys don't know what you're doing," said Cliff Roberts, the New York investment banker who was one of the president's favorite golf partners. "You've got to have drainage and you've got to have the right kind of soil." Roberts arranged for New York golf course designer Robert Jones, who had laid out the greens that Eisenhower played on at

Washington's Burning Tree Club, to come to Camp David and design a course complete with sand traps. Bulldozers cut a narrow clearing into the second-growth forest to provide more playing area. The course was designed as a miniature of both Burning Tree and Augusta National Golf Course, another Eisenhower favorite. The sod was donated by the Chevy Chase Club of suburban Washington. Local Cadillac-Oldsmobile dealer Floyd Akers and others provided funds.[10]

President Gerald R. Ford would find the small course frustrating when he came to it two decades later. "His basic relaxation was golf, and you couldn't play much golf up there," Richard Cheney, Ford's chief of staff, recalled. The course is a little bitty thing Ike put in. It's very short, almost a putting green."[11] Eisenhower said, "This is great," and started whacking balls. If it wasn't golf, said Beach, it was "a reasonable facsimile thereof." On one day, the president wagered his son, Maj. John Eisenhower, his daughter-in-law, Barbara, and Beach as to who could get closest to the green from the 140-yard second tee. Ike won and collected a dollar from each.

There were, however, many weekends when the president would walk restlessly out onto the porch time and again to find the rain still keeping him from his golf game. "Sometimes I feel so sorry for myself I could cry," he told his secretary, Ann Whitman.[12]

Like Mrs. Truman, Mamie Eisenhower took to using the camp to entertain women friends when her husband was away. Eisenhower authorized Aurand, who succeeded Beach as naval aide, to make the camp available to aides and Cabinet members. When Eisenhower took office in 1953, the camp could accommodate five couples, if one slept in a guest cottage living room. A rough cabin for the Secret Service could house twenty-two men. Most of the cabins were still unheated. By July, 1956, however, the two roughly finished cabins next to Aspen Lodge had been converted to more comfortable quarters, each with two beds and a private bath.

The naval aide had barracks and recreational facilities built for camp personnel, and ordered construction of a small family housing complex about two miles from camp. Until then, men with families had been renting homes in the Thurmont area and had frequently been unable to negotiate the icy roads in winter. A group photograph of Camp David personnel taken July 2, 1955, showed fifty-six Marines and sailors, with three noted as missing. By 1958, the Naval force had grown to ninety-four officers and men.[13]

In June of 1954, the mess hall at Greentop was struck by lightning and burned to the ground. So that the vacation for disabled children would not have to be canceled for the year, the Navy set up emergency cooking facilities at their camp, which was to be taken over by Camp David in the event of an emergency relocation of the White House.[14]

In the summer of 1954, Winston Churchill, back in power after a post-war interval in opposition, was again a visitor to the White House. This time there was no interlude in the Catoctins. In fact, Eisenhower found it a relief to get away to Camp David with friends for a long Fourth of July weekend after a depressing interval with the wartime ally who, enfeebled by years, repeated himself and strayed from the subject of discussion.

With Eisenhower on the outing were W. Alton Jones, president of Cities Service Company, and Ellis Slater, president of Frankfort Distilleries, with their wives; they were members of the close-knit group the president referred to as the gang. It was a typical Camp David weekend for Eisenhower, just as the visit with the Rosenmans and the Mac-Leishes had been a typical Shangri-La weekend for Roosevelt. The men played bridge and golf; the women went off separately to play bolivia, a then-popular card game, and talk. As always, Mrs. Eisenhower ran the home away from home with Army wife regularity — no liquor before six o'clock, dinner promptly at seven. Ike found it all so pleasant he arranged for everybody to stay an extra day, not returning to Washington until the Wednesday after the holiday.[15]

On that Fourth of July weekend, they went for a drive, as FDR and his guests had. Their destination was the farmhouse the president was building at Gettysburg, Pennsylvania, a little more than twenty miles away. For the Eisenhowers, Camp David was to become in many ways an annex to Gettysburg. After early 1955, when the house was ready, they spent most weekends and summer vacations at the farmhouse. Two Filipino housemen, Enrique and Lem, stayed in Navy barracks at the camp and commuted to the Pennsylvania farm.[16] Mrs. Eisenhower also asked the camp gardener to come to Gettysburg and give her advice. The gardener, "who was a damn good gardener . . . was delighted," Beach recalled. "He lived somewhere in between and, as far as he was concerned, it didn't matter where he went." To Beach, it was more of a problem: "I was concerned at one point that we not overstep the grounds of what I thought was the proper division between government property and private property. This could have become a politically touchy thing. I remember speaking to her about it and saying that we had to be careful and not let this get out of hand."

"What's wrong? He's the president, isn't he?" Mrs. Eisenhower asked.

"Yes, but, you know, the press will not let us get away with much."

The first lady responded, in effect, "Well, okay, you handle it if anything happens."

Feeling he had been put on notice that it was his fault if there was any bad publicity, Beach told the gardener, "Look, you are supposed to be here at Camp David. You're not supposed to spend all your time down there at Gettysburg. If you want to go there on weekends, why that's your business; you have weekends off." The gardener agreed to the restrictions but, Beach said years later, "I suspect he cheated a little."

It was also to the farm that Eisenhower went to recuperate after his first heart attack, which he suffered on September 23, 1955. When he decided to have a National Security Council meeting on November 21 and a Cabinet meeting the following day, they were held at Camp David, but only because there was no suitable room at the farm. As Naval Aide Beach saw it, there was not really a suitable one at Camp David either. When he became officer in charge in 1953, one of his goals was to make Laurel into a second lodge for the president's staff, adding a bathroom and an extra bedroom and installing a semicircular conference bench. His original plan was to have the work done in spare time as part of the regular camp maintenance. But with the message that there was to be a Cabinet meeting at the camp, Beach gave the word, "We have to have the Cabinet room ready, so let's get at it."[17]

Eisenhower told aides he did not want to be briefed in advance of the Cabinet meeting, because he felt he could better maintain his interest in the material if he had not gone over it beforehand. The night before the meeting, he played bridge at Aspen with his secretaries of state, John Foster Dulles; defense, Charles Wilson; and treasury, George Humphries.[18] At Laurel, Chief of Staff Sherman Adams "noticed that everybody in the room was studying Eisenhower intently, looking for a change in his appearance and in his actions. He was a little thinner, ruddy though not so tanned as usual, but his eye and his glance were sharp and he showed, perhaps a bit consciously and deliberately, an added force and energy in his comments and expressions of opinion. He was quick, decisive and keen. I could see that the Cabinet liked what they saw."[19]

As he had at the NSC meeting the day before, Eisenhower spent about an hour at the Cabinet session. "At its conclusion," he said, "I felt no fatigue or weariness, and concluded that I would soon resume the daily work schedule to which I was accustomed. Now I felt sure my recovery would be complete."[20] As members began to rise from the ta-

11. Recuperating from a heart attack in 1955, President Eisenhower met with his Cabinet in Laurel Lodge. An aide found him "quick, decisive and keen." *Left to right:* Secretary of State John Foster Dulles, Eisenhower, Defense Secretary Charles Wilson, and Agriculture Secretary Ezra Taft Benson. *Courtesy AP/Wide World.*

ble, Eisenhower signaled them to remain and thanked his Cabinet and staff for the way they had carried on in his absence. Vice President Richard Nixon, always sensitive to such matters, noted that "to my knowledge, he did not thank anyone personally."[21]

The meetings were the first in a weekly series at Camp David as Eisenhower's convalescence continued. During a walk in the woods after a December 8 NSC meeting, Dulles outlined plans to send a personal emissary to the Middle East to seek a peace agreement.[22] The emissary would not be the last to go on such a mission in the years of Middle East turmoil in which Camp David would play a growing part.

Eisenhower had come to the mountain hideaway by motorcade, like Roosevelt and Truman before him, but this was soon to change. On July 12, 1957, the president boarded a Bell Ranger helicopter at the White House and flew the sixty-three miles to Camp David in a little over thirty minutes. White House military and Air Force aides expressed concern about the safety of the helicopters, and Eisenhower said he would take the advice of Secret Service agent Rowley, "who has the legal responsibility of looking after the safety of my poor old carcass," and would use the helicopters only in emergencies. Naval aide Aurand, however, argued that the helicopters were safe for routine use. He evidently prevailed. Logs of Eisenhower's helicopter flights between July 3, 1959, and November 5, 1960, show seven trips between Camp David and the White House, code-named "Hotel," and seven between the camp and Gettysburg. Except in bad weather, it would no longer take two hours to travel between Washington and the Catoctins.[23]

It was on the first helicopter trip, part of a preparedness exercise called Operation Alert, that Eisenhower inspected the new bomb shelter at the camp. With the cold war at its height, bomb shelters were blossoming across America, and Beach had previously overseen construction of one at the White House. At Camp David one weekend, he told Eisenhower, "Look, Mr. President, really you ought to have a bomb shelter up here. If we're here when the bomb drops, we can't go back to Washington. We are going to have to have a shelter of some kind." The resulting refuge, hewn out of rock, was even smaller than the one at the White House, which had shocked Chief of Staff Adams with the closet-like size of his office. Once, during construction, a foreign dignitary visited the camp, touching off "a big affair to get the whole thing sort of covered over . . . an emergency move to cover our tracks." With the completion of the shelter, the Navy increased its complement of officers and men to 112.[24]

Meanwhile, there was trouble with the plumbing. Heating and water systems had been installed too close to the surface in the rocky soil of Shangri-La and, in 1957, many cabins were flooded when pipes burst during a cold spell. They were replaced in 1958 along with the sewer system.[25]

The retreat was still not fixed in the public mind as a place of presidential power. When Press Secretary Jim Hagerty announced that Eisenhower would meet at Camp David on March 20, 1959, with Britain's Prime Minister Harold Macmillan, one reporter asked where Camp David was.[26] Ike had invited Macmillan, the British government's emissary to his headquarters in World War II days in London, to discuss how to deal with Moscow's threats to shut off access to Berlin. On the way, they stopped at Bethesda Naval Hospital for a visit with Dulles, gravely ill with cancer, who argued heatedly that the West should "stick it out" in Berlin and the Soviets would not dare to intervene. After the thirty-six-minute flight from Bethesda into the Catoctins, Macmillan found the president "in capital form, clearly very glad to escape from the White House."

Showing the British leader to his room in Aspen, Aurand noticed with dismay that the corridor was decorated with old prints celebrating British defeats at sea in the Revolution and the War of 1812. It seemed obvious to the young naval officer that the prime minister had noticed, but Macmillan assured him he would not complain to the president.

Ike showed Macmillan the new bomb shelter. It was, the Briton wrote in his diary, "a sort of Presidential Command Post in the event of atomic war. It holds fifty of the President's staff in one place and one hundred and fifty Defence staff in another. The fortress is underneath the innocent looking huts in which we lived, hewn out of the rock. It cost 10 million dollars."

Their talks began at 3 P.M. on the sun porch, which was dominated by a massive sofa in beige silk brocade. At the north end of the room were bookshelves. One book had an ominous title: *Masters of Deceit*. The talks, however, were straightforward. Eisenhower, as Jimmy Carter would after him, favored the informal atmosphere of the Catoctin retreat for international meetings. At the White House, said Aurand, there was always "the pressure of time, the possibility of interruption, the press hanging around the outer doors."[27] Occasionally, the two wartime colleagues called each other "Harold" and "Ike," but most of the time it was "Mr. President" and "Sir Harold."[28] Ann Whitman noted the "real friendship that allows them to argue heatedly without having to couch everything in diplomatic language."

At one point, the usually stiff-upper-lipped Macmillan became emotional, his eyes moistening as he declared that his countrymen were unwilling to die over such issues as who stamped passes of what color for motor convoys to East Berlin. Eisenhower "reminded him that in case of general war, the United States would be the prime Soviet target. More Americans would die than British."

It was bitterly cold at Camp David and a stiff wind, common on the mountaintop in the winter and early spring, came up during the night. Whitman, in an office she described as "nothing but an extended shack," was awakened by a roar and found that the top part of the door had blown off.[29]

As for Macmillan, after a night in Aspen's Southeast bedroom — little changed from FDR's time with its unpainted oak paneling, fireplace and yellow-tiled private bath with call button — the Briton apparently thought better of his outburst. He apologized for the display of emotion, but Eisenhower, perhaps diplomatically, professed not to have noticed it. Nonetheless, Macmillan's agitated state had been plainly apparent to the president's son and military aide, John Eisenhower.

From time to time, Dulles telephoned from the hospital to see how the talks were going. During a drive to Gettysburg with his guest, Ike speculated on the likelihood that he might have to name a successor to the secretary of state. After his own and Dulles' illnesses, he wondered if it would be wise to appoint the arthritic Undersecretary of State Christian Herter, who needed crutches to walk and stayed in a room in Aspen equipped with a light raised and lowered by means of a weight.[30]

Back at the lodge, the talks became heated, with the Americans balking at British willingness to have an unconditional four-power summit meeting. Neville Chamberlain had gone to such a meeting before World War II, and Eisenhower would have no part of it. He and Macmillan agreed to sleep on it overnight and talk again in the morning.

Niceties were gone over at dinner, where the leaders sat beneath a circle of five gold stars, insignia of the president's General of the Army rank, mounted above the presidential seal surmounting the fireplace. That evening, Macmillan wrote in his diary, "We had a film, called 'The Great Country' or some such name. It was a 'Western.' It lasted three hours! It was inconceivably banal." The movie was *The Big Country,* a wide-screen color production that lasted 166 minutes and starred Gregory Peck, Jean Simmons, and Charlton Heston. Eisenhower, who relished watching Westerns at Camp David with friends, had already seen it at least three times.

In the morning, Macmillan "felt that the president had told his people to go as far as they could to meet us" on the issue of the four-power summit. The United States would agree to participate as soon as developments in the Foreign Ministers' meeting justified it. Then followed a long argument about emergency planning for Berlin in the event of the blockade that in fact ensued. Gen. Nathan Twining, Army chief of staff, winced as Eisenhower asked if the West should not consider "probing short of war" in response to provocative Soviet actions and exclaimed, "Why can't we do some of the things the Russians seem to do all the time with impunity!"[31]

On Sunday, the two leaders attended Trinity United Church of Christ in Thurmont, then joined their advisers at Laurel Lodge in a discussion of the Middle and Far East. They left Camp David by road at 4:00 P.M., with Eisenhower talking "at large about the future of the world." "He is certainly a strange mixture," wrote his companion. "With all his crudity and lack of elegance of expression, he has some very remarkable ideas."

Back in Washington, Macmillan said that "despite reports about the cold, all had really been quite comfortable." En route, they stopped to see the ailing secretary of state, at home on temporary discharge from the hospital. It would be their last meeting. Dulles resigned on April 25 and died on May 24.

Domestic affairs shared the president's attention with foreign policy, at Camp David as elsewhere. In July, 1959, during a motorcade trip to the camp, Eisenhower noticed a deep freeway construction gash on the outskirts of the Washington metropolitan area. Appalled, he called Budget Director Maurice Stans from Aspen, asking for an explanation. What Eisenhower evidently did not know was that the chief White House lobbyist, Jerry Persons, attempting to overcome big city opposition to the Interstate Highway Bill in 1956, had agreed to give cities a major share of construction outlays. When the president learned this, he expressed "concern that too much of the interstate highway money might be going into connections in the cities," but said it was too late to reverse course.[32]

It was foreign policy, however, that was to dominate Eisenhower's last months in office. At his July 8 news conference, the president was asked by Merriman Smith about a report from Moscow that Nikita Khrushchev had told visiting American governors that he was "available for travel and that he would like very much to visit the United States." When the news conference ended, Eisenhower telephoned Herter, whom he had appointed to succeed Dulles despite his misgivings about Herter's health. "If such an exchange were to come about," he told the new secretary of state, "a meeting in a fairly secluded spot would be desirable." The president spelled out the fairly secluded spot he had in mind in a carefully qualified message to Khrushchev, by way of visiting Soviet First Deputy Premier Frol R. Kozlov. If the foreign ministers meeting opening July 13 in Geneva made enough progress to justify a four-power summit, he said, "a meeting between Khrushchev and me at Camp David, near Washington, at a mutually suitable moment might be arranged." The message was given to Undersecretary of State Robert Murphy, who was to meet Kozlov at planeside as the Soviet official left for Moscow. Somehow, what Eisenhower said he wanted to convey wasn't what Kozlov understood Murphy to say. The president was stunned on July 22 to receive an acceptance from Khrushchev of an apparently unqualified invitation to visit the United States.

"An informal conversation between Khrushchev and me at Camp David, while some progress at the Geneva Conference might still occur, was one thing; an extended trip by Khrushchev around the United States and a personal conference between the two of us, after the foreign ministers had produced nothing, was quite another," he said. He considered canceling the trip, or at the very least canceling the invitation to Camp David, but decided against doing either. "For some reason," he said, "an invitation to Camp David had come to confer a special distinction upon a guest."[33]

Khrushchev's reaction, as recalled in his memoirs, was quite different. "I couldn't for the life of me find out what this Camp David was," he said. He recalled that after the Bolshevik revolution, when the Soviets were making their first contacts with the outside world, they had been invited to a place called the Princess Island where "stray dogs were sent to die." "I was afraid Camp David was the same sort of place, where people who were mistrusted would be kept in quarantine," Khrushchev said. "Not even our embassy in Washington could tell us for certain what Camp David was." He did find out, though, and learned that "far from an insult or act of discrimination . . . it was a great honor for me to be invited to spend a few days at Camp David with Eisenhower."

Dictating his memoirs in his old age, Khrushchev said, "I never told anyone at the time about not knowing what Camp David was. I can laugh about it now, but I'm a little bit ashamed. It shows how ignorant we were in some respects." (This was to change in a few years. When the SALT treaty was signed in 1972, Soviet Foreign Minister Andrei Gromyko gave Henry Kissinger the impression he "would be crushed" if plans for him to spend a night at the camp were dropped.)[34] At the time, after the misapprehensions had been cleared up, *Pravda* told its readers that Camp David "would seem to have been created for fruitful reflections by nature itself."[35] Nevertheless, the Soviets demanded and were granted an opportunity to inspect the camp in advance of the meeting.[36]

Khrushchev arrived in Washington on September 15 for brief talks at the White House, to be followed by a nationwide tour and then a longer meeting with Eisenhower at Camp David. The Soviet leader, plunged from the chill of Moscow into Washington's Indian summer, was pleased when the U.S. president told him that it would be cooler in the Catoctins.[37] Soviet officials resisted suggestions that Khrushchev be given a helicopter tour of the Washington area, but Ike wanted a chance to show his visitor the panorama of the capital and its surroundings from the air. "You know, I'll bet if I ask him personally, without any of his security people around, he'll go," he told Aurand.[38] Ten days later, when Khrushchev returned to the Oval Office, the chopper was waiting on the South Lawn. Eisenhower, ill with a cold, had spent the afternoon resting in the White House residence and returned to the Oval Office about an hour before Khrushchev's arrival.[39] When Ike asked if the Soviet leader would join him in the helicopter, Khrushchev nodded assent.[40] As they flew up the Potomac River, Ike pointed out to his visitor "a big green field where he told me he played golf" — the fashionable Burning Tree Club that had become a symbol of the easygoing lifestyle derided by the president's critics. Eisenhower asked Khrushchev whether he liked the game and told him it was a very healthy sport. The Soviet leader "didn't have the slightest idea what it was all about." Khrushchev was more impressed with the Sikorsky helicopter they were flying in, and asked Eisenhower's help in buying some of them for his government. In his memoirs, he credited the American president with helping clear away U.S. resistance and enabling the Soviets to acquire two of the craft.

"Leaving the city behind, we began to descend over a forest," Khrushchev recalled. It was 5:52 P.M., with dusk fast approaching.[41] "There were cars waiting for us when we landed. We drove past some structures resembling plywood barracks we used to put up for construction workers at building sites."

Outside Aspen, as photographers snapped away, Eisenhower said with a smile, "I am glad they don't shoot." Khrushchev, matching small talk with small talk, replied, "It's lucky Mr. Garst isn't here. He'd have tried to organize the thing in his own way." Two days earlier, when Khrushchev visited an Iowa farm, farmer Roswell Garst had thrown corn husks and silage at a horde of photographers. Said Eisenhower, "Everything seems to be quiet along this front."[42] A few moments later, the dark polished door of the weather-beaten one-story lodge closed behind the two leaders and the stage was set for what would be known, at least for a while, as the Spirit of Camp David. The World War II general and the veteran of provincial Soviet bureaucracy stood for a moment looking out the picture window, with a great bowl of yellow chrysanthemums on a table in front of it. Then they turned into the sun parlor to begin their talks.[43]

On one point at least, there was a measure of agreement. Unlike Macmillan, Khrushchev was an appreciative audience for Eisenhower's favorite form of movie entertainment. "You know, when Stalin was still alive we used to watch Westerns all the time," he said "When the movie ended, Stalin always denounced it for its ideological content. But the very next day we'd be back in the theater watching another Western. I too have a weakness for this sort of film." Eisenhower, more interested in the "fancy tricks" and the horses in the Westerns than their ideological content, said, "Good, we'll have some Westerns and other movies."

12. Presidential Press Secretary Jim Hagerty shakes hands with Soviet leader Nikita Khrushchev *(center)* as an aide helps Eisenhower from his car. Their 1960 meeting forged the short-lived "Spirit of Camp David." *Courtesy Dwight D. Eisenhower Library and the U.S. Navy.*

The Western for that night was chosen from a list that included, once again, *The Big Country,* as well as such classics as *Shane* and *High Noon.* By way of more serious fare, Khrushchev was shown, at his request, a film, dubbed in Russian, of the cruise of the U.S. atomic submarine *Nautilus* under the Polar seas. He also seized the occasion to talk with the U.S. president about Soviet films and later sent him three of them, *The Adventures of Two Cub Bears, Penguins,* and *The Fate of a Man.* Ike said he enjoyed them, particularly the ones about the penguins and the bears. As Khrushchev had slept poorly the night before and Eisenhower had a cold, they both went to bed about midnight.[44]

At breakfast, the shaven-headed Khrushchev, wearing a collarless white embroidered shirt, ate little. Instead, he leaned forward with both elbows on Aspen's medium-size dining table and told stories of his World War II experiences in Stalingrad and Odessa with an intensity that was a precursor of things to come.[45] The morning was foggy, so the helicopters were not flying. Science Adviser George N. Kistiakowsky, due to join the presidential party at 10:00 A.M., was driven up the interstate highway at speeds of up to ninety miles an hour in a White House car. Joining Atomic Energy Commission Chairman John McCone for coffee in the paneled living room of Aspen, Kistiakowsky could hear voices through the sliding partition that led to the glassed-in terrace. Inside, United States and Soviet officials were arranged in a large oval, with the president seated in an easy chair across from Khrushchev. Eisenhower and Khrushchev did most of the talking, neither speaking from notes. Vice President Nixon had joined the group as the meeting got under way at 9:00 A.M., but spoke little. At 10:45 A.M., the partition slid open. Eisenhower and Khrushchev emerged, followed by Herter and Soviet Foreign Minister Andrei Gromyko. They had failed to reach agreement on Berlin.[46]

The American president and his visitor then went for a mile-and-a-half walk, stopping off at Hickory, where they continued their discussion of Berlin while John Halferty, a Navy yeoman second class from Fennimore, Wisconsin, gave Khrushchev his first glimpse of American bowling. Both leaders autographed Halferty's score sheet, showing a 218 game out of a possible 300, but neither threw a ball. Khrushchev seemed more impressed with the bowling alley's new automatic pinsetter.[47]

After the walk, Eisenhower and Khrushchev met privately in the sun room for about half an hour. Eisenhower went to Herter's room to instruct State Department officials to prepare a memorandum summarizing the U.S. position, then returned and asked Khrushchev to join him for a private conversation. From then until 2:15 P.M., the two men sat on hard-backed chairs at a green-covered bridge table in the corner of the terrace, going over the State Department draft. "Because my purpose in these man-to-man talks was to learn more about his intentions, objectives, and personal characteristics, we used a single interpreter only—his own," said Eisenhower. "You've got to see things through the other man's eyes as well as your own," he told Gen. Andrew Goodpaster, the White House staff secretary. That afternoon, he learned quite a bit about how Khrushchev saw things. To Kistiakowsky, watching through the glass partition, it seemed the two leaders were "not raising their voices, but obviously not getting anywhere, judging by their expressions." Indeed they were not; Khrushchev found the State Department draft completely unacceptable.

A lunch of frankfurters, baked beans, and brown bread, originally scheduled for 12:30 at Laurel Lodge, was late. Although helicopter service was being provided on an hourly basis from the Pentagon, foggy weather required guests to drive from Washington instead. The lunch went no better than the meeting at the bridge table. Beginning with pleasantries, the conversation deteriorated rapidly. With all eyes on Khrushchev, the Soviet leader launched into a bitter attack on the U.S. exposition in Moscow that had been the scene of his rancorous "kitchen debate" with Nixon.

The vice president had come close to being left out of the Camp David meeting. Eisenhower had asked him some time before to be in Washington at the time of the Khrushchev talks, and Nixon had canceled plans to dedicate a dam so he could be on hand. His secretary, Rose Woods, told Ann Whitman it would be embarrassing if, after all this, he was not included. Eisenhower told his secretary that the State Department was inviting Nixon for Saturday. At the lunch table, both the vice president and Llewellyn Thompson, the United States ambassador to Moscow, defended the exposition, but Khrushchev said he found it "rather silly" and accompanied his diatribe with personal remarks directed at the vice president. Nixon, attempting to smooth things over, asked Khrushchev whether he preferred using a rifle or a shotgun when hunting birds and big game. Khrushchev curtly replied that Nixon obviously didn't know anything about hunting, since rifles were used for game and shotguns for birds. The Spirit of Camp David was off to a rough start.

Eisenhower tried changing the subject, asking his visitor whether he was free of work while on vacation or was followed by telephones. "Khrushchev again became almost violent, stating that telephones were even installed on the beach when he went swimming, and that he could assure us that soon they in the USSR would have more and better telephones than we have and that we will then cut off our telephones since we are always afraid of comparison." To the Ukrainian-born Kistiakowsky, it seemed that Khrushchev's interpreter, Oleg Troyanovsky, son of a former Soviet ambassador to the United States and graduate of Washington's fashionable Sidwell Friends School, toned down the offensiveness of Khrushchev's remarks without changing their substance. Eisenhower sat red-faced and silent during the tirade.[48]

After lunch, as his doctors insisted, Eisenhower rested for an hour.[49] Within an hour, again with their one interpreter, the president and his guest had climbed into a helicopter. Like any other of Ike's visitors, Khrushchev was in for a tour of Gettysburg. Behind them at the camp they left "a general feeling that the meeting will end in nearly complete failure." At the farm, however, things were looking brighter. By the time they returned to Camp David, Khrushchev had conceded that he would not insist on a time limit for negotiations on Berlin. The presi-

dent said he would regard this as acceptable. Nevertheless, at a 9:00
P.M. briefing in the Gettysburg High School gymnasium, Jim Hagerty
told newsmen that the Berlin situation had not been changed by the
talks.[50]

As always, there was an exchange of presents. Capt. Aurand
brought to the camp as a gift for Khrushchev a model, obtainable in toy
stores, of the *Polaris* nuclear submarine. In their talks the two leaders
turned to real, not toy, weapons in words that foreshadowed
Eisenhower's farewell warning in 1961 against "the acquisition of un-
warranted influence . . . by the military-industrial complex." "They
both agreed that they were getting the same arguments from their re-
spective military advisers," said Goodpaster. "They both held the view
that it should be possible to reduce the level of armaments."

As Khrushchev recalled the conversation, Eisenhower asked him,
"Tell me, Mr. Khrushchev, how do you decide on funds for military
expenditures?" But before Khrushchev could answer, he said, "Perhaps
I should tell you how it is with us . . . It's like this. My military leaders
come to me and say, 'Mr. President, we need such and such a sum for
such and such a program. If we don't get the funds we need, we'll fall
behind the Soviet Union.' So I invariably give in. That's how they wring
money out of me . . . Now tell me, how is it with you?" And
Khrushchev replied, "It's just the same."[51]

New York Times reporter Harrison E. Salisbury was surprised by
"the extent to which General Eisenhower and Mr. Khrushchev took the
course of the talks into their own hands and the amount of time they
spent by themselves." In these talks, Eisenhower said, his visitor "kept
belittling most of our differences and gave every indication of wanting
to find ways to straighten them out through peaceful compromise."
When Khrushchev had Gromyko and other advisers with him, he said,
he became more reserved and would often say he would have to take
matters up with his government before deciding. Alone, the president
told Hagerty, "We were able to have a real bull session." To Ike it
seemed that the Soviet chairman, whose relative openness to the West
had encountered resistance at home, had "much less confidence in himself than Stalin had."[52]

Despite the bull sessions, the trappings of a major international
conference had come to the Catoctins. Except for Eisenhower,
Khrushchev, Herter, and Gromyko, everybody had to have a special
Camp David conference pass, issued at the gate or the Pentagon, to get
in. There was a direct telephone line from the Soviet Embassy to Gromyko's bedroom in Aspen, with a nonringing extension in Khrushchev's

room. Dinner menus were printed in Russian as well as English. Dinner music was selected from a list that ranged from "The Sleeping Beauty Waltz" to "Jeannie with the Light Brown Hair."[53]

On Sunday morning, the president and Goodpaster attended services at the Gettysburg Presbyterian Church, stopping en route to pick up John Eisenhower near a Stuckey's restaurant on Highway 15. Ike asked Khrushchev to come along, but the leader of the officially atheistic Soviet Union said his people would be shocked.[54] While Eisenhower worshiped, the visiting leader and his foreign minister were up early for a walk on a secluded path, alone except for their bodyguards. They could have talked in their cabin, but were taking precautions against being overheard through American listening devices.[55]

After church and the walk, there was more talk of a four-power summit and of a possible Eisenhower visit to the Soviet Union. When Khrushchev said he did not want the communiqué at the end of the meeting to mention his offer to withdraw a deadline for a Soviet-Germany peace treaty, Eisenhower said, "This ends the whole affair and I will go neither to a summit nor to Russia." In the end, they compromised on separate announcements in Washington and Moscow.[56] With the party behind schedule and the weather still not clear enough for helicoptering, the two leaders motored back to Washington at eighty miles an hour.[57]

At a press conference on November 4 in the Executive Office Building in Washington, Eisenhower was asked if there was a "Spirit of Camp David." "I have heard this expression, 'The Spirit of Camp David' and I don't know what it means," he replied. "I think the 'Spirit of Camp David' as they used it, and I must say I have never used it, must simply mean that it looks like we can talk together without being mutually abusive."[58]

As the spring of 1960 unfolded, so did preparations for the summit. Harold Macmillan, back at Camp David on March 28, wrote in his diary, "All the omens are good."[59] But the spirit of hope fostered on the sun porch at Aspen with Khrushchev was not to last.

For Macmillan's March visit, Eisenhower left the choice of movie entertainment up to Aurand. With some trepidation, he picked the Peter Sellers comedy *The Mouse that Roared,* which poked fun at both United States and British officialdom. Eisenhower and Macmillan both seemed to enjoy the show, but in his diary the prime minister noted only that dinner had been "followed by the inevitable film."[60]

On April 30, the movie at Camp David was *April Showers,* a sentimental account of a vaudeville family's rise to Broadway. As the president watched it with family and friends, drama of a different sort was taking shape half a world away. At an airfield in Pakistan, a former Air Force lieutenant, Francis Gary Powers, was preparing to take off for a flight over the Soviet Union in a high-flying reconnaissance aircraft called the U-2. His flight would shatter the Spirit of Camp David and permanently affect Americans' perception of their government. Although the Soviets had known for years of the high altitude overflights, Khrushchev had not raised the issue in his talks with Eisenhower. Thus, the CIA had continued to plan further penetrations even as plans went ahead for the Paris summit.

The next morning, Ike was kept inside by a driving rain. When it stopped, he and friend George Allen hit some golf balls and then walked over to the skeet shooting range.[61] At his home in Alexandria, Virginia, Goodpaster received a telephone call from the Central Intelligence Agency. The U-2 was overdue and was undoubtedly down in Soviet territory. The staff secretary drove to the White House and called the president on a secure telephone line. In the balance of Eisenhower's term, he warned, "the winds will blow." "You're probably right," said Ike.[62]

U.S. officials put out a cover story about an accidental border crossing by a weather research plane. At a meeting of the Supreme Soviet, however, Khrushchev announced that not only had the U-2 crashed in Soviet territory, but Powers had parachuted and was in Soviet hands. After a series of confusing statements, Eisenhower's administration had to concede it had misled the American people. When the leaders arrived in Paris in mid-May Khrushchev thundered, "We caught the American spy like a thief, red-handed."

There would be no summit. Goodpaster's telephone call to Eisenhower at Aspen had spelled an end to good omens.

4

John F. Kennedy
Camelot in the Catoctins

John Fitzgerald Kennedy was only slightly interested when Dwight Eisenhower briefed him on the operations of Camp David on December 6, 1960. The sophisticated, cosmopolitan president-elect and his elegant wife, Jacqueline, were convinced they would not want to spend their weekends in any place that had suited the plebeian tastes of the Eisenhowers. Even before the inauguration, they had rented Glen Ora, a French villa in the Virginia hunt country. "I don't plan to use Camp David very often," the new president said at a February 8 press conference. Aware both of Eisenhower's continuing popularity and his own slender election victory, Kennedy deflected a reporter's suggestion that he might rename the retreat Shangri-La. "I think the name should be kept Camp David," he said. "But I doubt if I will go there very often."[1]

He would go there soon, but not for relaxation. On April 17, 1961, a U.S.-organized paramilitary force of approximately two thousand Cuban refugees landed at the Bay of Pigs in Cuba, where the Marxist administration of Fidel Castro had fallen into increasing disfavor with the United States. Without air cover or reinforcements, the invaders fell easy prey to Cuban troops who burst from a nearby swamp and overran the beach. U.S. intelligence had been faulty, and the debacle spread a stain on the new administration. Kennedy called Eisenhower and asked if the former president would come to the Catoctin retreat for consultation. Eisenhower quickly agreed and flew to the camp by heli-

13. After the Bay of Pigs debacle, President Kennedy talked with Eisenhower on the steps of Aspen. *Courtesy John F. Kennedy Library, photo no. KN 17618.*

copter on April 22. Kennedy, helicoptering to the camp after a National Security Council meeting at the White House, met him at the helipad. It was the first time the new president had seen the place. He and his guest went to the terrace at Aspen to talk. Kennedy did not ask for specific advice and, it seemed to Eisenhower, was not seeking "to find any scapegoat, because the President does seem to take full responsibility for his own decision."

Kennedy aide David Powers, recalling the meeting years later, said, "When I saw them together that day, April 22, 1961, a week after the Bay of Pigs, I was thinking of President Kennedy, the youngest man ever elected at the age of 43, and President Eisenhower, the oldest man up to that time ever elected president of the United States. And as I watched them I was thinking of the advice that President Kennedy was going to receive that day, not from President Eisenhower, from General Eisenhower, the old warrior."

Be that as it may, the youthful new president did not escape rebuke from his predecessor as the two men left Aspen and began strolling around the grounds. It struck Eisenhower, never much impressed with Kennedy, that the new president "looked upon the Presidency as not only a very personal thing, but as an institution that one man could handle with an assistant here and another there." To the former president, his successor seemed "very subdued and more than a little bewildered."

"No one knows how tough this job is until after he has been in it for a few months," said Kennedy.

"Mr. President, if you will forgive me, I think I mentioned that to you three months ago," Ike said.

"I certainly have learned a lot since then."

Kennedy then told Eisenhower he had held back on air cover because he had been advised to keep the U.S. role in the affair from showing. This was too much for the tart-tongued old soldier. "How could you possibly have kept from the world any knowledge that the United States had been assisting the invasion?" Eisenhower snapped. "I believe there is only one thing to do when you get into this kind of thing. It must be a success." Kennedy vowed that any such operations in the future would be. Eisenhower said he was glad to hear it. Ike was there for an hour and forty-four minutes. After he left, Kennedy inspected the bomb shelter his predecessor had installed and then helicoptered to Glen Ora.[2]

In the wake of the Kennedy-Eisenhower meeting, the question of a possible name change for the camp came up again. Reporters had noticed two things. First, the "Camp David" sign was gone and the camp was again designated only as Camp #3. Second, the White House yacht, formerly known as the *Barbara Anne* for Eisenhower's granddaughter, had been renamed the *Honey Fitz* for Kennedy's grandfather. Was a similar change in the works for the Catoctin retreat? No, said Presidential Press Secretary Pierre Salinger, it would remain Camp David.[3]

The president and Mrs. Kennedy continued to make little use of it, however, preferring to spend their weekends at Glen Ora. Kennedy went to Camp David only twice more in the first two years of his presidency, making an overnight visit with Jacqueline on November 12 and 13, 1961, and stopping overnight on his way back to the White House from Philadelphia on July 4, 1962.[4] Then, in the spring of 1963, the Kennedys lost the lease on their Virginia estate. Its owner, Gladys Tartiere, had been reluctant to lease to the president in the first place, not wanting the Secret Service in her house. She agreed for two years only, and now the two years were up. So the Kennedys decided to build a

14. In one of the best-known Camp David photos, the young president and his predecessor walked in the woods. *Courtesy AP/Wide World.*

house of their own near Middleburg, Virginia, and call it Wexford, for the president's ancestral county in Ireland.[5] While it was being built, they weekended at Camp David. Much to their surprise, they liked it. Jacqueline had her horses brought in a van. She was at the camp on June 22 when her husband dropped in for a two-hour visit before taking off for Germany. The president used the three-hole golf course. He had the Navy build a pony ring for his daughter, Caroline, and her

15. Kennedy held his son by the hand as his daughter, Caroline, rode her pony, Macaroni, on a Camp David trail. *Courtesy John F. Kennedy Library, photo no. KN 27612.*

pony, Macaroni. On Sundays, the nation's first Roman Catholic president boarded an electric golf cart and went to Mass in the military mess hall.[6] "If only I'd realized how nice Camp David really is, I'd never have rented Glen Ora, or built Wexford," Mrs. Kennedy told White House head usher J. B. West.

Kennedy visited the camp sixteen times during his last year in office. "He'd . . . have a drink before lunch and talk, and he might take a walk in the afternoon," said journalist and Kennedy friend Charles Bartlett. "And then he'd take a nap and have dinner." Like the FDR of Churchill's description, however, he was overtaken by swiftwinged messengers, so that "by Sunday afternoon, when he was getting ready for that helicopter, why, then the whole thing sort of came back . . . As soon as he got on the helicopter, they'd always hand him a sheaf of papers and he'd be signing and reading papers all the way out."[7]

Concerned about his small children feeling that they had to be constantly guarded by someone carrying a gun, Kennedy had the Secret Service take the place of the Marine guard at Aspen.[8] After the children went to bed, the Kennedys would watch movies. British Ambassador David Ormsby-Gore, an old friend, and his wife were frequent visitors.

16. John F. Kennedy, Jr., climbed into the cockpit of Marine One, the presidential helicopter, in the Camp David hangar. *Courtesy John F. Kennedy Library, photo no. KN 27682.*

So was Secretary of the Navy Paul Fay, a World War II companion in the South Pacific, and his family.

One weekend, Kennedy made a surprise helicopter trip to Antietam Battlefield with his guests, much as Truman had led the press on a tour of Gettysburg. As he toured the battlefield in an open Park Service convertible, followed by nervous Secret Service agents in a White House limousine, tourists watched and snapped pictures.

He had the Navy make home movies, complete with a musical sound track, of Caroline and Fay's daughter riding Macaroni; of his son, John, and the family dog romping with a soccer ball; of Jacqueline Kennedy trying her hand at skeet shooting.[9]

But Kennedy was to see sadly little of FDR's Shangri-La. On November 22, 1963, Kenneth Plummer, Sr., a Chambersburg, Pennsylvania, building contractor who was to do work at Camp David for many years, sensed an air of unrest as he drove up to the gate. A guard gave him the news: "The president's been shot." Unable to get more details, Plummer drove to the camp commander's office. As he and members of the staff watched the news on television, it was confirmed that Kennedy had died at Parkland Hospital in Dallas. "There were a lot of tears being shed," Plummer, an active Methodist layman, said. "I thought it would have been better if we had had somewhere to go, a chapel of some kind."[10] It would take nearly three decades, but the chapel would be built not far from where they sat.

5

Lyndon B. Johnson
Camp David and Vietnam

The times and titles were altered strangely for Clark Clifford when he sat down at Camp David on July 25, 1965, with Lyndon Baines Johnson and Robert Strange McNamara. No longer the inexperienced naval aide who signed passes to Shangri-La, Clifford was a prosperous Washington attorney and one of President Johnson's key advisers outside of government. He would later succeed McNamara as secretary of defense.

What had brought them to the Catoctins was the war in Vietnam, where Eisenhower had sent military advisers to shore up a government threatened by Communist insurgents and Kennedy had authorized the advisers to fight with their units. It was not the first time Southeast Asia had been on a Camp David agenda. At his meeting with Eisenhower after the Bay of Pigs, Kennedy brought up the subject of embattled Laos and Eisenhower urged him to strengthen the defenses of Thailand.

Now Clifford had been summoned to the Catoctins to argue the case he had made in a May 17 letter to the president, arguing that U.S. ground forces in Vietnam should be kept to a minimum to avoid slipping into "a quagmire . . . without a realistic hope of ultimate victory." He did not get a reply to his letter, but did get a last-minute invitation to Camp David. On July 21, at the White House, he and McNamara outlined their deepening differences on Vietnam. On Friday, July 23, White House Press Secretary Bill Moyers, sympathetic to Clifford's point of view but unable to speak out because of his position, telephoned Clifford to tell him the president appeared to be accepting McNamara's arguments for escalation. About the same time, Moyers was telling reporters there were no plans for Johnson to have anyone but a few staff members with him at the presidential retreat that weekend. Just before 7:00 P.M., however, the president called to invite Clifford and his wife, Marny. He said the McNamaras would also be there.

The next morning the Cliffords and McNamaras shared a helicopter flight to Mount Catoctin with Johnson's daughter, Luci, and her husband, Pat Nugent. Vietnam was never mentioned. They spent part of the afternoon playing tennis. McNamara's wife, Margie, took pictures. At dinner with the Johnsons, Clifford found the president more subdued than usual.

Sunday morning, Clifford went over the notes he had prepared. At 5:00 P.M., Johnson asked Clifford and McNamara to join him in Aspen Lodge. They assembled at a rectangular dinner table on the left side of the living room. The president sat with his back to the fireplace. Two of the ever present Filipino stewards served Fresca to Johnson and club soda to Clifford. Others were present — Supreme Court Justice Arthur Goldberg, who was to be sworn in the next day as ambassador to the United Nations; and Jack Valenti and Horace Busby, key members of the White House staff.

But "McNamara held the key," said Clifford. "His formidable intelligence and reputation were the critical variables." Facing such an adversary, the skilled advocate let out all the stops. Fifty-five thousand men would be lost in a stepped-up war in Vietnam, he told the president. It would last five or more years and cost hundreds of billions of dollars. "It will ruin us," he said. "I can't see anything but catastrophe for my country."[1]

Johnson said he shared Clifford's worries, but that "we could not simply walk out" and he would continue to press for negotiations. "The basic issue is not to get thrown out under fire," he said.

The meeting ended and the beautiful summer evening deepened. Johnson, so often oblivious to the glories of his surroundings, drove around Camp David for an hour, then walked around the grounds alone for nine minutes. At dinner with his guests, he did not mention their debate. They returned to Washington late that night. At the White House the next day, Johnson asked Clifford to repeat his presentation. But the die was cast. The president was speaking by now of the number of men to be sent.[2]

Clifford's words were prophetic. On March 31, 1968, buffeted by bad news from the war front and protests at home, Johnson announced he was restricting the bombing of North Vietnam and would not be a candidate for reelection. On April 8 he flew by helicopter to Camp David, relieved "to get away from the noise and carbon monoxide of downtown Washington." After changing into comfortable clothes at Aspen he sat in the living room with National Security Adviser Walt Rostow. After they had talked for some time, preparing for the full-scale meeting Johnson had called for the next day, the weary president dozed off in his chair until dinner. In the morning, the helicopters arrived. Clifford, by now secretary of defense, was there.[3] So was Averell Harriman. Harriman had last been at Camp David when, as Roosevelt's special emissary to Churchill and Stalin, he reported to FDR on the meeting of the two leaders in Moscow, but found him preoccupied with plans for the North African invasion.

Also on hand were Secretary of State Dean Rusk and Ambassador to Vietnam Ellsworth Bunker. The president took the wheel of a convertible and chauffeured his guests to Aspen, where they talked over breakfast and then moved to the sunlit patio, gathering around a glass-topped table. Bunker reported that South Vietnamese President Nguyen Van Thieu had "moved ahead on a great many fronts" and the Vietnamese forces were doing better than the press indicated. If they continued to improve, asked Rusk, would the news coverage improve? "Oh, Lord, I don't know," said the weary Bunker. Clifford concluded that the seventy-four-year-old ambassador, a straight-laced Yankee patrician, "would be a serious problem to those seeking to end the war." In the end, Bunker did prevail, as he and Rusk convinced Johnson that Harriman's authority in forthcoming peace talks should be severely limited. A message went to Vientiane for delivery to Hanoi, suggesting Geneva as a meeting place. The talks were to come to nothing; the war would drag on for five more years and end in capitulation and despair.[4]

Although he preferred his ranch in Texas, Johnson used Camp David twenty-nine times in five years and six months. When he did go to the camp, he was restless. Sometimes he went walking, lunging along trails at his customary hard-to-follow pace.[5] On one visit, a Cabinet member came upon him on the telephone at Aspen talking with a friend in Texas about the returns from local school board elections.[6] In movies, he generally went to sleep. Jogged awake by his wife or daughter, he would ask, "Well, how was it? Did you all like it?"[7] It was also Johnson who first installed a taping device on his phone at Camp David, a forerunner of the system that would contribute to Richard Nixon's downfall.[8]

His first visit to the camp was on a snowy weekend in January 1964, less than two months into his presidency. On Sunday morning, he drove to Catoctin Furnace outside Thurmont to attend Episcopal services at Harriet Chapel. Although he was a member of the Disciples of Christ Church, he had chosen the chapel because the camp commander was a parishioner. "I am sorry I did not have the get-up-and-get to go with him," Lady Bird Johnson, an Episcopalian, wrote in her diary. Instead, she and Margie McNamara walked in the twelve-degree weather "with every breath blowing out in front of us like a banner." In the woods of Camp David, Mrs. Johnson found "an insulation that keeps you from being terribly worried about what's going on in the outside world." But, as always, the outside world intruded. There were frequent telephone calls to the Catoctins from Washington about the crisis in Panama, where anti-American rioting had just ended with twenty Panamanians dead, four American soldiers killed, and many wounded.

Democratic Sen. Richard Russell of Georgia, then the chairman of the Senate Armed Services Committee, arrived about 11:00 A.M. Like Roosevelt's undersecretary of war, Russell was inspired by the location to rehash the battle of Antietam. After a late lunch, a nap and a little bowling, Mrs. Johnson turned on the television to watch an interview filmed the previous week with journalist Nancy Dickerson and found herself looking "old . . . frenetic . . . tired and . . . unprepared."

The trip to the bowling alley at Hickory that day was Johnson's first taste of the sport. The president threw himself into it with his customary energy, stepping forward to send the ball hurtling down the alley after first watching his guests bowl a few frames. He downed seven pins. A friend congratulated him on his initial effort, but it was not good enough for Lyndon Johnson. He quickly threw a ten-pin strike, and on his few subsequent visits was not satisfied with less.[9]

That same month, Johnson received a recommendation from his staff that the camp be renamed Shangri-La on Jan. 30, President Roosevelt's birthday. "I think we had better not do this at this time," he replied.

He did not again visit the camp for more than a year. By July 8, National Security Adviser McGeorge Bundy, after spending a weekend there with his family, was writing the president,

> It is absurd, of course, to think of keeping Camp David open simply for the convenience of an occasional staff officer, and if you are sure you are not going to use it in the immediate future there can be no

17. President Lyndon B. Johnson at the glass-topped table on the Aspen patio, where a crucial meeting on Vietnam policy was held on April 9, 1968. *Courtesy Lyndon Baines Johnson Library.*

argument against a temporary closing. But for the longer pull I do think this is a place we ought not to give up without some thought . . . I feel confident that there are many conferences and meetings which could properly and wisely be held there with just a little encouragement. But most of all, I have a feeling that the Johnsons would like the place if they gave it another try at some auspicious moment.[10]

18. Inside the lodge on April 9, 1968, Johnson glowers at his ambassador to Vietnam, Ellsworth Bunker. *Courtesy Lyndon Baines Johnson Library.*

The suggestion had limited effect. Johnson wrote to Dwight Eisenhower at Gettysburg that he and Mrs. Johnson could make "only an occasional weekend visit" to the camp but he knew it had "a special meaning" for Eisenhower. They would be pleased to have the Eisenhowers make use of the retreat any time.[11] The invitation was never acted on.

When an Arizona constituent of Sen. Carl Hayden wrote for information about Camp David, presidential aide Mike Manatos sent word that the camp was "maintained primarily as a site for important government conferences." He said that a small military cadre stationed there full time was reinforced with "a few additional personnel" when the president was there. The few consisted of a military aide, a doctor, a medical corpsman, helicopter crews numbering eight to twelve, eight or nine stewards, twenty-eight Marines, eight to ten White House communications workers, and eight to twelve Secret Service agents; altogether, sixty-three to seventy-four additional personnel.[12]

As the 1968 congressional elections approached, members of the

Senate Democratic Campaign Committee were looking for a place to hold a retreat for Democrats up for reelection. The name of Camp David came up and Sen. Edmund Muskie, the committee chairman, asked if it might be available. Johnson said no. Manatos, the president's administrative assistant, suggested an outing to the camp for Democratic senators and their wives.[13] Nothing came of it.

In the spring of 1965, Johnson introduced his beagles, Blanco and Him, to the camp. On the first weekend in April, as he met in Aspen with Canadian Prime Minister Lester Pearson, discussing nettlesome differences over Vietnam and other matters, the dogs ran in the woods, chased chipmunks, and barked at sentries. Alighting from the helicopter on the White House lawn that night, the thirty-sixth president asked, "Where do I get a job as a dog?" At the camp again on April 24, he reported that Him "had a big time." On May 8, he was upset because Him was at the veterinarian's and he couldn't take him to the camp. The next weekend, he not only took Him to the camp but took the dog to Berryville, Virginia, to attend a party for Sen. Harry Byrd. Blanco, the more troublesome of the two dogs, was sent back to the White House in a Secret Service car. Agents at Camp David reported they had trouble running Blanco down, and some were afraid of being bitten. On June 20, the feisty dog had a narrow escape. As the beagle patrolled the camp chasing chipmunks and squirrels, a Marine on patrol shouted, "Halt, who goes there?" and heard no reply. Just as the Marine was about to shoot, the dog barked.[14]

Johnson was at Camp David in April, 1965, when he got the first word of the Dominican Republic crisis that he would deal with by dispatching United States Marines. He had flown back to Washington and transferred to the Catoctin helicopter shuttle on Saturday, April 24, after crowning his daughter Luci as queen of the Azalea Festival in Norfolk, Virginia. Arriving at Aspen, he found that Thomas Mann, recently promoted to undersecretary of state from assistant secretary for Inter-American affairs, was trying to reach him. Within an hour he had returned the call and been told troubling news from the U.S. Embassy in Santo Domingo. Army officers had risen in a coup against the Dominican government. Crowds were in the street. On Sunday, Johnson kept in touch by telephone with Rusk and McNamara in the White House Situation Room and ordered ships of the Atlantic Fleet to steam toward Santo Domingo. He had already summoned key advisers to fly to the retreat by helicopter that afternoon to discuss Vietnam. Quickly, he added the Dominican Republic to the agenda. Even Lyndon Johnson could not command the weather in the Catoctins, however. Fog on the mountaintop ruled out helicopter landings and the president had to motorcade to Thurmont and then board his own helicopter for the return flight to Washington.[15]

On July 17, 1965, Rev. Billy Graham conducted a religious service at Hickory for the Johnsons, their guests, and Navy families. After church, the Johnsons joined Deputy Attorney General Nicholas de B. Katzenbach and novelist John Steinbeck and their wives on the grass around the pool. Conversation ranged over Russia, books and what to do about crime in the District of Columbia. That afternoon there was another trip to the bowling alley, where Mrs. Johnson urged television newsman John Chancellor to consider seriously the president's offer to become head of the U.S. Information Agency. He said he would but in the end he declined. Mrs. Johnson thought Chancellor the best bowler in the group except for the president.

Steinbeck found Camp David "very beautiful, a kind of large camp in a deep oak forest on top of a mountain, cool and sunny and wonderful."[16]

Back at the White House, Johnson startled Washington by naming Justice Goldberg to succeed Adlai E. Stevenson as ambassador to the United Nations. Goldberg hated to leave the court, but with Stevenson's death, Johnson badly needed a prestigious figure at the United Nations. Goldberg reluctantly agreed, and that weekend Johnson invited him and his wife to Camp David to ease the shock. Press Secretary Moyers said the president expected to return to Washington Sunday night or early Monday.[17] Actually, he stayed all day Monday, listening to Clifford and McNamara debate over Vietnam.

Returning to the White House at midnight, Johnson groused to daughter Lynda, who had arrived an hour earlier from a western camping trip, that they could have stayed at the camp longer if she had agreed to go with them.[18] It was not the first time Lynda's parents had expressed a desire to have her with them at the camp. During the early visit in January 1964, Mrs. Johnson telephoned her daughter about Senator Russell's Civil War history lecture and told her, "Honey, that is one of the reasons I want you up here . . . I want you to listen to these people I listen to."[19] Two decades later, it was Lynda who said, "Daddy didn't use Camp David as much as I would have liked." Both Lynda and her younger sister Luci used the camp to entertain their own friends. Lynda often drove to Harriet Chapel, remaining after the Easter service on March 26, 1967, to distribute flowers to the Sunday school children.[20] Luci, who had converted to Roman Catholicism with her marriage to Pat Nugent, attended Mass at the camp.[21]

On May 21, 1966, fire broke out aboard a helicopter as it was preparing to leave the White House lawn for Camp David with "four dogs and some people" aboard, as Traphes Bryant, the presidential kennel keeper, reported. The people turned the dogs loose, got off, and caught another helicopter. There was worse to come for the presidential dogs. On June 15, a driver for Luci ran over Him as the dog chased a squirrel near the Southwest Gate of the White House. "My God, what a day!" wrote Bryant. "Poor Him is dead." Furthermore, an agent returning from Camp David reported that "the way Blanco roams around there, it will be a miracle if he doesn't end up shot by the military guards."

But there were other hazards on the table at Camp David. On October 1, Johnson summoned his senior advisers to the Catoctin retreat in the wake of talks between Secretary of State Rusk and Soviet Foreign Minister Gromyko in New York about efforts to stem the spread of nuclear weapons. The talks, after dinner in Aspen, convinced him that the Soviet Union was sincere in such efforts but would nevertheless use the negotiations to sow discord in the NATO alliance. The next morning, walking through the blazing autumn woods, the president and his advisers agreed the talks should proceed cautiously and in consultation with U.S. allies.[22]

There were the usual foreign visitors to be entertained. On June 17, 1967, Australian Prime Minister Harold Holt and his wife were weekend guests and accompanied the Johnsons to Harriet Chapel, staying long enough afterward to join them in chatting with the congregation and playing with the children. The two leaders toured the camp in a golf cart, showed each other home movies and discussed the Vietnam war. During that visit, the president loaned the prime minister a pair of swimming trunks. Unfortunately, Johnson wore a larger size than Holt and the prime minister's borrowed trunks came undone on his first dive into the pool.

The Johnson-Holt meeting was to have been held at the Texas ranch, but Johnson wanted to stay close to Washington because Soviet Premier Alexei Kosygin was in New York and he hoped to meet with him. There was to be no Kosygin visit to Camp David, however.[23]

During Pearson's visit in 1965, the Canadian joined LBJ in a press conference on the lower patio of Aspen and said they had discussed "the state of the world, which isn't as happy in some places as it should be." Pearson had suggested a pause in the U.S. bombing of North Vietnam, which Johnson opposed, but the two papered over their differences. "There's something about Camp David that makes you feel

19. Johnson, who riled dog lovers by being photographed picking up one of his beagles by the ears, sailed into visiting Canadian Prime Minister Lester Pearson in April 1965 over their differences on Vietnam. *Courtesy* Toronto Star.

softer," said Johnson aide Jack Valenti. Nevertheless, on Pearson's return to Ottawa, the *Toronto Star* ran a cartoon of LBJ picking him up by the scruff of the neck while a bandaged beagle said, "Lucky it wasn't his ears."[24] A photograph of the President lifting one of his pets by its ears had enraged dog lovers.

Global negotiations at Camp David became a problem for the telephone companies. On July 30, 1968, A. L. Simpson, general staff supervisor for the Chesapeake and Potomac, wrote to his boss that he was worried about being able to provide the needed facilities. "Almost without exception we receive less than 24 hours notice," Simpson said. "Provision of the minimum additional services under such conditions has been extremely costly." Just that April, he said, some 150 correspondents had been on hand to report the expected momentous news of a peace conference. Even providing minimum communication facilities within their time limit was touch and go, he said. At Simpson's recommendation, twenty-five long distance loops from Camp David and Thurmont to Frederick, as well as other facilities, were added. During World War II, the telephone service that brought FDR his "newspaper" at Shangri-La consisted of two private lines overseen by White House operator Louise Hackmeister in a cabin dubbed "One Moment Please." Now, Camp David communications were being readied for major conferences to come.

One of the Johnsons' last trips to Camp David was on the afternoon of October 24, 1968, less than two weeks before the election of Richard Nixon. It was, said Mrs. Johnson, "a gray and cheerless autumn day. But the flight had been beautiful, and we had looked down on the Catoctin Mountains — a magnificent show of gold and bronze and green, and every now and then the scarlet of maples. To me Camp David is more a psychological journey than a physical one. I leave my troubles outside the gate."[25]

A week before Nixon's inauguration, on his last Camp David weekend, Johnson took care of a long-pending piece of business. Shortly after Robert F. Kennedy's assassination in 1968, the president was asked to approve a small appropriation, less than $500,000, for a permanent gravesite near President Kennedy's in Arlington National Cemetery. Johnson, who had feuded bitterly with Robert Kennedy when he was alive, refused to put the money into the budget despite pleas by Clifford, McNamara, and others. But on Jan. 12, 1969, in his study in Aspen, he ordered the Bureau of the Budget to request $431,000 for the final resting place for the man he had so often denounced as an upstart.[26]

6

Richard Nixon
Refuge from Watergate

In the Eden that Eisenhower had renamed from Shangri-La, Richard Nixon saw a snake. Pat Nixon saw the serpent first. She and old friend Ruth Buchanan spotted the creature curling up in the sun a few feet from their chaise longues as they relaxed on the flagstone terrace of Aspen Lodge. Vice President Nixon had come to the Catoctin retreat to work on the acceptance speech that would launch his first campaign as the Republican nominee for president. Mrs. Buchanan suggested that they tell their husbands about the snake. Nixon and Wiley Buchanan, the wealthy Texan serving as chief of protocol in the Eisenhower administration, excitedly summoned Marine guards to carry the intruder off in a truck. Most likely it was a black rat snake, an ominous looking but harmless variety common in the vicinity.

Menaces other than snakes in Paradise were on Nixon's mind on that Sunday, July 2, 1960. "Dick really is worried about K (John F. Kennedy) winning the Democratic nomination," Ruth Buchanan wrote in her diary. "He's sure that's who he'll have to beat and he doesn't feel too easy about it." He had reason for uneasiness. He would not visit Camp David again until, after eight years in the political wilderness, he returned in triumph after his election in 1968.

Some time in the interim, the "Camp David" sign had come down. Driving into the camp with her mother and father in the presidential limousine after the inauguration, Nixon's daughter Julie saw only a large, rustic wooden sign that said, "Camp #3." Nixon asked if the old sign could be found, and by sundown the name Eisenhower had given the camp was again hoisted at the gate.[1] The old general was not to visit there again, though. On March 28, 1969, two weeks after his third heart attack, he died at Walter Reed Army Hospital in Washington at the age of seventy-eight. Nixon decided to go to the Catoctin retreat to work on the eulogy he was to deliver, by Eisenhower's wish, as the former president lay in state at the Capitol. Pat Nixon was against going to Camp David at such a time. Mamie Eisenhower, however, visiting with Julie at the White House, told Nixon in a telephone conversation that she was glad he was making use of the retreat her husband had come to enjoy so much. Ill with a bronchial infection, Nixon was in and out of bed for much of the weekend. By the fire in Aspen, he told speechwriter Raymond Price, "Everybody loved Ike. But the reverse of that was that Ike loved everybody. In politics, the normal reactions are to have strong hatreds one way or the other. But Ike didn't fit that format. There were many who disagreed with him, but nobody hated him. And the reason was that Ike didn't hate anybody. He was *puzzled* by that sort of thing."[2]

Much that might have been puzzling to Dwight Eisenhower lay ahead, but the immediate task was to shape the new administration and its image. Chief of Staff H. R. Haldeman arranged for Jeb Stuart Magruder, the former merchandising manager he had chosen as deputy communications director, to meet at Camp David with Henry Kissinger, then the president's national security adviser, and John Ehrlichman, who was emerging as chief adviser on domestic affairs. "We felt we faced special problems in selling the Nixon program," said Magruder. "Our man lacked the warmth of an Eisenhower, the charisma of a Kennedy, or the flamboyance of a Johnson. He wasn't supporting the sort of domestic programs that had immediate popular appeal. So, as Haldeman and I stressed to Ehrlichman and Kissinger, we would have to work for everything we got."[3]

Haldeman's concern for the presidential image extended to Camp David itself, secluded from the public gaze though it was. He told White House aides that the retreat wasn't "presidential" enough.[4] And in a four-page memo of April 21, 1969 — "more Haldeman nit-picking, I'm afraid" — he took up the subject of movies. "If we are going to the trouble of providing the service of movies at Laurel, and especially at Aspen, we should do it right," he told Col. Don Hughes, then head of the military office. The selection of films available for the previous weekend, he said, had for the most part ranged from "poor" to "pretty good." Eventually, Mrs. Nixon had selected the highly praised *Dr. Zhivago*. But the trouble had not ended. Because the projector was aimed off to the side, one edge of the picture ran on a curtain all night instead of on the screen. Switching from one projector to another after each reel caused the size of the picture to fluctuate, "which is, to say the least, somewhat disconcerting." The focusing and volume were bad. The film had to be stopped and restarted because the picture was jumping up and down on the screen. The chief of staff suggested bolting the projectors down, locking the picture size in with a set screw and sending some members of the permanent Camp David crew to projectionist school. "Movie theaters throughout America manage to project the films night after night without this kind of problem, and there is no reason why it can't be done at Camp David," he told Hughes. The situation did not immediately get any better. On May 23, as Haldeman watched *A Man for All Seasons* with the Nixons, a "panic-stricken" projectionist "screwed up again, with the topper of getting the reels in the wrong order."

Other changes were afoot. The original swimming pool, dating to the FDR era, was inconveniently located in a service area and had been little used by previous presidents. Nixon wanted a pool near the stone sun terrace outside Aspen. "He would like a small pool with rocks built in around it and perhaps a little island in the middle of it," Haldeman wrote. A week later, he reminded Hughes that the president "is pushing very hard on the pool at Camp David" and "is anxious that you bring in someone who really knows how to build swimming pools." Nixon had changed his mind about the location and wanted it "right in the natural oval that is there in front of the main terrace and the rock garden which would be just to the left as you came down the steps."[5] This location, however, was right over the bomb shelter. No one wanted to say, "Mr. President, you can't do that," Bill Gulley, then an aide in the White House military office and later its director, recalled.[6]

Building contractor Kenneth Plummer found the proceedings "a little unusual. Evidently they were being pushed to do it in a hurry, because instead of the Navy designing it, as the Navy designs 99 percent of the work up there, they asked me if I could get a design for them, so we submitted a design to them, and a price on it. We wanted to make sure we used the same stone that Aspen has around it, which is a native stone that is found in a quarry on the Park Service land. And so the Park Service gave us permission to open the quarry up again and quarry enough stone to build the dressing room there and the walls around the pool."[7]

The pool and other improvements to Aspen cost $238,583, not counting $261,417 for reinforcement of the underground shelter—a total more than twenty-five times the original cost of Shangri-La. By August 1970, Haldeman was telling Camp Commander J. L. Dettbarn that the long cords on the telephones by the pool were "extremely helpful so that people can get a phone by them when they are spending a lot of time on a number of calls." At the same time, he said it would be helpful to have a big outdoor clock and a supply of towels. White House aide Larry Higby, who routinely passed along Haldeman's wishes, asked Hughes to make it standard summertime practice to have the pool furniture set up by the pool. The president personally took an interest in the camp menu, telling Haldeman that the steaks served were too large and a great deal of meat was being left on people's plates. Orders went out to serve smaller portions.[8]

While Nixon and his aides fussed over movies, poolside furniture and cuts of meat, Vietnam was high on the still-young administration's agenda. The war continued to spread, spawning protests on college campuses, and elsewhere in the United States, throughout 1969. In October, Press Secretary Ron Ziegler announced that Nixon would make a major address on Vietnam on November 3. The president went to Camp David on October 24 to begin drafting on his customary yellow legal tablet. By the end of a week at Camp David and the White House, the speech had gone through twelve drafts.

Late the next Friday night, back in Aspen, Nixon read a memorandum from Senator Mike Mansfield of Montana, Johnson's successor as majority leader, saying, "The continuance of the war in Vietnam, in my judgment, endangers the future of this nation." About 4:00 A.M., he wrote the passage for which the speech would be remembered, calling for the support of "the great silent majority of Americans" for his policies. Then he went to bed. Unable to sleep, he got up and worked until 8:00 A.M. That afternoon, sounding relaxed, he telephoned Haldeman and told him the "baby's been born." In his memoirs, Nixon called the speech "a milestone and a turning point for my administration," but said he was "under no illusions that this wave of Silent Majority support could be maintained for very long."[9]

Meanwhile a new communist offensive in Cambodia posed the danger that Vietnam could be threatened from the west as well as the north. On Friday, April 25, 1970, Nixon canceled a National Security Council meeting on the issue and went to Camp David for the weekend. On Saturday, he asked Kissinger to join him by helicopter. As the president swam in the new pool and the national security adviser walked along the edge, Nixon told him he had reached a decision: he would order American troops into Cambodia. The decision touched off a new wave of campus unrest and peace remained elusive.

Two years later, Kissinger was still continuing his fruitless shuttle diplomacy with North Vietnam's Le Duc Tho. On May 2, 1972, he broke off the Paris talks and returned to Washington. On Friday, May 5, Nixon helicoptered to Camp David with Julie and told her he had decided to bomb military targets in Hanoi and mine Haiphong harbor. She "seemed concerned about it in terms of whether it would work." Tricia and her husband, Ed Cox, joined them that evening and Nixon told Tricia the next day. His older daughter's reaction "was immediately positive." Friday night, the president watched a Bob Hope movie with his family, then went to Birch, where he dictated the first draft of a speech announcing the mining and bombing. When he returned to Aspen, he saw the light on in his wife's room and went in. "Don't worry about anything," Pat Nixon told her husband. His announcement, however, set off a new firestorm in Congress and the war continued to go badly.

On August 19 at Camp David, Kissinger told Nixon that the North Vietnamese had not yet accepted a proposed settlement, and South Vietnam's President Thieu was intractable. The president took notes, asked questions, but made no decisions. The bombings and the negotiations were to continue. Just after midnight on Sunday, October 22, Nixon received a cable from Kissinger that was telephoned to him at Aspen as he was getting ready for bed. "We have just finished two-hour meeting with Thieu that was tense and highly emotional," Kissinger said. "However, I think we finally made a breakthrough and can keep to the original schedule with his support." Kissinger told reporters, "Peace is at hand." Again, however, the agreement broke down.[10]

On the snowy, cold night of December 6, while Nixon swam in his superheated pool outside Aspen, Haldeman showed Ehrlichman a cable from Kissinger suggesting that the president go on television to explain why the talks were being broken off. Ehrlichman opposed the idea: "The president should explain successes. The staff explains failures." As Ehrlichman watched clouds of steam rise from the pool, Nixon came in from the terrace in a bulky terry cloth robe, drying his hair as he exploded, "That damn 'Peace is at hand'!" Kissinger, he said, had weakened himself by his press conference statement. "I'm telling Henry to finesse," he told Ehrlichman as he handed Col. Richard Kennedy, one of Kissinger's aides, a typed draft and dictabelt containing presidential instructions. Looking into the fire after Kennedy left, he said, "There

20. President Richard Nixon looks out at what aide John Ehrlichman described as the "fenced-in snow" of Camp David. *Courtesy National Archives Nixon Project.*

are no good choices, you know. But, by God, we won't let them humiliate us."[11]

On December 31, aide Charles Colson read to Nixon, over the telephone from Washington, a column by James Reston of the *New York Times* suggesting that Kissinger had opposed the bombing and had only reluctantly gone along with it. "You tell Henry he's to talk to no one, period! I mean no one," the president said, slamming down the telephone in Aspen. He was so upset, it seemed to valet Manolo Sanchez, that he did not even enjoy watching the Washington Redskins beat the Dallas Cowboys, 26 to 3, in that evening's televised championship football game.[12] A few minutes before midnight on New Year's Eve, however, Nixon wrote in his diary that "while the end of the year was somewhat marred by the need to bomb Hanoi-Haiphong, that decision, I think, can make the next four years much more successful than they otherwise might have been." After continued jockeying, the last Americans left Vietnam in 1975. In 1976, the country was reunited as the Socialist Republic of Vietnam, with its capital in Hanoi.

Like Eisenhower reflecting shock at unsightly freeway construction as he drove toward Camp David, Nixon could not keep the business of government out of his mind as he moved back and forth to the mountain retreat. Looking down on the CIA headquarters in Langley while his helicopter turned to or from the White House, he noted the size of the building and the number of cars parked around it. When he appointed James R. Schlesinger as director, he reportedly told him to "clear it up and clean it out."[13]

Nixon outlined his domestic agenda in the two years leading up to the 1972 presidential election in a telephone call to Ehrlichman from Camp David in November, 1970, calling for steps dealing with the interests of labor, youth, and Catholics. Of Jews, he said, "We won't get many, but don't write them off. We'll get most of the intelligent ones." He knew he had only "a small chance of a breakthrough with the Negroes," but urged, "Continue to pay attention to them. Do what is right."[14]

In June, Tricia and Ed Cox honeymooned at Camp David, with the president joining them there on June 24. Cox, a young New York lawyer, had come into Nixon's study in Aspen on Thanksgiving weekend and formally asked permission to marry his daughter.[15]

The economic news was grim, and there were increasing demands for action. Then, in the second week of August, the British ambassador asked the Treasury Department to convert $3 billion into gold. A crisis was at hand. Granting the request might create similar demands, and the United States might not be able to meet them. On Thursday, August 12, William Safire received a telephone call from Larry Higby asking him to be available for the weekend. The next day Higby called again. Safire was to take a car to the helipad in Anacostia, the staff takeoff point for Camp David, but not to tell his wife or secretary where he was going. Similar calls were going out all over town. Secretary of the Treasury John Connally was called back from a weekend in Texas. All in all, fifteen economic experts, as well as speechwriter Safire and other White House aides, were summoned. As the sessions began in the Aspen living room, Nixon told the group sternly, "One of the reasons we are holding this meeting at Camp David is for security. There are to be made no calls out of here . . . between now and Monday night, when we announce our decisions, everyone here is to button his lip."

The group quickly agreed on a ninety-day freeze on wages and prices, reinstatement of an investment tax credit, and the removal of the excise tax on automobiles. A touchier point was the proposal made by Connally and Budget Director George Shultz to close the "gold window"—the willingness of the United States Treasury to exchange gold for dollars at a fixed price of $35 an ounce, in effect making the dollar

the standard for other currencies. After four hours, most of the participants were dismissed. Nixon, unsmiling through most of the session,
met for an additional hour with a smaller group that included Connally
and Shultz. Undersecretary of the Treasury Paul Volcker then told Safire to write a speech on the assumption that the gold window would be
closed. Nixon had decided to let the dollar float.

The next question was when to make the announcement. Federal
Reserve Board Chairman Arthur Burns suggested Sunday night instead
of Monday. Nixon feared Sunday would create a crisis atmosphere and
was reluctant to antagonize television viewers by preempting the popular *Bonanza*. Retiring to his own cabin, Old Birch, Safire wrote most of
the night, walking across the road at 7:00 A.M. to Witch Hazel, the
cabin where Rose Mary Woods, the president's secretary, stayed. To his
surprise, she was vigorously typing. "Is there another speechwriter
here?" Safire asked. She nodded and pointed to Aspen Lodge. Nixon
had arisen at 3:15 A.M., made notes on both sides of three sheets of
paper, and dictated a draft into a recording machine. "At five forty-five,
he put on a robe and walked out of Aspen into the swimming pool area
holding the dictation tape in his hand, startling a Navy chief who was
surreptitiously taking a dip in the Boss's pool. The president said good
morning and asked the panic-stricken chief to take the tape over to
Rose Woods' cabin and leave it inside the screen door." Nixon had
changed his mind about the timing, sending word through Haldeman,
"Sunday, not Monday." He wanted the news out before the financial
markets opened for the week.[16]

In the short run, the package as a whole seemed to work. But after
controls came to an end in 1974, the economy went into a recession.
The decisions at Camp David would come home to roost in the administration of Gerald Ford.

By the summer of 1972, the reelection campaign had taken center
stage. At an hour-and-forty-five-minute Cabinet meeting at the Catoctin
retreat on August 8, Deputy Campaign Director Frederick Malek
warned that the effort being mounted by Democratic nominee George
McGovern posed a serious threat.[17] Three days later, meeting with the
president at Aspen, former Michigan Governor George Romney submitted his resignation as secretary of housing and urban development, saying his views on the crisis confronting the nation's cities were being
ignored.[18] Two days before the GOP convention was to open in Miami
on August 21, Nixon helicoptered to Camp David to finish his acceptance speech. Walking with Kissinger on a camp trail at night, he
stumbled and splintered a bone in his foot. For months, he was both-
ered by a limp.

On a clear blue day in early September, with the formality of his renomination behind him, the president lay on his back in the pool at Aspen and looked up at the leaves. "I expect the situation to get rougher in the next week and throughout," he wrote in his diary.[19] About this time, Safire, arguing that the president should be seen at work at the White House and not on a mountaintop, suggested to appointments secretary Dwight Chapin that Nixon should spend less time at Camp David during the campaign. "Do you want to be the one who tells the president he can't go to Camp David?" Chapin asked the speech writer. "Because it sure as hell isn't going to be me."[20]

After his overwhelming reelection, Nixon abandoned all reluctance to make use of the camp openly, beginning a pattern in which he would disappear behind its fences for days and even weeks at a time. "I find that up there on top of a mountain, it is easier for me to get on top of the job," he told reporters. Recalling words of his Whittier College football coach, he reflected that after a few days at the camp he felt ready to "hunt bear with a switch."[21] One of his first tasks was to reorganize the executive branch, shaking up personnel and using his executive powers to make structural changes he had tried in vain to get Congress to put into law. The job would keep him and his top aides preoccupied for weeks in a setting Ehrlichman described as "the fenced-in snow" of Camp David.[22]

Seated at a meeting in the Aspen living room on November 14, wearing a black checked jacket, open blue shirt, and bell-bottomed purple trousers, Nixon outlined a plan calling for four "super-Cabinet" officers based at the White House, supervising a broad range of government activities.[23] First, however, there were the personnel changes to be made. While secretaries and heads of agencies paraded to the camp, Ziegler briefed reporters in a trailer set up at the guarded gate. He gave little information.[24]

Colson was the first aide summoned to the camp. Over a before-dinner drink in an alcove off the Aspen living room, he told Nixon he wanted to return to law practice, although he had indicated earlier that he wanted to remain. Nixon first asked him to stay on as counselor, then said that maybe he could do more good on the outside. After dinner, they agreed he would stay for a few months. Colson was "gripped by this sort of sensation that all of a sudden the Presidency has changed . . . that the Presidency is now in exile up at Camp David." As on all his trips to Camp David, he said, he had "bad vibrations."[25]

At Aspen, the name of George Bush, then ambassador to the United Nations, came up for deputy secretary of the treasury, secretary of the interior, ambassador to NATO, and head of the Arms Control and Disarmament Agency. Rogers Morton, then secretary of commerce, was decided upon for the interior post. Romney was to be offered nothing. In the end, when Bush was called at the United Nations on November 17 and told to come to Camp David, he was asked to be Republican national chairman, replacing Kansas Sen. Bob Dole. Bush said taking the job would kill his political prospects in his home state of Texas. But, he told Nixon, "I'll do what you tell me. I'm not all that enthralled, but I'll do it." Dole, also summoned to the camp, told Nixon, "If I came up here for the hanging, I at least want to say a word in my own defense." To avoid political damage in Kansas, he wanted to avoid the impression that he was being fired. Consulting during a weekend sleet storm, aides worked out a deal. Bush would stay at the United Nations through the General Assembly session and Dole would remain at the Republican National Committee through its January meeting.[26]

Robert Bork, a Yale University law professor later to be an appeals court judge nominated for the Supreme Court by President Reagan and rejected by the Senate, was tabbed for the post of solicitor general. "Wears a beard!" said Ehrlichman's notes. Nixon, talking with Bork about the post, "gave me a discussion, quite lengthy, about what he viewed as the proper function of a judge and what judges shouldn't do. And it was pretty good. I mean, you know, I thought some professors I knew could do better, but I think for a busy president to sit down at Camp David, it was a damn good talk."[27] Only a few months later, Bork would be thrust into the center of the Watergate maelstrom when it fell to him to fire Special Prosecutor Archibald Cox while Bush battled to stave off political damage at the party headquarters.

The future of Spiro Agnew was also on the agenda as the reelected president sat in the corner of his den at Aspen on a rainy day, with clouds hanging low on the hilltop like fog and steam rising from the pool outside the windows at his back. "He's the first question we have," Nixon said. "I'm not sure he's the one to succeed me in 1976 — but we may be stuck with him. He wants it, but we will not help him."[28]

As Nixon spoke, events were under way that would prove the former Maryland governor's undoing. That fall, the U.S. attorney in Baltimore had begun an investigation of shakedowns and bribes from Maryland contractors. Grand jury testimony implicated Agnew. On July 31, 1973, Agnew's attorney was notified that the vice president was under investigation. On August 6, as Agnew sought a meeting with Nixon, the president, reportedly "floored by the news," flew to Camp David. Agnew and his chief of staff, Art Sohmer, stood by in the vice president's suite of offices expecting a telephone call summoning them to the mountaintop. At about 9:00 P.M., Sohmer stepped into the vice president's office and said that the *Wall Street Journal* would publish the story the next morning. "There's something else," Sohmer said. "We are not going to Camp David. The president is sending Bryce Harlow here to see you — tonight." Harlow, the chief White House lobbyist, arrived about fifteen minutes later; Alexander Haig was with him. The president's chief of staff told the vice president that Nixon wanted him to resign.[29] Agnew resisted, but on October 10, as the grand jury investigation continued, he submitted his resignation and pleaded no contest to a felony charge of income tax evasion. He was fined $10,000 and placed on three years' probation. At dawn on October 12 at Camp David, Nixon chose his new vice president. His choice was Gerald Ford.[30]

Meanwhile there were the visitors from abroad to entertain at the Catoctin retreat — Prime Minister Gorton of Australia; President and Mrs. Pompidou of France; Yugoslavia's Tito and his wife; President Echeverria of Mexico.[31] To Nikita Khrushchev, reading or hearing of them in his forced retirement, they brought back memories of "the presidential dacha where I met with Eisenhower."[32] In July, 1970, Britain's Prince Charles and Princess Anne were guests for an evening of bicycling, skeet shooting, and swimming followed by hamburgers and steaks on the Aspen terrace, with banana splits for dessert.[33] In February, 1973, Nixon invited British Prime Minister Edward Heath to Camp David on the second day of a Washington visit. On the way, their helicopter had to land at Catoctin High School in Thurmont because a heavy fog had enveloped the mountains, and they went the rest of the way by motorcade. Nixon, no better at small talk than the diffident Heath, told Henry Kissinger that the trip in the back seat of the presidential limousine was "tough going." Once on the mountaintop, things got only a little better, and the two leaders failed to break any new ground. Sir Alec Douglas-Home, who was foreign secretary at the time, later speculated that Heath may have been circumspect because British officials had learned of Nixon's taping system.[34]

On June 16, 1973, it was Soviet Premier Leonid Brezhnev's turn. Arriving at Andrews Air Force Base, Maryland, for talks on nuclear weapons, Brezhnev was taken directly to Camp David to spend two days resting and adjusting to the time change from Moscow. Nixon telephoned him from Key Biscayne, Florida, and "had never heard him sound so friendly and completely uninhibited."[35] The next day, Kissinger traveled from Key Biscayne to Camp David, where the Soviet leader kissed him. "The only time in our acquaintance," the secretary of state said.[36]

21. President Nixon and British Prime Minister Edward Heath found their talks no more cheery than the weather during the Briton's Camp David visit. *Courtesy National Archives Nixon Project.*

After two days of talks at the White House, Brezhnev made a second helicopter flight into the Catoctins, this time with his host. He seemed delighted with the customary gift of a blue Camp David windbreaker with his name on it, and wore it most of the time. Knowing Brezhnev's fondness for luxurious automobiles, Nixon also presented him with a dark blue Lincoln Continental donated by the manufacturer. Brezhnev jumped in, motioned Nixon into the passenger's seat, and took off for a spin around the camp. They approached a steep slope marked "Slow, Dangerous Curve." Nixon knew it well. Driving the road in a golf cart, he had been forced to use the brake to avoid going off the sharp turn at the bottom. Brezhnev, driving a Lincoln Continental, was going more than fifty miles an hour. "Slow down, slow down," said Nixon. Brezhnev, paying no attention, slammed on the brakes and made the turn. "This is a very fine automobile," he said. "It holds the road very well."[37]

Automobiles were not Brezhnev's only weakness. Approaching the premier's cottage for their first meeting, Nixon encountered "a very attractive, quite full-figured young woman" leaving. Brezhnev's transla-

22. Soviet President Leonid Brezhnev, wearing a windbreaker given to all Camp David guests, chats with Nixon beside an ornamental pool near the presidential lodge. *Courtesy National Archives Nixon Project.*

tor introduced her as the premier's masseuse. The president recognized her scent as Arpege, Pat Nixon's favorite.[38] Gulley remembered it a bit differently. He said that although most of Brezhnev's aides doubled up because of the limited space, one woman described to him as a stewardess had a cabin to herself. Shortly after midnight, two KGB men escorted the woman down the path to Brezhnev's cottage. At dawn, they escorted her back.[39] Brezhnev stayed in Dogwood, the cabin where Tricia and Edward Cox had spent their honeymoon, which had been refurbished in 1971 as part of the biggest face-lift Camp David ever received.

Not long after Nixon took office, Haldeman learned of a fund that would make it possible to rehabilitate the aging camp in relative secrecy. Don R. Brazier, a deputy assistant secretary of defense, outlined the fund in testimony in 1973 before a subcommittee of the House Committee on Government Operations: "The moneys that are in the defense budget that are under the management of the military assistant to the president are put into our budget at the direction of the Office of Management and Budget in a lump sum. We are merely told to lodge a certain amount of money in a certain account for the use of the White House and that is the extent of our knowledge of the item." John H. Buchanan, Jr., a Republican representative from Alabama, pursued the point: "Is that amount itself classified?" Brazier said, "Yes, sir; it is."[40]

Armed with what Hughes told him about the fund, Haldeman expanded what had originally been a rather modest proposal. Charles "Bebe" Rebozo, a close friend of Nixon's who was regarded by the White House staff as speaking with the president's authority, told the military office aides, "Before you go out and get boards and nails, let's devise a master plan for Camp David."[41] On April 13, 1970, Hughes submitted such a plan to Haldeman. "Fungus, termite damage, moisture and age have resulted in severe deterioration, particularly in the cabins surrounding Aspen lodge," he said. "Aspen itself appears to be in good shape." Despite Ned Beach's work in the Eisenhower years, Hughes said the conference and dining facilities in Laurel Lodge were no longer adequate for Cabinet or National Security Council meetings. Hughes outlined a five-year building plan he said would ensure that "by 1976 the entire camp will be in excellent shape for perhaps another twenty years." The new buildings, like the old, were to have rough-hewn siding and shake roofs. Under Pat Nixon's supervision, the interiors were to be similar to the existing ones but "better coordinated." Nixon, examining the proposed new design, ordered a small lounge in Laurel converted into a presidential office with a desk and flags. Most cabins would have two bedrooms and a sitting room, but some would have four bedrooms. Most of the cabins FDR had built would be torn down.[42]

The cost of the first two buildings, Dogwood and Birch, was estimated at $145,000. The rebuilt Laurel, scheduled for completion in April, 1972, was to cost $700,000. All this threatened to break the two-million-dollar discretionary fund, so Harlow talked to Rep. George Mahon of Texas. The Appropriations Committee chairman agreed to increase the fund. Utilities, bachelor officers quarters, and other Navy support were requested and granted through Navy Military Construction appropriations, bypassing customary procedures.[43] In 1973, the Pentagon's Brazier told the House subcommittee that operating and maintenance costs for Camp David had risen from $148,000 in 1960, the last year of the Eisenhower administration, to $640,000 in fiscal year 1973.[44] The refurbishing received some help from private enterprise when Nixon supporter Donald Kendall, chairman of the board of Pepsi-Cola, donated a new tennis court. The money went through the Navy under a law that permitted the military departments to accept gifts for their installations.[45]

From the day Shangri-La was established, presidents and their aides were sensitive to the political danger of spending too much money on a weekend retreat. "I heard them state any number of times they didn't want to create any cause for complaint by spending a lot of money for someone's vanity or what not," Rigdon recalled of the Roosevelt era.[46] Nixon spent the money but tried to keep it secret, not always successfully. Aides were able to keep construction of the swimming pool out of the newspapers, but Washington society reporter Maxine Cheshire was writing by January, 1971, about the five-year plan to replace eight cabins. She said it might cost as much as $75,000. This was a ridiculous underestimate, but Deputy White House Press Secretary Gerald Warren told reporters it was "rather high." Magruder, asked to stem such leaks, replied, "First, there is no real way to stop reports about construction: there is only one road in and out of the camp and construction trucks must use that road." Nevertheless, he suggested to military aides that they make it clear to those using the camp that they were not to discuss the building program. When Higby requested and received floor plans from the General Services Administration for the entire new Laurel lodge, he was told by Commander Craig Campbell that "we could be criticized for not allowing open bidding on the furnishings or each separate portion of the construction" and was admonished, "In the future, no information on Camp David should be released without checking first with the Military Assistant's office."[47]

There was reason for the secrecy. Presidents and their families have persisted in describing Camp David as a simple, bucolic hideaway in the woods. As late as 1987, Nancy Reagan would say, "It's very simple; it's very rustic; it's not elaborate or fancy at all, not at all."[48] In Roosevelt's day, it was not, but, gradually improved over the years and then drastically reshaped under Nixon, it was far from most people's idea of rustic. "It's rustic compared to the White House, but you're not exactly living in log cabins and peeing in the woods," said the Reagans' son, Ron.[49] "The cabin where the writers stay is rustic," said Safire; the rest he described as "Catoctin Hilton."[50] Maureen Dean, who accompanied her husband to the camp in the depths of Watergate, wrote: "You can't believe Camp David until you see it. I suppose that when a man gets there he feels like a king, because when I arrived I felt like a queen." The young wife of the White House counsel was impressed by the swimming pools and bowling alleys, the bicycles and golf carts, the movie theater with a projectionist available at all hours. Dining on

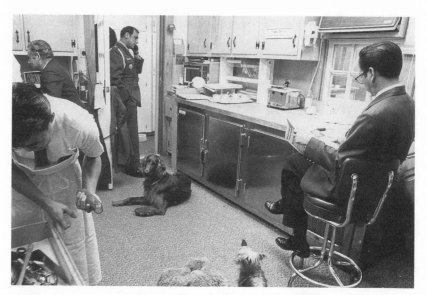

23. Backstage at Camp David. The dogs relax in the kitchen while the staff prepares dinner and a military aide makes a phone call. *Courtesy National Archives Nixon Project.*

Long Island duckling and Baked Alaska under the cathedral ceilings of the spacious Laurel dining room, she noticed fresh flowers and candles on every table, although only one was occupied. The cabins, she said, were "not plush, but . . . oh, so comfortable" and "all we had to do to order a cocktail, or lunch or dinner, or wine, or anything at all was to pick up the telephone. Immediately, a steward would materialize in front of us."[51]

"It's like a resort hotel where you are the only guests," said Tricia Nixon Cox.[52]

The president's cabin was equipped with a 35-millimeter projection booth for movies and a large stereo system. It had four bedrooms, just as FDR had sketched it three decades before, but the screened porch had been converted to a glassed-in dining room with a table to seat twelve.[53] The kitchen was still small, only about ten feet by sixteen feet. In a newly added presidential study, Mrs. Nixon placed a replica of her husband's favorite brown easy chair and ottoman, covered in blue raw silk.[54] Even the unused bomb shelter, reached by an elevator just to the left of the front door, was redone with new beds, bedspreads, pictures, paint, and office furnishings at a cost of $250,000.

The other cabins, while still of the original green-painted board and batten construction, were substantially changed inside. A visitor to new Maple described it as "larger, more elaborate, and more modern than the older ones, with a vaulted ceiling, a large living room with a high glass wall opening onto a patio in the woods, two bedrooms, a huge fieldstone fireplace with a large supply of extra logs, neatly cut, arranged by the door."[55]

Outside, the walls of what had once been Shangri-La were posted with new, small unsigned notices that read, "No Stopping, Slowing, Turning or Standing Here." Simon Winchester, a Washington correspondent for the *Manchester Guardian,* described the newly reinforced fence: "It is just like Berlin. There are in fact three fences. One, tall and silvery new, tipped with barbed coils. Another, smaller, with porcelain insulators on the supporting stanchion and just visible signs with red lettering, behind that another taller, mesh fence, and more barbed wire." Park Ranger Don Gaver told Winchester, "The forests are always crawling with security folks nowadays. It's not like it used to be here."[56]

Communications were also upgraded. On Labor Day, 1971, Nixon addressed the nation by radio from old Maple, a short walk from Aspen. Even though the room had been carefully selected and equipped to flatten out the sound, aides detected "a certain bass-sounding edge and hollow quality" in the presidential voice. For Nixon's Veterans' Day radio address, they checked out and rejected the Hawthorn sitting room and the camp library and then settled on the small dining room at Laurel, with woolen waffle-type carpet padding on the walls and an acoustical tile ceiling. Another office was decorated with the thought of Nixon doing television appearances, but was never used.[57]

The beeper came to Camp David also. Higby gave orders that one be provided for Haldeman whenever he was there.[58] Outside, telephone cables streaked through the woods and microwave dishes connected the camp with the Pentagon's underground outpost twenty miles northward on the Pennsylvania border.[59] Gone were the days when the telephone line from Shangri-La went through a switchboard at Thurmont; by the time Nixon came to office, the calls were routed through an Army Signal Corps board. This changed after Nixon was unable to reach Adm. John McCain to ask him about a possible court martial of elite Green Beret soldiers in Vietnam. Within half an hour, Secretary of Defense Melvin Laird telephoned Ehrlichman at Aspen to find out why the White House wanted to talk to McCain. Ehrlichman wondered how closely Laird monitored Camp David calls: "Did he just keep track of whom we called, or did he also know what was said?" From then on, calls were routed through the White House switchboard.[60]

In May 1972, the secret Service hid a microphone in the president's study and attached two others to telephones on his desk and his table. They were wired to Sony 800B recorders in a room under the presidential cabin, following up on the decision the previous year to install taping systems in the presidential offices in the White House and Old Executive Office Building. The device was removed when any foreign visitor was invited to stay at the lodge. The microphone hidden in the study was disconnected on March 18, 1973. The ones on the telephones were left until July 18, 1973, two days after Alexander Butterfield revealed their existence in testimony before the Senate Watergate committee.[61]

Nixon was using the camp more and more. In his first year in office, he went twenty-five times, staying a total of sixty-one days.[62] By October, 1973, he had made 149 visits, more than three times as many as Eisenhower made in his eight years in office. He had entertained eleven foreign visitors, compared with two each for Roosevelt and Johnson, five for Eisenhower and none for either Truman or Kennedy.[63] In the early years of his presidency, Pat Nixon often accompanied him, describing herself as "starved for exercise" in the White House and seizing the chance to don slacks and a windbreaker and hike the camp trails. As his troubles deepened, the president more often went to the mountain without her. Curiously, he would order a fire started in an Aspen fireplace even in the heat of August. On some nights he would turn out the lights, so that his study was lit only by the flames. In this setting, Haldeman once heard him say, he did "all his big cogitations."[64]

As usual, a visit to the Catoctins could be a reward, its denial a rebuke. Industrialists Clement Stone and John Mulcahy, the two biggest contributors to Nixon's 1968 campaign, were both invited to social affairs at the camp.[65] In the first year, ten of the twelve Cabinet officers visited. When disgruntled Secretary of the Treasury John Connally threatened to resign, Nixon ordered aides to offer the Catoctin retreat to him for a weekend.[66] By his second term, however, Nixon was telling Ehrlichman that Cabinet meetings "will be just substance, and we'll do no more social things like dinners at Camp David."[67] On May 22, 1972, aide Butterfield told Brig. Gen. Brent Scowcroft, the president's military assistant, that policy on use of Camp David had been revised. Ehrlichman was to be scheduled whenever he wanted it, but acting director L. Patrick Gray would "have to plan to hold his conference with top FBI officials elsewhere."[68]

Apollo astronauts were invited to the camp four times to relax after their flights, but on the second occasion Higby told Butterfield that "their children should not be included this time." On a weekend in October when a number of aides and families were invited to the retreat, Higby noted that the occupants of Walnut and Maple were being switched "to keep the baby away from the President."[69] The family setter, King Timahoe, was also a frequent visitor, arriving in the back seat of a blue Chrysler with a black vinyl roof a few hours after his master had made the trip by helicopter.[70]

Like all presidents, Nixon was billed for food served to him and his family and personal guests, whether at Camp David or at the White House. Unlike others, he tried to get a tax writeoff for it. The president claimed deductions of $16,480.65 in 1969, $7,152.82 in 1970, $11,465.28 in 1971 and $12,316.24 in 1972 for "expenses incurred in the performance of official functions as President of the United States." The Congressional Joint Committee on Internal Revenue, looking into his tax returns, said the expenses appeared to have been incurred at Camp David, at Nixon's home in San Clemente, California, aboard the yacht *Sequoia* and at other places away from the White House. The White House counsel's office advised the committee staff that it "could not supply any substantiation of the business purpose for any of the expenses deducted." The deduction was disallowed.[71]

Nixon, a man of intimidating formality, wore a suit and tie at Camp David more frequently than any other president. Not an outdoorsman, he made little use of the camp recreational facilities except for the pool. Conscious of his stiff public image, he suggested that Ziegler slip word to the press that he had taken up bowling in the alley at Laurel. He had never bowled before except for a couple of times at the camp in 1960. Five months after taking office, he was averaging scores of 130 to 140 and had bowled one 204 game. For petite Tricia, he ordered an unusually small bowling ball.[72] At the request of Clifford Evans, White House correspondent for the RKO radio stations, he spent an afternoon at Camp David compiling, with David Eisenhower's help, an all-time baseball All-Star team. Stiff image or not, the notes he wrote to accompany the list showed that he knew his baseball.[73]

More than anything else, however, it was Watergate that drove the thirty-seventh president to the Catoctin hideaway. The furor that would engulf his administration began on the night of June 16, 1972, when the office of the Democratic National Committee in Washington's Watergate Building was broken into. On November 13, E. Howard Hunt, the former CIA agent who organized and carried out the break-in, telephoned Charles Colson to say he and the six other defendants in the case had "a great deal of financial expense" and, "After all, we're protecting the guys who were really responsible . . . now is the time when some moves should be made." Colson taped the conversation and gave his tape to John Dean.

By Dean's account, he took a cassette of the tape to Camp David on November 15. Walter Minnick, a White House lawyer, sat beside him in their limousine. They did not talk about Watergate, but about the executive branch reorganization.[74] When he reached the camp, Dean went to the president's little-used office at Laurel lodge, almost bare except for one American flag and a presidential flag on each side of the empty desk. He played the tape for Haldeman and Ehrlichman. The chief of staff winced. Ehrlichman doodled. "Well," said Dean "this tape is a beauty." At Ehrlichman's suggestion, they told the others at the camp that they were discussing the reorganization. Nothing was done at the time about Hunt's demand for money, and Ehrlichman and Haldeman later denied that Dean had played the tape for them.

At an Oval Office meeting on March 22, 1973, Haldeman urged Dean to "hole up for the weekend" and start drafting a report that Nixon and his aides hoped would put Watergate behind them. "Why don't you use Camp David?" asked Nixon. "I might do it," said Dean. "I might do it."[75] The next day, a White House limousine picked the Deans up at their home and drove them to the presidential retreat, getting lost on the way. While they were on the road, Judge John Sirica read in open court a letter he had received from Watergate defendant James McCord. "There was political pressure applied to the defendants to plead guilty and remain silent," McCord said. "Others involved in the Watergate operation were not identified during the trial, when they could have been by those testifying." The heat was on. No wonder Haldeman would say, joking about how to avoid a subpoena, "We move to Camp David and hide! They can't get in there."

On the trip into the Catoctins, John Dean read a newspaper and spoke little. At the gate to Camp David, his wife found his eyes "glazed and unseeing." Staring out at the brown Catoctin mountainside, he fantasized about "a helicopter snatching Mo and me at Camp David and taking us to some little-used Air Force base, then on to Latin America."[76] There was to be no such escape. The next morning, Dean began taking notes on a legal pad, eventually covering twenty-six pages, broken down into the period before and after the break-in. It was tough going. He called an assistant, Fred Fielding, and arranged to have his secretary come up the next day. Still, he made little headway.

On Sunday, March 25, Ziegler called to say that Monday's *Los Angeles Times* would have a front-page story saying that Dean and

Magruder had advance knowledge of the break-in. Dean called Magruder, taping the conversation by holding the microphone of a dictating machine to the telephone receiver. "I'm taking a bum rap, Jeb," he said. Telling his wife he would go to the prosecutors with what he knew, he arranged to retain a criminal lawyer. On Wednesday, March 28, Haldeman summoned him down from the mountain. His report would never be finished.

For John Ehrlichman, the first hint that the end was approaching came when the president went to Florida for Easter. "Pointedly he suggested that Haldeman and I use Camp David while he was gone, instead of coming with him." A trip to the Catoctin retreat, so often taken as a sign of presidential favor, was something else in the atmosphere of Watergate. "Nixon had begun to cut us loose."[77]

At 9:35 P.M. on Friday, April 27, Nixon flew to the camp himself. It was foggy the next morning. After breakfast on the porch, the president went to his small library to work. At about ten o'clock he wanted a cup of coffee and stepped into the living room looking for Manolo Sanchez. Instead he found Tricia sitting on the couch. She said she had been talking with Julie and David and with her mother. They had asked her to tell him that they all believed that Haldeman and Ehrlichman should go. Bill Rogers, no longer his secretary of state but still a key adviser, arrived at 11:30 A.M. He agreed; leaves of absence would not do. Nixon said he had come to the same conclusion. That night he had a telephone call from Ehrlichman. The blunt-spoken lawyer from Seattle told him that all the illegal acts ultimately derived from the president, directly or indirectly. To Nixon, it seemed that Ehrlichman was suggesting a presidential resignation. At 12:13 P.M. on Sunday, he telephoned Haldeman at his Georgetown townhouse. As Haldeman recalled it, Nixon said, "I've thought it through all the way. It's got to be a resignation." As Nixon recalled it, he did not say the words, but was sure that Haldeman got the message. Yes, Haldeman replied, both he and Ehrlichman would come to Camp David. They wanted separate meetings with the president. Nixon agreed reluctantly, but asked Haldeman to talk to the prickly Ehrlichman on the way up and "explain to him what the situation is."[78]

Flying over Georgetown in a White House helicopter, Haldeman could pick out his townhouse below. Over the roar of the rotors, he shouted, "It's resignation, John, not leave of absence." Ehrlichman, by his own account, was "barely civil" to the outgoing chief of staff when they took off, but his mood eased "as we flew low over the Maryland landscape, which was turning a bright spring green." To Haldeman he still seemed angry as they arrived at the camp and were taken to Laurel. Haldeman was to see the president first. Ehrlichman opened his brief-case and took out a yellow pad — presumably, thought Haldeman, to prepare his argument — and Haldeman left with Ziegler for a brief walk in the woods before going to Aspen. Ehrlichman sat on the Laurel ter-race and telephoned his Christian Science practitioner, who had been counseling him in the hard times.

Haldeman chose to ride a bicycle to the place where he would be dismissed. The fog and clouds had lifted, and, as he stepped into the living room at Aspen, he had a last view of the masses of green de-ciduous foliage below. Nixon, wearing a checked sports coat, tapped him on the shoulder and suggested they walk outside onto the terrace. There they attempted small talk, discussing the beauty of the tulips planted in rock gardens on the mountain slope; then they turned to business. "Last night before I went to bed, I knelt down and this time I prayed that I wouldn't wake in the morning," said Nixon. "I just couldn't face going on." Haldeman was touched that the president would bare his soul to him in this way. Four years later, watching Nixon recreate the scene in a television interview, he was hurt to hear the former president repeat the words but ascribe them to his meeting with Ehrlichman. The president also told his long-time aide that Camp David would always be available to him, but Haldeman knew at once that this was a meaningless gesture. He said he accepted the president's decision even though he did not agree with it. Then he stepped out the front door, twenty-two minutes after he had arrived, and pedaled back to Laurel.

Ehrlichman, for his part, walked the two hundred yards to Aspen and entered the living room without knocking. Nixon entered from the bedroom and the two men stood, the president's eyes red-rimmed and puffy. After Nixon did indeed tell him of praying for death during the night, Ehrlichman put his arm on the president's shoulder and Nixon turned and walked out onto the terrace. Following him, Ehrlichman, too, noted that the bulbs were in bloom. "Just explain all this to my kids, will you?" Ehrlichman asked. "Tell them why you had to do this?" At the end they hugged each other. The fired aide was wiping his eyes with his handkerchief when he left. "I could see that he had said all he had to say and that was the end of it," Ehrlichman reflected. His meeting with the president had lasted thirty-six minutes.[79]

Looking out the window of his bedroom at new Maple, where he had set up a typewriter to work on the speech in which the president would announce the resignations, Ray Price saw Ehrlichman "striding along the footpath as he left the President's lodge, arms swinging, his head facing grimly forward, looking neither to right nor left." To Rose Mary Woods, looking back on the weekend, Haldeman had taken it "more like a man."

At Laurel, Haldeman and Ehrlichman waited nearly two hours for Rogers, who had returned to Washington, to arrive to work out the details of their resignations with them. Ehrlichman made detailed notes of his conversation with the president. On the difficult helicopter ride back to the capital, he and Haldeman did not compare notes. It was dark when the helicopter arrived in Washington. A few minutes later, Nixon and Rogers sat down to dinner in front of the fireplace at Aspen.

The next day, Price came to the president's lodge to discuss the speech. He had never seen Nixon "so unraveled or so distraught." At one point, the president dropped the papers he was working on and they lay on the floor beside him unregarded. "Maybe I should resign," he said. "Do you think so?" Price told him he had a duty to stay in office. As they discussed the shoals of foreign policy, Nixon became more animated and decided to go for a swim. Price, still concerned about the president's state of mind, saw him safely to the pool and then dashed off to put the finishing touches on the speech. Rose Woods was waiting in her cabin to type it.[80]

On July 23, a federal grand jury and the Senate Watergate committee subpoenaed the tapes of Nixon's White House conversations on Watergate. Three times in the next three weeks, Nixon retreated to Aspen to work on responses to the increasingly insistent questions. On August 15, in an address to the nation, he said it was time to turn the matter over to the courts.

On Friday, September 28, Nixon instructed Haig, who had succeeded Haldeman, to arrange for a review of the tapes at Camp David. Gen. John C. Bennett, an aide to the new chief of staff, called Fred Buzhardt, the special White House counsel in charge of the tapes. Buzhardt walked over to Bennett's office with two legal-sized mimeographed sheets listing the subpoenaed tapes. Bennett went to an electronically locked room in the basement of the Executive Office Building, asked the Secret Service to let him in, and spent an hour and a quarter looking through the four or five locked cabinets there to find the tapes he needed. Back in his own office, he went over the tapes with aide Stephen Bull to make sure they were the right ones. Bull spotted one that he did not think he would need, and Bennett sealed it up in an envelope and put it in his safe. They put the rest in Bull's briefcase which Bennett also locked in his safe, giving Bull the combination.

Nixon called Rose Woods and asked if she would mind going to Camp David to transcribe the tapes. "I said, of course not, and I canceled my plans thinking, of course, I was going to get it all done that weekend," she later testified. Saturday morning, she and Bull went to Bennett's office, got the tapes out, counted them, and rode to Camp David in a White House limousine with the tapes and three Sony tape recorders. They did not discuss the tapes during the ride because the driver could overhear their conversations. Miss Woods read the daily White House news summary.[81] At 9:10 A.M., Haig called the camp, but they had not arrived. When they did, they went to Dogwood. In one room, Miss Woods set up a black machine with oversize earphones; in another, Bull marked the first tape with a piece of white paper showing where the critical passage began, and brought it to her. The tape contained conversations Nixon had with Ehrlichman and Haldeman in the president's office in the Executive Office Building on June 20, 1972, less than three days after the break-in. At about 9:50 A.M., Haig was to testify, he called again and Bull told him he was having trouble matching up conversations on the reel with the first item on the subpoena.

This would be the only tape from which Miss Woods would transcribe that weekend. She started at about eleven o'clock, sending out for her lunch. Three minutes after Nixon arrived at Aspen that afternoon, he was in Dogwood to see how she was doing. He listened to the tape for five or ten minutes, pushed the buttons on her machine back and forth, commented that he could hear two or three voices speaking at once, and told her, "I am sorry this is such a terrible job." He came back again for about half an hour between six and seven o'clock and invited her to join the family for dinner.

That evening, while the president, Pat Nixon, and Julie Eisenhower watched the somber baseball movie, *Bang the Drum Slowly,* Miss Woods returned to her cabin.[82] She worked until 3:00 A.M., rose again at 6:00 A.M. and worked all day Sunday. Altogether, she spent twenty-nine hours at the task that weekend alone. Bull telephoned Bennett that he still could not find the tape of Nixon's April 15, 1973, meeting with John Dean after Dean's visit to Camp David to write his report.[83] Bennett came to Camp David and brought a back-up tape, but it did not contain the conversation either.[84] When an eighteen-and-one-half-minute gap in the tape became known in November, Miss Woods said it could have happened by accident as she leaned over to answer a telephone call while working with the machine. The mystery was never solved.

On Friday, October 12, the United States Court of Appeals for the

District of Columbia Circuit, by a vote of five to two, ordered Nixon to turn the subpoenaed tapes over to Judge Sirica for his examination. The next afternoon, Nixon, accompanied by the first lady and Julie, flew again to Camp David, where he reached the decision that he would put into action, after a pause to seek a compromise, a week later. He would fire Archibald Cox, the Harvard law professor turned special Watergate prosecutor; this prompted the resignations of Attorney General Elliot Richardson and his deputy, William Ruckelshaus, and would become known as the Saturday Night Massacre.

By spring, the House Judiciary Committee wanted the tapes, too, and set a deadline of April 30. On Saturday, April 27, Nixon told Ziegler that on the following Monday he would publicly release the first tape transcripts, then flew to Camp David to work on a television address he planned to make Monday night. Haig, Ziegler, Price, Patrick J. Buchanan, and the president's counsel, James D. St. Clair, helicoptered to the camp Sunday afternoon. They set up headquarters in Laurel.[85]

Haig walked to Aspen, where Nixon, sitting by a cold fireplace, said he had changed his mind; there would be no televised speech, just a simple statement accompanying the transcripts. Price went to Hawthorn to draft the statement, eating a sandwich as he wrote. Haig took the draft to Nixon, who penciled in changes, then invited Price to join him in a martini on the Aspen terrace. "Evening was falling. The spring air was crisp but comfortable. Below, the lawn sloped gently, peacefully, down toward the enveloping forest."[86] The scene recalled by Price would be one of the last serene moments of the Nixon presidency.

On May 4 at Camp David, a depressed Julie Eisenhower told her father, "Everything is so dreary." Nevertheless, she later said, when the president outlined the case for his resignation the family urged him to stay on. On May 5, with new special prosecutor Leon Jaworski still seeking additional tapes, Nixon returned to Washington from the Catoctins, went to his hideaway in the Executive Office Building, and listened for the first time to the tape of June 23, 1972. This was the "smoking gun" in which Nixon instructed Haldeman to have the Central Intelligence Agency step in and halt the FBI's Watergate investigation. The next day, he notified St. Clair and Buzhardt that he would give up no more tapes.

Walking along a muddy nature trail at Camp David that spring, Nixon reflected "that from now on until approximately the first of August when the Supreme Court will rule, the thing to do is to just treat every day as basically the last one and not be constantly concerned about what may happen in the future." On July 24, the court announced its decision: Nixon must give up the tapes. On Thursday, August 1, the president told Haig that he planned to resign. On Saturday, he took the helicopter to Camp David with Mrs. Nixon, Ed and Tricia Cox, David and Julie Eisenhower, and Rebozo. Even in the mountains it was hot and humid, so they went for a swim, then sat on the terrace looking over the valley, sharing "a sense of the mystery and the beauty as well as the history and the tragedy that lay behind our weekend together in this setting."[87]

Haig flew to the camp on Sunday with St. Clair, Price, Buchanan, and Ziegler. They discussed the planned release on Monday of the June 23 tape. According to one account, Ziegler "desperately sought alternatives" to a presidential resignation in his talks with the other four. He received none.[88]

On Monday, August 5, Nixon flew back to Washington, where he would resign three days later. Among the items left behind in his desk at Camp David was a green Halloween mask. Before the former president's papers and memorabilia were opened to the public at the National Archives, they were screened by his representatives. The mask, like much else, was withheld from public view.[89]

7

Gerald R. Ford
Camp David Meets the Press

Throughout much of the Nixon administration, the sign on the press trailer outside the Camp David gate, mocking the botanical names Mamie Eisenhower had given the comfortable cabins inside, read, "Poison Ivy Lodge." With the elevation of Gerald Ford to the presidency, the sign was changed to "Honeysuckle."[1]

Ford, who came to the presidency in the wake of Watergate promising to be "as open and candid as possible," probably made Camp David as accessible to the press as it has ever been,[2] which isn't saying much. The sign on the trailer notwithstanding, many traces remained of the secrecy that had surrounded the presidential retreat from its beginnings.

Despite the occasional leaks, Roosevelt's Shangri-La was kept almost entirely under wraps during World War II. Reporters who covered the White House knew about it, but followed a wartime code of voluntary censorship. They became as irritated as anybody when leaks appeared on society pages, complaining that the society writers thought the code "applied to everybody but them."[3]

"To my knowledge, it was kept a secret officially and by connivance of the press because of the war, as were his other movements," journalist Chalmers Roberts, who was with the Office of War Information at the time, recalled years later. "He went all across the country on trips and visited a lot of war plants and everything and it was only announced after the trips that he had done these things."[4]

Mary Freeze, whose Cozy Motel in Thurmont would be a haven for countless reporters in years to come, agreed: "Very few people knew anything about what was going on."[5]

Although photographers and reporters were permitted in for a quick look during the Truman administration, the camp remained generally a closed operation. On July 31, 1949, Truman's press secretary, Charles Ross, told the editor of the Hagerstown, Maryland, *Morning Herald* that "it would be against the policy of this office to permit any exclusive stories or pictures of Shangri-La."[6] Sixteen years later, the *Herald* was faring no better. George E. Reedy, press secretary to President Lyndon B. Johnson, told editor Arnold Miller on April 8, 1965, "Camp David is the President's personal retreat and is treated in a personal way and our policy is not to permit picture stories."[7]

In March, 1959, shortly before Eisenhower's meeting with Macmillan, selected reporters were given what was probably the longest press tour ever conducted, including a walk-through of Aspen lodge. It was thorough enough that a reporter could write, in a memo to an editor, "The entry is through a dutch door. Flanking it on the exterior are two ship's masthead lights. Through the entry is the main living room, perhaps 13 by 25 feet, maybe a bit bigger, running north and south. At the left or north end is a large stone fireplace. Beyond that is the kitchen and butler's pantry. In front of the fireplace is a table and chairs of beautifully grained walnut in a somewhat modern style. The table extends to seat 12." And so on for six pages.[8]

Reporters were admitted to the grounds to watch the arrival of Eisenhower, Macmillan, and the other principals, and Ann Whitman wrote in her diary that "the first hour or so we simply stood around and talked to newspapermen."[9]

Foreign visits brought reporters from not only throughout the United States but throughout the world into the Catoctins. During the Khrushchev visit later in 1959, the front seats at Jim Hagerty's press briefing in Gettysburg had these four place cards in a row: "*Pravda* . . . *Pravda* . . . *Pravda* . . . *Christian Science Monitor*."[10]

Even for American reporters, the experience was a new one. They sought assignments to the small pool of reporters admitted inside the gate for twenty-five minutes after Khrushchev's arrival. At one of Jim Hagerty's briefings at Gettysburg, one of the reporters who didn't make it asked if there was "any chance of getting up into that area as far as the guards." Hagerty gave him no encouragement.[11]

Two weeks before the Eisenhower-Khrushchev meeting, four men in a car registered to an official of the United Arab Republic Embassy encountered a Camp David sailor on his way down to Thurmont for supplies. They asked the way to camp and, when they got there, took pictures of the sign at the gate. They said they were covering the story for the Egyptian press and wanted to know if they could take pictures after Khrushchev arrived. Naval aide Aurand reported the incident to Hagerty and the Secret Service.[12]

When Kennedy called on Eisenhower to confer with him at Camp David after the Bay of Pigs, coverage was more open and forty reporters and photographers waited in the hazy sunlight in front of Aspen. After lunch, Kennedy, scuffing the ground with his toe, told the journalists he had "invited the President . . . to get the benefit of his thoughts and experience." As photographers jostled for position, the former president who had ordered the Normandy landing cracked, "This is damn near an invasion, isn't it?"[13]

Frank Cormier, who was White House correspondent for the Associated Press from the Kennedy administration into the Carter years, recalled landing at the camp helipad with Kennedy when the president returned from a trip, but said this was unusual. Cormier and other reporters watched from inside the chopper as Kennedy got out and was greeted by his wife. Then the helicopter returned to Washington with the members of the press pool.

More customary was the routine that evolved over the years of tedious waiting at the motel, being on hand to greet the helicopter's arrival, or following the president in his motorcade in bad weather. A pool report filed by Ellen Warren of Knight-Ridder Newspapers during the Reagan administration gives the flavor of such assignments: "Presidential motorcade lurched through rush hour traffic leaving angry motorists in its wake. Motorcade stopped dead in traffic 7 times, arriving here in 2 hours—40 minutes longer than usual travel time. Otherwise uneventful."

Major news organizations rented rooms at the Cozy, installing their own telephones and darkroom equipment. For years, reporters and photographers spent weekends at the Thurmont motel while the president was in camp. It was dreary duty for the most part, standing by at the motel for calls that seldom came. Only the advent of the electronic pager gave them more freedom. Michael Putzel, who came to the White House for the Associated Press in the Carter administration, took his family with him to the Cozy and went hiking with them in the woods near Camp David, knowing his beeper would go off if he was needed.

For the most part, the journalists left their weekend headquarters only to stand behind a barrier dubbed "the duck blind" and watch the helicopter land or take off. The photographers were on hand to take pictures of anything unusual, such as a helicopter crash, but otherwise were not allowed to shoot. Many thought that in the event of a crash their film would be confiscated anyway. The increasingly unproductive practice was largely discontinued by the news organizations in the Reagan administration, but reporters and photographers continued to accompany the president in his motorcade when weather prevented making the trip by helicopter. When the presidential party entered the grounds, they were left outside, where they could call their offices from special telephones near the gate. Shortly before the 1972 presidential election, Nixon proposed building a small press briefing room and lounge at the camp, but nothing came of it.

Occasionally, there was news to cover. "Johnson had us up to Aspen Lodge a couple of times, I think, not inside, but outside, on the patio by the pool," said Cormier. Nixon held news conferences in the helicopter hangar during his 1972 governmental reorganization meetings. By the end of his administration, even access to the helipad had been cut off. "Ford opened that up when he came in," said Cormier. "He would often come by and stop and chat with us on the way to the helicopter. He didn't do it every time, but you never could tell."[14]

In October 1974, Ford agreed "in principle" to an interview with Walter Cronkite, and other filming by CBS television at the camp. Press Secretary Ron Nessen, a former NBC White House reporter, said he "checked and found there are no technical or security problems." The plan called for Cronkite and the president to walk around the grounds, "talking about personal things," followed by a half-hour interview — on the terrace outside Aspen if the weather permitted, inside Laurel Lodge if it did not.[15] The network turned down the opportunity because it would have occurred during the congressional election campaign.

On October 26, Harry Reasoner, then with ABC, conducted a similar interview with Ford at the camp. ABC said Ford became available for the program on short notice, apparently after the turndown by CBS.[16] As Reasoner and the president strolled along a blacktop trail that leads from the helipad past the commanding officer's quarters, with the nameplates of Cedar and Rosebud cabins in the background, Ford spoke of the camp as "a place where you can really live as a family." Outside Aspen, decorated with corn husks and jack o'lanterns for Halloween, he observed that for the first time recently he had gotten eight hours of sleep the night before.

The formal part of the interview was conducted with the men, both wearing Camp David jackets, seated on plaid-upholstered couches in

24. President Gerald Ford was frustrated by the "little bitty" three-hole golf course Eisenhower had installed. *Courtesy Gerald R. Ford Library.*

Laurel. Reasoner told viewers that Ford had "decided the public ought to have a look" at the presidential retreat but also that "there are many other sights to see at Camp David which we were not permitted to film for security reasons—such things as the inside of the president's lodge, his swimming pool, his three-hole golf course and his view of the mountain valley, which he told us was strikingly beautiful."

In the interview, Ford said changes would have to be made in the original agreement to forward Richard Nixon's tapes and papers to the former president, but defended withholding some of the tapes from the public.[17] William Sheehan, president of ABC News, decided that the president's comments went beyond those of a tour guide. Although originally scheduled for the Tuesday before the election, the broadcast was put off until November 16 to avoid a possible demand for equal time from the Democrats.[18]

Meanwhile Bob Boyd of Knight Newspapers, who had been turned down when he asked to take a photographer to the camp to do a feature story, got wind of the Reasoner visit and renewed his request. The answer was no "on the basis that it is a classified area and the military was opposed to such stories." Dirck Halsted of *Time* fared no better on his bid to do a color picture spread on the presidential retreat. Nessen told Halsted he could not "be promising for any time in the near future."[19]

When Republican Sen. Ted Stevens of Alaska asked for a "quick tour" of the camp in May, the president's military assistant, Navy Capt. L. S. Kollmorgen, said, "We are still paying a toll for the Harry Reasoner interview last fall." A White House memo urging rejection of Stevens' request spelled out an essentially unchanged policy: "For the most part, Congress, the press and the public are not aware of how extensive the facilities are at Camp David. The Press Office and the Military Office have expressed the view that there is no value in advertising the extensiveness of the camp's development."[20]

The attitude continued to prevail. When William G. Renner, the workman who recalled witnessing FDR's first glimpse of Shangri-La, sought to revisit the site, he was first turned down, despite the efforts of Republican Sen. Charles McC. Mathias of Maryland. When Mathias persisted, the request was granted but the visit was kept "very low key because we don't want to open the floodgates on Camp David."[21]

During the Reagan administration, Maryland Public Television, putting together a TV special on the camp, was not allowed inside at all. Producer-director Lori Evans was delighted when told that the narrator of the special, broadcast journalist Ann Compton, would be allowed to do her standups in front of the "Camp David" sign, which would at least put them right outside the gate. No such luck. The Navy had switched signs, putting the "Camp David" one on a standard a couple of hundred yards away from the gate which normally said "Camp #3."[22]

One of Ford's news conferences at Camp David came on September 1, 1975, and was marked by an unusual glitch in White House communications. Howard Benedict of the Associated Press was in his room at the Cozy when he got a telephone call from Nessen saying Ford would make an announcement at the camp at around noon and it would probably deal with the Middle East. Benedict picked up his telephone to call editor Richard E. Meyer, on duty in the AP's Washington bureau. Instead, he found himself listening to a conversation between Ford at Camp David and Henry Kissinger in Jerusalem. "Good work, Henry, good work," Ford was saying. "That's really good news." The president told his secretary of state he was having the press come up to Camp David so he could make the announcement. A few moments later, the conversation ended.

25. President Ford and Secretary of State Henry Kissinger on a sofa in Aspen. *Courtesy Gerald R. Ford Library.*

"I was sitting there shocked listening to this thing, in the Cozy Motel, a supposedly secure telephone conversation between Ford and Kissinger," Benedict recalled. He had only one problem. Neither Ford nor Kissinger had said what it was they were going to announce. "All I knew was that they were going to have some good news. Then I got through to Rick and I told him about it and we didn't know what the heck to do with it." Not knowing what news they had, they decided to wait for the announcement. At noon, in a telephone hookup that reporters were deliberately allowed to listen to, Ford spoke with Kissinger, Prime Minister Yitzhak Rabin of Israel and President Anwar Sadat of Egypt and announced an Egyptian-Israeli troop disengagement agreement.[23]

On August 6, 1976, the second anniversary of Ford's ascension to the presidency, the journalists got inside Aspen again. Sitting on an overstuffed sofa in the presidential lodge, the president was interviewed by Benedict and his Associated Press colleague Dick Barnes and by Helen Thomas and Dick Growald of United Press International. As a fire flickered in the fireplace, Ford defended his pardon of Nixon and said he felt confident he would turn back a challenge from Ronald Reagan at the GOP convention in Kansas City. He also predicted he would defeat another former governor, Georgia's Jimmy Carter, in November.

Sipping iced tea, the president laughed often and occasionally shooed his golden retriever, Liberty, from the room. Outside, his daughter, Susan, tossed apples into the pool for the dog to fetch. Despite overcast weather, the reporters were struck by the view over the valley from the picture window. "Afterwards we had a drink or two and we talked about his little three-hole golf course and a couple of other things and then we made our way down the hill and dictated our stories," said Benedict.[24]

Others were writing about the camp from a distance, and getting advice from the White House. In an article for the November, 1975, *Reader's Digest,* Peter Michelmore said that Ford "looks upon the retreat as a family sanctuary reserved for exercise, meditation and long talks with his wife and children." Long-time Ford aide Robert T. Hartmann, to whom the article was submitted for review, jotted "study?" in the margin beside the word "meditation." In the article as published, neither word appeared. Hartmann circled Michelmore's statements that the camp had 150 military personnel and cost an estimated $350,000 a year to maintain. Both figures were dropped.[25]

In December, 1975, Captain Kollmorgen wrote to Warren Silver, associate editor of the *World Book Encyclopedia,* suggesting that a proposed encyclopedia article make clear that the camp golf course was only a three-hole one to "prevent any mistaken impression of grandeur." The draft article had also called the camp "the official place of rest of the President of the United States." Kollmorgen wrote Silver, "I wish to assure you that no former presidents are interred at Camp David; nor, to my knowledge, does President Ford intend that as his final place of repose. Therefore, may I suggest something less terminal to describe the President's retreat." The encyclopedia article as published specified "three-hole golf course" and called the camp "the official retreat of the President of the United States."[26]

Ford had visited Camp David a couple of times in the Nixon administration, spending part of a day each time and staying at Birch Cottage. He first went there as president on August 31, 1974, for a weekend of swimming, golf, tennis, skeet shooting, and horseback riding with his family. Betty Ford wrote in her diary, "Camp David is the best thing about the White House. Except you gain too much weight up there, because the staff is so glad to have you come that they prepare all these delicious meals."[27]

26. Betty Ford, at the door of Aspen, found Camp David "the best thing about the White House." *Courtesy Gerald R. Ford Library.*

On Labor Day, they returned to the White House. The president told a letter writer that Mrs. Ford talked with Mamie Eisenhower over the weekend and that President Eisenhower's widow "was unable to join us at Camp David over this past week, but she is looking forward to joining us very soon."[28] Mrs. Eisenhower was not to visit the camp again, however.

Ford's next trip to the Catoctins was October 25–27, the weekend of the Reasoner interview. The first lady was recovering from breast cancer surgery by this time and, after a publicized return to the White House from Bethesda Naval Hospital, encountered "still another Welcome Back. The whole staff hugged and kissed me when I came in the door of Aspen." She found the fare less appetizing this time, eating the liver and onions that had been prescribed for her. For the first time, they brought Liberty, and the dog created a stir by chasing a doe.

That weekend, the president, in slacks and a red Marine Corps sweatsuit, studied a report on Kissinger's latest meeting with Brezhnev, but laid it aside to take up with his wife a matter closer to home. Their son, Steve, had enrolled in a school for rodeo ropers in Wyoming. Mrs. Ford wanted them to try to stop him, but her husband said, "I've given him some good advice. Get gentle cows and old horses." The first lady, an aspiring dancer in her youth, accepted the situation: "What Martha Graham had been to me, horses are to Steve."[29]

Meanwhile, with the economic news increasingly troublesome, Chief of Staff Donald Rumsfeld urged the president to convene a meeting at Camp David to discuss long-range goals for his administration. Ford considered such a meeting, but felt it should deal with nuts-and-bolts legislative proposals and budget items rather than the broader issues Rumsfeld had in mind. In the end, he skipped it, going instead to Vail, Colorado, with his family for their annual Christmas and New Year's vacation amid the ski slopes.[30]

Despite his words to Reasoner, going to Camp David appears not to have been a favorite recreation for Ford, any more than it was for Truman. He visited the camp seventeen times in his thirty months in office, seldom sleeping there for more than two nights in a row.[31] When he did, he indulged the habit of sleeping late on weekends and enjoying a traditional family Sunday breakfast of waffles, strawberries, and sour cream.

The affable Ford befriended members of the camp crew. In January 1976, he wrote to Richard Cheney, who had succeeded Rumsfeld as chief of staff: "Our family thought a great deal of Chris (one of the stewards at Camp David). We have noticed he has been bumped from Aspen. What is the story?" The camp commander advised Bill Gulley that Chris was becoming "too familiar with the family and perhaps taking advantage of the situation." But Gulley said Chris would be reassigned to Aspen immediately if the president wished.[32]

The retreat was also being put to use for business. Budget Director Roy Ash's proposal for a budget-cutting session of congressional leaders in September was vetoed as unwieldy, but in December energy advisers met at the camp to make recommendations on coping with oil shortages and related issues.[33]

The rule had been that Cabinet officers and White House staff could use the camp when the president was away from the Washington area. About this time, this rule was changed. Now they could also use it when he chose to stay at the White House. The Cabinet officers were told they could take their families. When staff or guests were invited, business sessions should be included.[34] Visitors were told that irons, ironing boards, hair dryers, toilet articles, and swimming suits were available from the camp duty officer. Taking photographs was not allowed and, despite Liberty, guests were discouraged from bringing pets because of the numerous squirrels, rabbits, raccoons, opossum and deer on the grounds. Bicycles were available outside the cabins and at Laurel

27. President Ford, out for a snowmobile ride, offers a paw to the family's golden retriever, Liberty. *Courtesy Gerald R. Ford Library.*

and Holly. An archery range could be set up near the field house on request. A nature trail took off from near the entrance and wound through outlying areas. A list of available movies, with synopses of each, could be picked up at either Laurel or Holly. There was a shuffleboard court next to the old swimming pool behind the water tower. The pool, by now heated, was also available for their use, although there were no lifeguards. Cribs, strollers and high chairs could be obtained at Chestnut. "Baby sitting service is not available at the camp," the visitors were cautioned. However, "occasionally it is possible to arrange for teenagers in the area to care for smaller children in the cabins."[35]

In January, Secretary of the Army Howard H. Calloway sought permission to use the camp for an "executive retreat," but was told he could not because the Secretary of the Army was not considered a Cabinet member.[36] Even Cabinet rank didn't help Attorney General Edward Levi when he tried to reserve three rooms at the camp for Thanksgiving: Levi was told the White House did not reserve Camp David for holidays.[37] Hartmann, returning from a year-end vacation in St. Croix, found a note from Ford, just back from Vail, urging him to devote full time to the 1976 State of the Union message and saying, "Isolation at

Camp David with a group is a possibility." Hartmann found that the camp had been reserved for a group of foreign visitors.[38] In June, nearly three years before the disaster at Three Mile Island, a three-day meeting at Camp David explored the adequacy of safeguards to assure the safety of nuclear power plants.

One conference that was held at the camp caused trouble. On September 2–4, 1975, the Presidential Clemency Board, charged with considering clemency for Vietnam-era draft evaders, met at the retreat to prepare its final report to the president. Lt. Cmdr. Gerard A. Zimmerman, who had recently taken over as commanding officer of Camp David, reported to the White House military office that "this group was unusually souvenir-conscious and had taken an uncommon amount, and type, of items." Despite press inquiries about reports of "damage" at the camp over the weekend, the matter languished in the White House bureaucracy. In 1976, retired Marine Corps Gen. Lewis W. Walt, a former member of the board, tipped Rep. John Ashbrook of Ohio, a foe of the panel who feared Carter would reconvene it if elected. On August 31, Ashbrook wrote to the FBI demanding an investigation, saying conference participants "took such items as towels, bed sheets, ash trays, the Presidential Seal from the President's Office, silverware and china. Also, they shot over 400 rounds of skeet ammunition and did substantial damage to the surface of the tennis court." The FBI referred the matter to the Naval Investigative Service, but the Military Office's Gulley ordered a White House investigation instead.

Charles R. Torpy, security adviser to the Military Office, reported that nothing had happened "which a reasonable person would categorize as unruly, boisterous, destructive, etc." He said the conference-goers did party well into the evening, but no more so than most others who used the camp. They did "consume" thirty-two vinyl pad holders, twenty-four felt tip pens, thirty pairs of bowling socks, nine ash trays and thirty golf balls, but this "will not be considered by camp personnel to have been excessive, given the number of persons aboard for the conference." Golf balls considered to be "consumed," Torpy wrote, included those lost in the woods. As to the presidential seal that was taken, it was a thin metal one costing less than a dollar that had been glued to a golf cart. The claylike surface of the tennis courts had to be dragged, rolled, and watered as usual after heavy use when the weather had been damp, but had suffered no other harm. "In brief summary," said Torpy, "the use of Camp David by PCB Conference participants does not appear to have involved excesses of behavior, services required or consumables retained, save a golf cart seal." The case was closed.[39]

The Sunday morning papers of March 2, 1975, brought disturbing news to Betty Ford on the Fords' fourth visit to the camp. *Family Weekly,* the syndicated Sunday supplement, carried an article about the first lady's personal assistant entitled, "Mrs. Ford's Best Friend: Nancy Howe." Howe, a garrulous woman with the habit of calling her employer "Petunia," was described by writer Frances Spatz Leighton as the first lady's "personal shopper, confidante and part-time clown." Mrs. Ford was not amused. In a tearful telephone conversation, she told press secretary Sheila Rabb Weidenfeld, "She is *not* my best friend." The first lady said that as she spoke she was rolling up the article and throwing into into the Aspen fireplace and that Howe would be fired. Howe, staying in a guest cabin during the three-day weekend at the camp, was upset at the first lady's reaction. In telephone conversations with both women, Weidenfeld sought to pour oil on the waters. When Mrs. Ford put presidential photographer David Kennerly on the phone, he promised that he, too, would try to calm the first lady. As it happened, Weidenfeld did not regard Nancy Howe as her best friend either, but she managed to persuade the president's wife to keep her on.[40]

On another weekend, the Fords watched television in Aspen as Nessen appeared as a guest host on NBC's zany "Saturday Night Live," whose star, comedian Chevy Chase, was making a small career out of lampooning the president as a clumsy oaf. Ford had provided an introduction for the segment at a taping session in the Cabinet Room a few days earlier, deadpanning, "Ladies and gentlemen, the press secretary to the president of the United States." Now, as he and his family watched in Aspen, Chase as Ford and Nessen as his press secretary swapped wisecracks.[41]

Ford used Camp David only once to meet with a foreign visitor, less even than the two such meetings held by Johnson and far short of Nixon's record of eleven or Eisenhower's five. Indonesian President Suharto's visit in July, 1975, was brief and marked by a small diplomatic contretemps over the size of his traveling party. Ford's national security adviser, Brent Scowcroft, objected when the State Department requested three White House helicopters to transport Suharto, his party, and fifteen members of the Indonesian press. A party of twenty ended up accompanying the visiting head of state into the Catoctins. Thirteen others stayed behind at Andrews Air Force Base. In a toast during his return visit to Suharto in Djakarta that December, Ford recalled their "productive series of talks at Camp David." The toast was polite persiflage. Their brief encounter was of little diplomatic importance.

For Easter, 1976, the Episcopalian Fords decided to make the seventeen-minute, nine-mile drive from Camp David to Harriet Chapel, as Johnson had done in 1967. Advance man Jim Cavanaugh inspected the 143-year-old stone church and told his boss, Terry O'Donnell, "Nothing fancy — Nice inside, sort of nondescript outside." What Cavanaugh didn't mention was that for years the church had been home to a colony of bees. The Reverend Charles Shaffer knew from experience it was time for them to swarm. Alerted by Father Shaffer, the camp sent an exterminator who sprayed the outside of the building twice, leaving dead bees all over the floor and more bees buzzing in the sanctuary. When a young woman insisted on going through with her Easter eve wedding in the church, the priest felt bees crawling on his ankles as the bride and groom repeated their vows. By the time the couple were man and wife, Father Shaffer had been stung on both calves. After all Holy Saturday services had ended, the exterminator came back to fog the interior. The church was kept closed until midnight to allow the insecticide to work. Overnight, a military clean-up crew swept up dead bees, shampooed the carpet, and replaced a bee-stained linen on the altar. Secret Service agents checked under the organ pedals for bombs. The Fords arrived at 10:30 A.M. and the service went off without mishap.[42]

As the pace of the campaign year quickened, Mrs. Ford became concerned about her husband's prospects. With all of the presidential primaries over, Ford led Reagan in delegates but neither had enough for the nomination. On June 16, Missouri, the first state to hold a delegate nominating convention, gave Reagan eighteen and Ford one. Heading for Camp David that weekend, the first lady planned a heart-to-heart talk with the president. "If you ask me, his big problem isn't his speaking; it's his loyalty," she told Sheila Weidenfeld. "He's digging his own grave. They're giving him lousy speeches. Hartmann is head of his speech department. He should kick Bob upstairs and bring in a real professional, a guy who can produce good speeches. And overscheduling. He does too much. I can't get him to take a break." Obviously, she had a lot on her mind. The next night, however, returning from the weekend in the Catoctins, she said, "The opportunity to talk never came up." To her press secretary, she sounded hurt.

On August 9, pollsters, strategists and top staff people gathered at the camp for a preconvention session. When the subject of a running mate was brought up, pollster Rob Teeter said his surveys indicated one thing clearly: the idea of a woman was out. "The country is not ready for it." Ford's running mate should be an "attacker." In fact, the eventual choice, Kansas Sen. Bob Dole, would win an enduring reputation as a "hatchet man" with his slashing campaign for the Ford ticket.

The following day, a Saturday, was devoted to filming for "Ford the Man," a campaign documentary to be shown in Kansas City. As the cameras whirred in the Laurel conference room, someone in a darkened corner of the building shouted, "Reveal your human side, Mr. President." That was the idea, but it wasn't working. Ford's performance grew more wooden with each retake. Things got a little better when his son Jack moved in to do some of the interviewing. Next came the family scene, with the Fords sitting around the dinner table. Susan, who had been scheduled to arrive on Friday, showed up that morning after a heavy date and seemed, to her mother's press secretary, to have a "morning after" air about her. To Mrs. Weidenfeld's practiced eye, the scene somehow fell short of the desired campaign celebration of the all-American family.[43]

As he predicted, Ford disposed of Reagan rather easily, but Carter was something else. When Ford again had the leisure to visit Camp David, it was as a defeated candidate. On a November 21 visit, as Weidenfeld and her husband got in some skeet shooting with Jack Ford and some of his friends, the Secret Service agents regaled them with tales of their mistreatment by President Johnson. They had fonder memories of Ford. "When agents were shivering outside at Camp David, he would sneak them an egg sandwich when the boss wasn't looking," agent George Rush recalled later. "He'd wink and say, 'Boy, it's cold out here. I'll get you a cup of coffee.'"[44] On the way back from the skeet range, they passed the jungle gym the Kennedys had built, and Jack Ford told the Weidenfelds, "Amy Carter will soon be playing on those swings."

Soon most of the camp was closed for cleanup. The Fords made one more visit on January 15. The record of that final weekend closes with a telling vignette: As he waited for the last helicopter ride back to Washington, the thirty-eighth president of the United States stood in an empty fieldhouse near the helipad, practicing his golf swing.[45]

8

Jimmy Carter
Arab and Jew at Camp David

Jimmy Carter, home in Georgia for a weekend break, was on a fishing trip to St. Simon's Island when he made the telephone call.

Two days earlier at the White House, he and his national security adviser, Zbigniew Brzezinski, had explored a new approach to the ever-vexing problem of the Middle East. Egyptian President Anwar Sadat had electrified the world with his unprecedented visit to Jerusalem in November, 1977. After two months, however, there still seemed little chance of the Geneva conference for which Carter had hoped.

Why not invite Sadat and Israel's hard-line Prime Minister Menachem Begin to Camp David?

Now the president picked up the phone on the offshore Georgia island and called Brzezinski. Carter was indeed leaning toward such a summit, either at the Catoctin retreat or in Washington. He wanted to have a meeting about it at the White House that night. To Brzezinski's surprise, when the meeting took place, Rosalynn Carter was there. She was also to be at Camp David.

At the White House meeting, Secretary of State Cyrus Vance argued against an immediate summit, saying that the outcome would be too uncertain for the risk. Brzezinski, too, had cooled to the idea. Carter argued forcefully for a three-way meeting, but in the end decided to invite Sadat alone. So on the first weeekend of February, he and the Egyptian president met with their advisers in the conference room at

28. President Jimmy Carter invited Egypt's Anwar Sadat to the Catoctin retreat in February 1978 to pave the way for the Camp David accords. Walking behind the two presidents is Carter's son Chip. *Courtesy Jimmy Carter Library.*

Laurel and forged a strategy. The Egyptians would make a proposal and lay it open to Israeli attack. That would pave the way for an American compromise.[1] The wintry weekend in the Catoctins also gave the president and first lady a chance to get acquainted with Anwar and Jehan Sadat, going snowmobile racing together and forming a relationship much closer than Carter would ever establish with Begin.[2]

At a July 20 White House breakfast with advisers, Carter again broached the idea of inviting Begin and Sadat to a summit. Looking at a terrestrial globe in his study, he talked of the possibility of a meeting in a dramatic setting overseas. He mentioned Spain and Portugal. Brzezinski, recalling FDR's wartime meeting with Allied leaders at Casablanca, favored Morocco. Ten days later in Aspen Lodge, Carter told advisers he had made his decision. Camp David it was to be.

"If one is looking for a place to lock up a group of distinguished officials for an extended period of time and deny them easy access to anyone on the outside, it would be hard to find a better one than Camp David," Carter's press secretary, Jody Powell, would recall.

Carter agreed that "it was necessary we be completely isolated from the press so that neither Begin nor Sadat nor their representatives would feel constrained one or more times every day to explain what they were doing, what modifications were being made to previous promises or commitments. I think we would have been doomed to total failure had we had a daily report to the press."

There were no facilities at the camp for briefing the horde of journalists who were expected, and in any event, said Powell, "the last thing we wanted was several hundred reporters roaming around the area."[3] Plenty of them wanted access. Both Eddie Adams of the Associated Press and David Hume Kennerly of *Time* sought exclusive photos. ABC asked for a "brief cook's tour before the meeting" to get "leaves-on-the-trees" pictures. Walter Cronkite of CBS wanted to "roam the grounds with a camera." Lt. Cmdr. Ralph Cugowski, the camp commander, responded that "we do have classified installations up here" and it would be difficult to control where cameras were pointed. Cugowski recommended using White House photographers. The White House photo office urged maximum coverage because of the meeting's historical importance and added, "If we get lucky . . . and a settlement is *reached* we want to be in a position to visually remind a quickly-forgetful American public when the President runs again."

Media adviser Jerry Rafshoon agreed that photo coverage should be limited to the beginning and the end, but emphasized to Carter the importance of "showing you with the two leaders early, in control and striking a demeanor that prevents people from thinking that you are being manipulated by these two master showmen and manipulators."[4] Powell proposed a daily photo opportunity inside the fence for the news organizations. Carter, prompted in part by a letter from Mamie Eisenhower, vetoed the idea. President Eisenhower's widow, possessive about the camp and proud that it bore the name of their grandson, wrote the president that she was pleased it would be the site of a peace conference but at the same time wanted its privacy preserved.[5] Privacy or not, there were several hundred people who held White House press passes, and the State Department had issued 495 badges for summit coverage.[6]

On the recommendation of a White House advance and communications team that scouted the area, the press secretary leased the Thurmont American Legion Hall to house a press filing center, staff offices and a briefing room. The rent was $4,200 for twenty-one days, including one extra day because the Legion had to cancel a scheduled dance.[7] Eighteen teletype machines and two hundred special telephone lines, including a direct line to Cairo for the Egyptian press, were installed. There were even twelve phones at the foot of a tree near the small wooden "Camp David" sign just outside the gate. "Everyone has been taking pictures of the sign like mad," an internal press office memo reported on August 30. Later, the sign was ruled off limits and the telephone lines were extended to a point further from the camp entrance.[8]

Camp David was, of course, not new to international conferences. FDR and Churchill had conferred there about the Normandy landings, Eisenhower and Khrushchev had forged the ill-fated "spirit of Camp David," Leonid Brezhnev had stayed in Dogwood as Richard Nixon's guest. But it was not until Carter's meeting with Begin and Sadat that the camp gave its name to a major international accord.

Vance was sent to Cairo and Jerusalem with the formal invitations, which Sadat and Begin quickly accepted. On August 8, with Vance still in the Middle East, the White House announced that the summit would begin the first week in September. Inside the compound, elaborate preparations were made for the Egyptian and Israeli leaders and their hundreds of aides.

Although it was Carter's custom to walk to Aspen from the helipad, when he flew to the Catoctins with Begin, they rode, in deference to the Israeli leader's frail health. Begin stayed in Birch. Sadat was assigned Dogwood, a few hundred feet away. Both cabins were just across a winding driveway and through a grove of trees from Aspen.

Others had more crowded quarters. In Red Oak, for instance, Israeli Foreign Minister Moshe Dayan slept in one of the two bedrooms, while three other Israeli officials shared the other. "There were really not enough houses to go around," said Mrs. Carter.

Holly, the cabin normally used as a recreation center for camp personnel, became the meeting place for the peace talks. "Ideally located between Laurel and the cabins of the three principals, it had a small cozy reading room that made an ideal conference room and was far better suited for the mood we wanted to create than the formal, cold conference room at Laurel," the first lady said. Even so, Carter and Begin often met at the Carters' cabin, using the small private office Nixon had built down the hall from the main living room.

Most members of the American team were assigned to the camp's Marine barracks, because the more desirable accomodations had been used up as Israeli and Egyptian advance teams both demanded more space than originally allocated. Key aides had better quarters, but doubled up. Brzezinski and White House Chief of Staff Hamilton Jordan bunked together, depositing their dirty laundry in the middle of the bedroom floor.[9]

Sadat brought his own chef because his doctors had put him on a diet consisting primarily of boiled meat and vegetables and honey-flavored mint tea. A section of the kitchen at Aspen was set aside for the pots, pans and dishes used in preparing kosher food for members of the Israeli delegation. As matters were planned by the Carters, the principals would eat in their own cabins and the others would eat at Laurel, the staff dining hall. As it turned out, Begin often ate at Laurel with his staff, and the cooks at Aspen hurried to the big dining hall with a golf cart loaded with extra kosher food.[10]

Carter set the style in dress, wearing a pair of faded blue jeans. Vance sported an oversized sweater, and others in the American delegation were equally casual. All delegates received blue wind jackets lettered "Camp David" in gold and were told they could dress as they chose. Begin wore a coat and tie, making the point that he was not a head of state as the two presidents were, and therefore should stick to protocol. Sadat usually went tieless, but wore immaculate sports clothes. Dayan, who had no jeans, wore the khaki slacks in which he gardened at home.[11]

For recreation, Carter followed his usual routine — running, swimming, riding a bicycle, or playing tennis, often with his wife. Some of the American delegation relaxed in the camp bowling alley. Few of the Israeli or Arab participants were bowlers or tennis players. Israeli Defense Minister Ezer Weizman did mount a bicycle, but it was the first time since his childhood. As Margaret Truman had before him, he found the camp claustrophobic and gloomy. Begin sent Dayan on a reconnaissance mission and, when his foreign minister reported back on the forbidding security fence, dubbed the place a "concentration camp de luxe." Sadat would say later that he felt himself "under house detention" at Dogwood.[12] The Israeli leader, no athlete, got around the camp on a golf cart. Sadat most often walked. Each morning, he donned a jogging suit and went for a brisk three- or four-mile hike.

Carter, a Baptist, ordinarily set aside the camp's theater in Hickory Lodge to serve as a chapel on Sundays, with a military field altar and hymnals provided by the chaplain at nearby Fort Ritchie. During the

Camp David meetings it was reserved as a private place for Sadat to say his Moslem prayers and was made available to Begin and his delegation for Rosh Hashanah. A movie projector was set up, along with a billiard table, in a room in Holly adjoining the conference room, and fifty-eight films were shown before the summit was over.[13]

Dayan, who scorned the cinema, contented himself with a daily walk around the perimeter of the camp. He found the landscape beautiful but said the lush greenery and the carpet of fallen leaves "failed to move me as does the wild and primitive desert." He enjoyed the stiff uphill climbs, and found himself recalling boyhood hikes through Galilee, the Jordan Valley, and the Negev Desert.

Begin played chess with Brzezinski, but, as Dayan saw it, "the game proved less a form of peaceful relaxation than a battlefield confrontation, with each one trying desperately to defeat the other." The national security adviser reported that his adversary played "a very good, systematic, somewhat aggressive, but strategically very deliberate game." They split four games. Jordan told Begin: "Thanks for beating Zbig. If he'd won all four games, he would have been impossible to live with."[14]

The leaders had not come to Camp David, however, to play chess, or see movies, or ride bicycles, or even to pray. On August 11, after returning from the Middle East, Vance and aides had gone to Averell Harriman's estate at Middleburg to prepare a briefing book in the quiet of Virginia's hunt country. An attachment to the document warned Carter: "Sadat resorts to generalities as a defense against decisions which are difficult for him to make, and it will frequently be necessary for you to summarize what you have heard him say. Whereas Begin has a tendency toward literalism and an obsession with detail, Sadat is often imprecise with words and has little patience for precision and for real negotiating. In this situation, the danger of genuine misunderstanding, followed by feelings of betrayal and recrimination, is very great."[15]

Elsewhere, the flamboyant Weizman summed up the differences between the two leaders more pithily: "Both desired peace. But whereas Sadat wanted to take it by storm, capitalizing on the momentum from his visit to Jerusalem to reach his final objective, Begin preferred to creep forward inch by inch. He took the dream of peace and ground it down into the fine, dry powder of details, legal clauses and quotes from international law."

At a National Security Council meeting on September 1, Carter said he thought the sessions should take one week at the most. The White House set aside three days, and kept the calendar clear for four more if needed.[16] In the end the participants were to spend, in Carter's words,

29. Carter studied a briefing book and wrote two pages of notes to prepare for his meeting with Sadat and Israel's Menachem Begin. *Courtesy Jimmy Carter Library.*

"thirteen intense and discouraging days, with success in prospect only during the final hours."

The president flew to Camp David by helicopter on Monday, September 4, after telling well wishers on the south lawn of the White House: "Compromises will be mandatory. Without them, no progress can be expected."[17] Summer held full sway in the Catoctins, with bright sunshine and a cloudless sky, as the Carters arrived. Preparing for the meetings, the president studied the bulky briefing book and wrote by hand two pages of notes. At the end of one page, he jotted, "First Egyptian-Jewish peace since time of Joseph." Then, always a careful Bible scholar, he reconsidered. He crossed out "Joseph" and wrote "Jeremiah."

Less biblical considerations were close at hand. The Egyptians and Israelis, evidently assuming their rooms were electronically bugged, held their meetings outside on the porches. Brzezinski had in fact proposed

HEY, FOLKS! THIS SUMMER SEND THE KIDS TO...

CAMP DAVID

WHAT FUN THEY'LL HAVE LEARNING TO...

CANOE...

...AND COOK OUT... ALL UNDER THE WATCHFUL EYE OF OUR TRAINED COUNSELORS!

HORSEBACK RIDE...

TIE KNOTS...

30. A cartoonist for the *Los Angeles Herald Examiner* took a more lighthearted view of the Sadat-Begin meeting. *Courtesy The Hearst Newspapers.*

installing listening devices, but Carter overruled him. "I agreed with the decision, but I must confess that my position had more to do with the expectation that word of the eavesdropping would leak than with a refined sense of propriety," Press Secretary Powell said.[18]

Sadat chose to rest the first night, but Begin wanted to start work immediately. In a meeting with Carter at Aspen, he proposed that the conference be confined to general principles, with the details to be worked out later. Carter insisted on nailing down specific decisions on the major issues. Later that evening, Carter, Vance, and Brzezinski sat on the porch at Aspen and talked about strategy for the second day.[19] Brzezinski did not feel "at all nervous or concerned," but by early morning breakfast Carter "kept shaking his head and expressing his disappointment" at the start of the talks.

31. Rosalynn Carter greeted Sadat on his arrival for the September meeting as the president looked on. Sadat stayed in Dogwood Lodge. He did not use the bicycle. *Courtesy Jimmy Carter Library.*

That morning, at a coffee table on the Aspen patio, Sadat read aloud the full text of the eleven-page Egyptian proposal. It demanded that all Israeli settlements be removed from captured lands, that East Jerusalem be returned, and that Israeli troops pull out of the West Bank. Begin was equally intransigent, and Carter found him "brutally frank" in his assessment of the Egyptian proposal. "How do we know that you can be trusted?" the Israeli asked Sadat. Carter noted "bitter discussions" interspersed with occasional laughter. The men joked about kissing television reporter Barbara Walters and about trade in hashish.[20] Privately, Sadat handed Carter three typewritten pages of concessions, marked for the president's eyes only, to be used as needed. The strategy the two had agreed on in the Catoctin winter was taking shape in their summer meeting. When Vance and Brzezinski joined the president after an afternoon tennis match, the national security adviser found him, to his surprise, "very cheerful and pleased."[21]

Back at his cabin, Begin told an adviser: "At least Sadat didn't say the settlements had to be burned down." The next day, he flatly rejected the Egyptian proposal, saying it smacked of "a victorious state dictating to the defeated." A member of the Israeli delegation approached William B. Quandt, the National Security Council official responsible for dealing with the Arab-Israeli conflict, and told him that "Begin was beginning to harden his position and was already thinking of how the summit could end in failure without his being blamed for it."[22] In a telephone conversation with his wife in Paris that day, Sadat complained, "Begin is being very difficult. That man is so complexed." More time would be needed.[23]

Saturday was the fifth day. After an early morning round of tennis with the president, the U.S. political team decided to try to break the impasse by presenting an American proposal. Vance walked to the lodge where the professional team was working. Carter joined the group in the afternoon and the proposal was put into final form. Late in the afternoon of the sixth day, Sunday, September 10, the Israelis were presented with the American plan. Among other things, it called for withdrawal of Israeli forces from the West Bank. Begin heatedly attacked it. They were in session until 3:00 A.M.[24] Carter invited Dayan to walk back with him to his cabin, where they talked for an hour, sitting on the terrace so as not to disturb Rosalynn and the Carters' daughter, Amy. "I knew that my answers to his questions — and his requests — did not satisfy him, but I hoped that at least I had presented a clear and reasoned account of Israel's position," Dayan said.

There were many such sessions between Carter, the man of detail, and aides to other leaders. "The fact of the matter was that the meeting at Camp David was not a summit meeting in the true sense of the term," said Dayan. "The leaders did not get closer to each other and found no common language. Indeed, the meetings between the three were the least productive. The solution to the knotty problems, the progress in the negotiations, and the subsequent agreements were achieved at other meetings, mainly in talks with members of the American delegation, headed by President Carter, who kept going back and forth between us and the Egyptians."[25] When he did talk directly to Sadat, Carter found they were often able to reach agreement in as little as fifteen minutes. Begin, by contrast, tended to start each session with a half-hour recitation of Jewish history.

Carter took both leaders to Gettysburg after Begin expressed interest in seeing the Civil War battlefield. On the way in the car, the president recited Lincoln's Gettysburg Address, as Churchill had recited Whittier years before. Press Secretary Powell "thought at the time that perhaps he hoped, with that visit to the place where fifty thousand men

32. At an opening get-together, Carter and Sadat chatted while Begin sat stiffly in a metal chair. During most of the thirteen-day negotiating session, Sadat and Begin did not talk to each other. *Courtesy Jimmy Carter Library.*

had fallen, to let Sadat and Begin know that he understood and to remind them of what was at stake."[26]

Early in the talks, a Secret Service agent saw Sadat, walking with his cane and smoking his pipe, and Begin, hands in his pockets, meet on an asphalt walkway and stroll off together into the woods. As he watched, Begin picked up a leaf and started rolling it in his hands. The agent felt that "something good was going to happen."[27] In the last ten days of the talks, however, although their cottages were only about a hundred yards apart, Sadat and Begin did not speak to each other. To Quandt, it appeared that they did "not get along personally at all."[28]

The negotiators did not rest on the seventh day, a Monday. Between eight and ten o'clock, as the Egyptians watched from their quarters about twenty yards away, members of the Israeli delegation ran or bicycled to Holly, handing new bits of language to Carter and his advisers at the table where they sat. Each time, an American would emerge from Holly a few minutes later and ride off toward the Israelis' cabin.[29]

On September 12, day eight, Carter wrote out on a yellow legal pad the first draft of a proposed accord on the Sinai. As later refined, it called for phased Israeli withdrawal from the triangular peninsula that Israel had seized in its 1967 war with Egypt. Begin and Dayan balked. "My right eye will fall out, my right hand will fall off before I ever agree to the dismantling of a single Jewish settlement," Begin told Brzezinski during a forty-five-minute walk in the woods. In the next two days there was little progress. Carter became increasingly annoyed with Begin's habit of interrupting. Rosalynn Carter told Brzezinski that her husband had become so discouraged that he called the Israeli a "psycho." Vance reassured the president and first lady that "in such negotiations there are always up and downs and that things eventually will turn out all right."[30] Vice President Walter Mondale, alarmed by reports from the meetings, flew to the mountaintop and persuaded Carter to soften his position on West Bank settlements.[31]

Powell, meanwhile, suspected that the Israelis were beginning to leak and manipulate news from the talks. Reporters complained to him that their counterparts were getting background briefings from both Israeli and Egyptian sources inside the camp. The press secretary, who had been giving deliberately uninformative daily briefings at the American Legion Hall, began to supplement them by talking with reporters more freely on a not-for-attribution basis.[32]

"After ten days of intense discussions and negotiations at Camp David, almost everyone believed the talks had reached an impasse," Quandt wrote. "Even Carter's belief that the tranquil atmosphere of Camp David would make it easier to reach an agreement was not holding up. Despite the lovely surroundings, claustrophobia was setting in. Almost everyone wanted to get away, if only for a few hours."[33]

Wednesday, September 13, was somber and rainy as Carter and his advisers worked on changes. Brzezinski feared the modifications, designed to sway Begin, might instead merely alienate Sadat. Other fears soon arose. At 4:15 the next morning, Brzezinski made his way to Aspen in his pajamas, awakened by a telephone call from the president. "Zbig, I am very much concerned for Sadat's life," Carter told him. The president had gone to see his Egyptian counterpart at about ten o'clock and been told that he was asleep. Because the light was on in his cabin and he normally stayed up late, Carter feared Sadat might have come to harm from hard-liners around him.[34] In fact, the Egyptian president was unharmed, but increasingly out of temper. Dayan had told him the Knesset would have to approve any action Begin took on removal of Israeli settlements from the Sinai. Sadat mistakenly believed that this

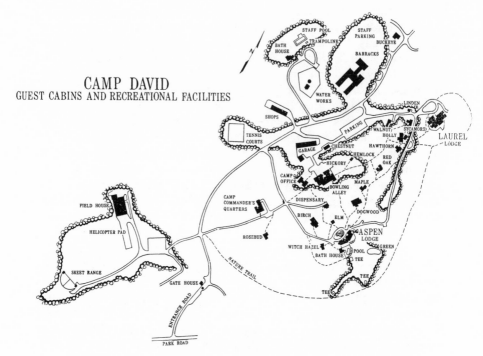

CAMP DAVID
GUEST CABINS AND RECREATIONAL FACILITIES

33. By the time of this 1971 map, Camp David was far from the little cluster of cabins in the woods that FDR inaugurated. Later, a chapel would be built along the road *(upper right)* leading to Laurel Lodge. *Courtesy National Archives Nixon Presidential Materials Project.*

meant Begin could not negotiate anything without Knesset approval. "Ezer, everything's collapsing," he told Weizman. Later that day, Vance received a telephone call from the Egyptian president and crossed the road to Aspen Lodge. His face was so ashen that Carter feared war had broken out. "Sadat has packed his bags," Vance said. "He has asked for a helicopter and he's leaving later with his entire delegation."[35]

The stunned Carter told Vance and Brzezinski to do nothing about the helicopter request without written authorization from him. Then he telephoned Sadat and asked to meet with him privately. Sadat said he saw no reason for a meeting. A few minutes later, Sadat's telphone rang again. It was Jehan Sadat calling from Paris. "Begin is being totally unreasonable," Sadat told her. "There is no point in continuing." Dismayed, Mrs. Sadat told her husband, "You can hear at least what President Carter has to say." In a strained voice, Sadat agreed.[36]

Back at Aspen, Carter changed into more formal clothes and walked to Dogwood. If the Egyptian president walked out of the talks, he said, "It will mean first of all an end to the relationship between the United States and Egypt. There is no way we can ever explain this to our people. It would mean an end to this peacekeeping effort, into which I have put so much investment. It would probably mean the end of my Presidency because this whole effort will be discredited. And last but not least, it will be the end of something that is very precious to me: my friendship with you. Why are you doing it?" Sadat replied, "You have imposed this and that on me, but OK. For peace, I agree." The conversation had lasted less than a quarter of an hour. Both men stood throughout.[37] When Carter walked back to Aspen, he told Vance, "Sadat will stay."[38]

On the next night, Carter and Sadat watched on television in Aspen as Muhammad Ali regained his heavyweight championship from Leon Spinks. With the Moslem leader of Egypt standing by, the Baptist president telephoned his congratulations to the Moslem fighter in Los Angeles.

Work continued on a speech Carter was to deliver on Monday if, as anticipated, the talks ended in failure.[39] The most crucial discussions came on Saturday night, September 16, in a session that lasted well into Sunday morning and focused on the West Bank and Gaza. By Sunday, the way appeared to be clear for an agreement. Powell summoned Hodding Carter, spokesman for the State Department, and members of his own staff from Washington to plan the announcement. Then, as the group conferred in their shirtsleeves on the patio at Laurel, Jordan walked up, motioned Powell aside, and told him the president wanted to see him in his cabin. There was a problem: in the billiards room at Holly, Dayan had told Carter and Vance that Begin could not accept the proposed language on the status of holy sites in East Jerusalem and he was threatening to break off the talks.

Powell hurried back to Laurel, ordered preparations for the announcement shelved, and returned to Aspen with Jordan. Through the windows from the terrace they could see Carter plunged in conversation with Sadat's flinty undersecretary for foreign affairs, Usama al-Baz, and Israel's Attorney General Aharon Barak. Carter spotted his worried aides pacing up and down on the flagstones, turned his back to the others in the room and flashed a thumbs-up sign. The Jerusalem problem had been solved. A few minutes later another sticking point arose, this time over details of a Knesset vote on removing settlements from the Sinai Peninsula.

Late Sunday afternoon, Carter went over a proposed final agreement with Sadat and al-Baz. After seeing Sadat to the door, he told Vance, "I was almost afraid to ask him, but yes, I think we have an agreement." They did — on the twenty-third draft of the American proposal. Rosalynn Carter favored having the accord signed right away, before either party could change his mind. The president told her not to worry. The documents had already been initialed. Rafshoon told Carter it would take four hours to arrange a signing ceremony. The president's watch read 6:08 P.M. "You have my approval eight minutes ago," he said. "Let's have the ceremony at ten o'clock." Rafshoon and Powell pleaded for more time, and the ceremony was set for 10:30 P.M. in the East Room of the White House.[40]

Summer had given way to the approach of fall as the meetings ran their course, but now one of the thunderstorms common in Catoctin summers came up and the camp was drenched with an ominous downpour. "The President sat in his chair, looking rather tired, with a wistful smile on his face, but not particularly elated," Brzezinski recalled in a note written two days later. "No one spoke up, no one cheered."[41]

Sadat and Begin exchanged visits. At Begin's quarters in Birch, they toasted each other. The Israeli drank wine, the Egyptian orange juice.

Reporters were assembled in the briefing room next to the American Legion bar. They were told there would be a full-scale briefing later that day in the State Department auditorium in Washington, followed by the signing ceremony.

In a sign of trouble to come, al-Baz and other Egyptian foreign ministry officials boycotted the signing. The Camp David accords would lead to a peace treaty between Israel and Egypt on March 26, 1979, but leave the Israelis still in a state of war for years with their other Arab neighbors. The accords would win the Nobel Peace Prize for Begin and Sadat, but not for the mediator Carter. When Carter visited the Middle East as a former president in 1987, Begin, out of office and living the life of a recluse embittered by the continuing strife in the region, refused to see him.

For his part, Carter told the Democratic National Convention in Atlanta in 1988, "Camp David is not just a weekend retreat; it is a symbol of the courage and determination of two great leaders."[42]

If the accords were the high point of Carter's experience at Camp

David, the domestic summit of 1979 may have been the low point. Just back from an economic meeting in Tokyo, Carter went to the camp on July 3 to prepare his fifth nationwide address on the energy crisis. He took with him a copy of a public opinion survey by pollster Patrick Caddell suggesting the need for a patriotic appeal to overcome unrest among the American people. After studying Caddell's memo, Carter sent for the proposed energy speech his staff had been preparing while he was in Japan. He and Rosalynn read it over. Carter wrote in his diary, "I told her I couldn't deliver it, that I had already made four speeches to the nation on energy and that they had been increasingly ignored." With his wife he decided "that we would stay at Camp David for a few days, and have some people come in whom we trusted to give me advice on where we should go from here." He telephoned aides in Washington and told them to cancel the speech.

Once again Mondale, alarmed at a plan that he was convinced could lead to political catastrophe, flew to Camp David. In a walk around the perimeter fence, Carter persuaded him to support the decision but not to agree with it. Over the next few days, the president met separately with small groups of political advisers, governors, local officials, congressional leaders, business and labor executives, economists, and energy experts. In one session, he sat on the floor of Aspen, propped against a cushion, taking notes. Some of the politically sophisticated guests found Carter's manner disturbing. "I think he believes, as I do, that he's not getting across to the people," said Clark Clifford, now a Washington lawyer again and still advising presidents.[43]

Outside the conference room, the elegant Clifford had his own problems when he mounted a bicycle for the first time in sixty years. Unfamiliar with hand brakes, he bailed out on a steep slope and got some Camp David dirt on his well-creased trousers.[44]

To Arkansas Governor Bill Clinton, Carter seemed to have aged a great deal since he had last seen him in February. Clinton, summoned from a governors' conference in Louisville where he had told reporters his former fellow governor was "in deep trouble," sat next to the president during a three-hour meeting of business, labor, and political leaders. At a news conference on his return to Little Rock, he said he spoke to Carter as a friend and "told him very frankly in what I thought was an emotional exchange that . . . his administration was too withdrawn, too stilted, too involved in the day-to-day administration."[45]

Carter's political advisers suggested changes in the cabinet that would be made. With Jordan and Powell out of the room, they suggested changes in the White House staff that would not be. They told

' Sounds great! Can I borrow it ?'

34. Arkansas Governor Bill Clinton said he gave Carter friendly advice at the president's July 1979 summit. A cartoonist in Little Rock satirized Clinton as Superman offering his cloak. *Courtesy Jon Kennedy Cartoons.*

Carter he "seemed bogged down in the details of administration." Privately, a top aide cautioned the president not to let the meeting "degenerate into a bitch session."[46] In his notes, Carter recorded what people told him. A young woman from Pennsylvania said, "I feel like ordinary people are excluded from political power." Another visitor said, "Mr. President, you're not leading this nation — you're just managing the government." Another, in a phrase that was to echo, told him, "There is a malaise of civilization."

The Carters wound up with unannounced trips to homes in Carnegie, Pennsylvania, and Martinsburg, West Virginia, and then joined eighteen editors, columnists, and television anchors for lunch in Laurel Lodge. As the journalists scribbled notes on big white pads at their

'Why, it's Mr. Moses and company, back from the mountain . . . what's the good word, Mose?'

35. Cartoonist Patrick Oliphant depicted Carter, Chief of Staff Hamilton Jordan, and Press Secretary Jody Powell coming down from the mountain. Some saw the summit as the beginning of the end for the Carter presidency. *Courtesy Patrick Oliphant.*

places, the Carters outlined the president's thinking on a "deep background" basis, meaning they could report on his thoughts and intentions without attributing the information to anyone. One of the writers, Meg Greenfield of the *Washington Post,* found "something slightly eerie about presidential power's having been transported to this place — a kind of well-tended woodland park, silent and almost uninhabited, seeming to exist outside the rhythms of real time." Another journalist at the luncheon, Jack Germond of the *Washington Star,* reflected after Carter left office that "the guests could not but wonder what the hell was going on."

Others wondered, too. The *Post*'s Haynes Johnson, not at the gathering, wrote, "The longer the silence from the summit, the greater the suspense. The more people consulted in secret, in or out of government, the greater the anticipation. One way or another, there will be a final act. Carter's fate will hang upon it."[47]

In his televised speech of July 15, Carter told the nation: "We were sure that ours was a nation of the ballot, not the bullet, until the murders of John Kennedy, Robert Kennedy, and Martin Luther King Jr. We were taught that our armies were always invincible and our causes always just, only to suffer the agony of Vietnam. We respected the presidency as a place of honor until the shock of Watergate . . . These wounds are still very deep. They have never been healed."

He did not use the word *malaise,* but it would be used against him with telling effect in the 1980 presidential campaign, as the buoyant, optimistic Ronald Reagan overwhelmed an opponent he portrayed as an apostle of American self-doubt.

It was from Camp David that on October 22, 1979, Carter instructed Vance to proceed with arrangements to bring the Shah of Iran to the United States for medical treatment, despite the recommendations of diplomats in Tehran who feared the Iranian response.[48] He was at the camp when he learned on November 4 that the American Embassy in Tehran had been overrun and hostages taken.[49]

A few weeks later, at Thanksgiving dinner in Laurel with White House aides and their families, the president led the group in prayer for the hostages' quick release.[50] He and his family spent a quiet Christmas in the Catoctins that year, because he had vowed not to light the White House Christmas tree until the hostages were freed, and chose to pass up holiday festivities in Washington.[51]

It was at the camp on March 22, 1980, that he met for five and one-half hours with Mondale, Vance, Brzezinski, and others, all dressed in jeans, for a discussion focused on an isolated patch of desert about two hundred miles south of the Iranian capital. From aerial photographs, it appeared that the sand there would be smooth enough for transport planes to land. Carter authorized the flight of a small airplane to the area to check. The reconnaissance led to the disastrous Desert One helicopter operation that cost eight lives and failed to free the fifty Americans. After continued negotiating efforts, they would be freed on Reagan's inauguration day.[52]

In times of crisis or not, the retreat in the Catoctins was important to Carter from the beginning of his presidency in January, 1977. As the outgoing and incoming presidents and their wives rode from the White House to the Capitol for the inauguration, first lady Betty Ford and Mrs. Carter chatted "mostly about Camp David, where the Fords had just spent their last weekend."[53] Carter, however, "felt he had been sent to Washington to do a job, not to relax away from the White House." At a meeting in his home in Plains, Georgia, a month after the election, he closely questioned Bill Gulley, then director of the White House Military Office, about the Catoctin retreat. Gulley got the impression that the president-elect wanted to close the camp.[54]

At about this time, Stephen Hess, a fellow at the Brookings Institution in Washington and a former Nixon aide, received a telephone call from Carter assistant Greg Schneiders while at home on Sunday. Hess, who had built a substantial reputation as a presidential scholar since leaving government service, had agreed to do a series of briefing papers for Carter on the organization of the White House. Nevertheless he was irritated by being called with a query about how to cut down on motor pools while he was watching the Washington Redskins on television. When he had cooled down, Hess wrote a defense of the trappings of the presidency.

"A president should be able to walk in the woods on a weekend if it helps him restore his spirit or rethink his concerns," he advised Carter. "Herbert Hoover and John Kennedy were able to buy themselves rustic retreats, but should we have to count on a president being rich? I have never been inside Camp David; judge for yourself whether it is too opulent. Do not dismantle it until you have determined that it does not serve a legitimate need."

"The advice may have been gratuitous, but I like to think that there could not have been a Camp David accord, the high-water mark of the Carter presidency, had he not followed my advice," Hess reflected later.[55]

Richard Nixon, living the life of a former president in New York, also heard that Carter was considering decommissioning the retreat that FDR had "accepted" on the Navy's behalf three decades before. He urged the president-elect to visit the camp before making a decision.[56] Carter and others who were with him denied that he ever planned to shut Camp David down.[57]

Whatever he thought about it in Plains, Carter liked the camp when he saw it. A little over a month after he took office, he directed his old friend and new budget director, Bert Lance: "Please do not permit any more construction at Camp David." He also told Lance "not ever to let me know how much it cost to operate it, because I didn't want to know."[58]

A survey ordered by camp officials a month after Carter took office, however, showed that age, moisture, drainage, and termites had caused structural damage to ten buildings. Repairs to Aspen, Hickory and Maple were quickly undertaken and others were renovated later. The most seriously damaged, the camp dispensary, was torn down and rebuilt at a site farther from the presidential lodge. Carter approved the project, although he said the $61,000 cost estimate seemed excessive because extra Seabees were being brought in to do the work.

Also in the first year, the Pentagon approved replacement of the camp's twenty-year-old steam heating plant, cautioning that "complete failure of the entire heating system is possible at any time." The $313,000 project provided electrical baseboard heating to seven support and residential buildings. A Defense Department rule against use of electrical heat for personal comfort was waived.[59] The Sheet Metal Workers International Association offered to install solar heat at no cost, but the White House said the deep woods and cool weather of the Catoctin retreat were obstacles.[60] Another then-fashionable mode of heating fared better. In line with his support for wood as an energy-saving fuel, Carter accepted the donation of wood-burning stoves for Aspen and five of the guest cabins.[61]

Carter made ninety-nine visits to the camp, totaling 6,647 hours and 50 minutes, or more than three-fourths of a year.[62] He also made it available to Cabinet officers and staff aides and their families, not without some resistance. When Secretary of Labor Ray Marshall asked permission to take his family and allow his children to bring their friends, Jordan okayed the family but vetoed the friends.[63] Presented with a suggestion for restricting use of the camp while he and his family were there, the president wrote on it, "A *few* other guests don't bother us."[64] A limit of two families in the guest cabins was imposed.[65] For the two months before the 1980 election, at Mrs. Carter's request, no guests at all were allowed while the campaigning president was there.[66]

Another time, in a memo on guidelines for use of the camp, Hugh Carter pointed out to the president how many people it took to maintain it whether anybody was using it or not. Wrong strategy, argued Jordan. The president would come back and say "too many — cut further." Jordan suggested "a different approach to the President if the desired result is he will let some of us have use of Camp David."[67] The president's private secretary, Susan Clough, pleaded that she should be allowed to take her children to give them "some insight and sharing of my work and the people, other than a tired mom." She was added to a list for special consideration.[68] Jordan urged Hugh Carter to "point out that staff persons who used Camp David would pay for meals just as we do at the White House."

They paid, in fact, for more than meals. When chief White House lobbyist Frank Moore brought his wife and four children for a weekend in the Catoctins as guests of the Carters, he got a bill for $250 for the helicopter ride. He didn't have to pay for himself, but it was $50 a head for the rest of the family. Some aides were outraged and stalled for weeks before paying up.[69] Rosalynn Carter disagreed with the policy, but it was reaffirmed.[70]

Sometimes the relaxation was overdone. In the new administration's first spring, Mondale's teenaged daughter, Eleanor, and a friend aroused concern by riding golf carts at breakneck speeds both on and off the narrow, hilly, and curved roads and trails. An officer of the camp said this not only was dangerous for the two young women but could damage the lawns. The conference table at Laurel was also put to a new use. Miss Mondale and her friend played shuffleboard on it with heavy crystal ashtrays, breaking one and scratching the table.[71]

In the next year, another incident brought a more serious investigation. It began with the discovery of some minor theft from the troop dining area. Two Marine suspects, reassigned to the Marine Barracks in Washington, admitted they were involved. One of them volunteered the information that he knew about marijuana smoking at Camp David. Sixteen Marines were identified in sworn statements, but inquiries showed only 12 were still at the camp. After investigation by the Navy, they were reassigned to the Marine Barracks for disciplinary action and stripped of presidential protection clearances. Despite efforts to keep the investigation low key, the administration was embarrassed when the story broke on network television and in Washington newspapers the following weekend. The Barracks commander said he believed a Marine made an anonymous call to the press, prompting queries to the Marine press office about the investigation.[72]

Invitations to the camp were, as usual, one of the perquisites that went with presidential favor. It did not escape Brzezinski that Vance, his rival for predominance as a foreign policy adviser, was invited to the presidential hideaway more frequently than he was.[73]

As in every Democratic administration since Eisenhower, the subject of making the name of the camp Shangri-La again came up. The Democratic Central Committee for Frederick County passed a resolution urging the change, saying many residents were "extremely disappointed" that the original name of the camp within the county's borders had been abandoned. Gulley, however, argued that the name Camp David had become "traditional, symbolic and instantly recognized by people throughout the country and around the world." Camp David it remained, and would remain. By the time of the Clinton administration, White House officials said no suggestions for a name change had been received. FDR's Shangri-La was a fading memory.[74]

During his first year in office, Carter and his family attended

churches in surrounding communities on the Sundays they were at
Camp David. After completing the rounds, they had the Army chaplain
from Fort Ritchie conduct services. They dressed informally, and invited
their guests to do the same.

When the Carters arrived by helicopter they would be met by the
presidential limousine but, unless the weather was bad, they passed it
up and walked through the woods to Aspen. They would read together
and the president would work on speeches or decisions. Sometimes he
didn't shave. Often they would have an early dinner and then watch a
movie with daughter Amy. In July of 1978, Carter invited Civil War
historian Shelby Foote to visit the camp and guide him on a tour of
nearby battlefields.

The Carters walked hand in hand on moonlit nights, jogged in their
warm-up clothes around the perimeter trail, and went cross-country skiing. On one skiing trip about a month before he left office, the president
fell and broke his left collarbone.[75]

He liked to run. On September 15, 1979, wearing number 39, black
socks, and a yellow headband, he took part in the 6.2-mile Catoctin
Mountain Race. As he neared the four-mile mark, about two hundred
yards from the entrance road to Camp David, he faltered, walked two
or three paces, attempted to run again, then staggered. Secret Service
agents grabbed his arms. Although he insisted that he was able to continue the race, he was assisted across the road to an electric cart in
which Secret Service agents had been riding. Pale and breathing heavily,
he was given oxygen.

"It really scared me," said John Frye of Hagerstown, Maryland,
who was a few runners behind Carter in the race. "I saw him fall over
and they were holding each arm. His legs were gone and they sat him
down on the concrete. He looked totally exhausted."

An ambulance was called and Marine One was removed from the
hangar to be ready for a possible evacuation. Dr. William Lukash, the
White House physician, who had been running with him, said he
wanted to take the president to Aspen in a spare car before doing anything else. At the presidential lodge, Carter was put to bed. Lukash,
assisted by a Navy nurse and two corpsmen, began medical tests and
administered fluids intravenously. According to a report by Assistant
Special Agent in Charge Roger D. Counts of the Secret Service, the president's vital signs had returned to normal within an hour. By 1:45 P.M.,
two hours after he dropped out of the race, "he had the appearance of
being fully recovered." At 2:00 P.M. he returned to the assembly area
and took part in a twenty-minute awards ceremony.[76]

Carter, an avid woodworker, made frequent use of the camp's carpentry shop.[77] At Hunting Creek, he sharpened his skills as a fly fisherman, catching fish where Roosevelt and Churchill had failed. "Of all the things about the presidency, I would guess going to Camp David now and then is the one I would miss most," he said later.[78]

As he prepared to leave, he saw to the careful crating of two bamboo rods he had kept at the camp. One was a gift, "the finest and most balanced rod I've ever seen," made for him after normal working hours by craftsmen of the H. L. Leonard Co. The other was an award from a sporting magazine for his efforts to protect Alaska wilderness.

When the crates arrived in Plains, after shipment from the Catoctins by way of the White House, it was found that the two rods were missing. Jimmy Carter, tormented by the hostage crisis, taunted with the echoes of "malaise," defeated for reelection as no president had been since Herbert Hoover, was not even to be able to keep his prized fishing poles. They had been stolen.[79]

9

Ronald Reagan
Horseback in Shangri-La

The president, at ease in an open-necked lumberjack shirt, took a gulp of hot water from a glass, put it down on the long table, and waited for an arm signal from personal assistant Jim Kuhn.

"My fellow Americans," he began.

As he had been so many times since he went to work for Station WOC in Davenport, Iowa, in 1933, Ronald Reagan was on the air. It was April 17, 1982, and Reagan was delivering the first of some 150 weekly five-minute radio messages that he would broadcast from Laurel Lodge. His subject was the Geneva arms negotiations. In later talks from Laurel, usually from the conference room, he would talk on themes ranging from United States-Soviet relations and the hotly disputed dispatch of U.S. Marines to Lebanon to the availability of summer jobs for students.

Nancy Reagan would be with him. Afterwards they would walk to the gym, where the president would lift weights, and his wife, after her breast cancer operation in 1987, would do therapeutic exercises.

The hot water was a throat-clearing trick Reagan said he had learned from a preacher and from his friend Frank Sinatra. The casual clothes were standard. Unlike Richard Nixon, Reagan was not one to wear a coat and tie on Saturday if he could help it; except when there were state visitors, Nancy, too, wore jeans.[1]

Reagan visited the camp in the Catoctins more than any of his pre-

36. President Ronald Reagan, who favored informal attire while at Camp David, broadcast some 150 of his weekly five-minute radio addresses from Laurel Lodge. *Courtesy Ronald Reagan Library.*

decessors, 187 times for a total of 571 days, compared with forty-four visits by Dwight Eisenhower, the only other president to serve two full terms since the retreat was built.[2] Reagan also used it more privately than any other president, seldom entertaining a foreign visitor overnight or holding a conference on affairs of state. Typically, he and Nancy Reagan came alone, usually leaving the White House about 3:00 or 3:30 P.M. on Friday and returning early Sunday afternoon or, when it was a three-day weekend, on Monday. Even his daughter, Maureen, although she spent most of her father's administration in Washington, made it only once — on a spring weekend in 1985 when her stepmother was away in California looking at a prospective home for the Reagans' retirement. Reagan did not offer the use of the camp to his staff when he was not there, as other presidents had done. "Even Ronnie's closest advisers were rarely there," said Mrs. Reagan.[3]

There was one compassionate exception. White House Counsellor Edwin Meese, an old friend of Reagan's from his days as California's

37. The presidential retreat, officially a Navy base, is staffed by sailors and Marines. Here they salute the commander-in-chief on a Fourth of July weekend walk in 1988. *Courtesy the White House.*

governor, was away from Washington in the summer of 1982 when he learned that his nineteen-year-old son had been killed in an accident. The automobile the youth was driving went out of control on the George Washington Parkway. Going straight from the airport to his office, Meese was moved when the Reagans quickly joined him, throwing their arms around him in his grief. Meese and his wife were invited to use the camp for several days "to get our lives back together."[4]

Pat Nixon, who should have known, told Mrs. Reagan before she became first lady, "Without Camp David, you'll go stir crazy."[5] The new president's wife was given a familiarization tour of the camp on January 29, 1981, nine days after Reagan's inauguration. The next day she and her husband helicoptered into the Catoctins for the first weekend visit of his presidency. Reagan had been at the camp once before, for political consultations during the Nixon administration.

The president was disappointed to find that Nixon had paved the riding trails, and quickly restored them.[6] He and his wife were pleased to look out the picture window on their first visit and see a delegation of eight white-tailed deer. The deer, almost exterminated in the area by heavy hunting before World War II, had flourished after establishment of the surrounding national park, and were now so plentiful that debate raged in the Park Service as to whether a hunting season should be created.[7] The dogwoods that once flourished in the park, by contrast, had nearly disappeared — victims of a disease spreading through the Appalachians.[8] The Reagans rounded out their first day by touring the grounds, meeting some of the staff and then, in what would become a Friday and Saturday night routine, inviting aides to join them in breaking out the popcorn and watching a movie at Aspen.

By now, the video cassette recorder had arrived at Camp David, and most movies were shown by VCR. At the president's lodge, however, the film reel and projector still held sway. The movies, too, were as often as not old ones from the era of Reagan's own Hollywood stardom. At first, new attractions were shown, but Reagan "began trying to sandwich in a few older movies from my generation." Soon the 1930s and 1940s were the mode in the Catoctins. "He would bring in the Secret Service and the other people around and give them a little education in what some of the great films of the past are," an associate recalled later. For his seventy-seventh birthday, Reagan watched his own performance as a highly fictionalized George Armstrong Custer in the 1940 film, *Santa Fe Trail*. In 1983, on the eve of unveiling his revised proposal for a nuclear arms treaty with the Soviets, he watched *War Games,* a film in which a teenager ties into the North American Air Defense Command computer and almost touches off World War III.[9]

Amanda Deaver, daughter of Deputy White House Chief of Staff Michael K. Deaver, had a fourteenth birthday dinner with her parents and the Reagans at Aspen and then watched *Bedtime for Bonzo,* the much-ridiculed 1951 comedy in which the future president costarred with a chimpanzee. Afterward, Reagan regaled his guests with stories about the hazards of making a movie with a monkey.[10]

Bonzo may have been boffo at Camp David, but Mike Deaver was to find that *The Kiss of the Spider Woman* was poison. Deaver had been moved by the 1985 film about the lives and deaths of a homosexual and a left-wing radical who meet in a South American jail, and recommended it to the president. The Reagans had a print delivered to Aspen, but turned it off halfway through the reel. "Mike, how could you recommend that film?" Nancy Reagan asked. "It was dreadful."[11] The incident came home to Deaver as a signal of the Reagans' mind set: upright, decent, and in so many ways fixed in the 1950s or earlier.

The Reagans made their second visit to the camp late in February, with Vice President George Bush and Supreme Court Justice Potter

38. More than any other president, Ronald Reagan used the camp for purely personal and family purposes. *Right to left:* Ron Reagan, Nancy Reagan, the president, and Ron's wife, Doria. *Courtesy AP/Wide World.*

Stewart and their wives as guests. Four months later, Stewart, a Yale friend of the vice president, would announce his retirement. The Reagans were back again on March 6, beginning their routine of going to the retreat whenever they were both in Washington and did not have weekend engagements.

After Reagan was wounded by a would-be assassin's bullet on March 30, 1981, he spent part of his recuperation at Camp David. On the telephone to Maureen on the morning of her April wedding in Beverly Hills, he told her from Aspen, "we all have every reason to celebrate."[12]

There were no horses stabled at the camp, but the National Park Service brought mounts for the Reagans to ride when they were there. The Secret Service reluctantly allowed them to ride on trails outside the fence, as Harry and Bess Truman had done in their jeep. Sometimes deer would frighten the horses.[13]

The president and his wife took their first Camp David horseback ride on June 6, two days before President José Lopez-Portillo of Mexico, also an avid horseman, arrived for working meetings and riding with

Reagan. The meeting was an exception. When Secretary of State George P. Shultz visited Moscow to pave the way for the 1987 Reagan-Gorbachev summit in Washington, he suggested that some discussions might be held at Camp David. As the summit meeting took shape, however, there was no trip into the Catoctins for the Soviet leader.[14]

Even Reagan's great friend from Britain, Prime Minister Margaret Thatcher, was invited only for lunch on her two visits. The first time, December 22, 1984, Reagan met her helicopter in a golf cart and took her to Aspen and then on to Laurel. Listening to the president outline his prized "Star Wars" program of space-based missile defense, Mrs. Thatcher found him "at his most idealistic," especially when he spoke of making the defense system available to all countries. "I was horrified to think that the United States would be prepared to throw away a hard-won lead in technology," she wrote later. She made good use of her time: in an hour and a half speech, she relied on her training as a chemist to lecture the American president on the obstacles to implementation of the system. Reagan conceded that "it would be some time before we knew it would work as we hoped." Before lunch was on the table, the two sides had agreed on a declaration that there would be negotiations before the system was actually put in place.

The British prime minister's second visit to the Catoctins was prompted by Reagan's proposal at the October, 1986, United States-Soviet summit in Reykjavik, Iceland, to eliminate all strategic ballistic missiles over ten years. Although the summit foundered on disagreements over "Star Wars," Mrs. Thatcher felt "as if there had been an earthquake beneath my feet" when she heard how far the Americans had been prepared to go. "I arranged," she said, "to fly to the United States to see President Reagan." Preparing for talks at Camp David, she showed shrewd knowledge of the president's strengths and weaknesses in the care with which she crafted her arguments. "These must be logically coherent, persuasive, crisp and not too technical," she wrote. In the end, Reagan agreed to a statement reaffirming support for a 50 percent cut in United States and Soviet strategic weapons over five years, but making no mention of eliminating them. "I had reason to be well pleased," said Mrs. Thatcher.[15]

The only other foreign visitor to be entertained at the camp was Japanese Prime Minister Yasuhiro Nakasone, who got along so well with Reagan that they took to calling each other "Yasu" and "Ron."[16]

In another scene that would seldom be repeated, Reagan invited fifteen Democratic congressmen to the mountaintop for lunch and a round of lobbying on behalf of what some Democratic critics were call-

39. Some aides thought Reagan should have used the camp more frequently to entertain members of Congress. Here, in his first year in
office, he regales visiting congressmen while his then secretary of the
treasury, Donald Regan, looks on from the right. *Courtesy the White
House, photograph by Bill Fitz-Patrick.*

ing a "rich man's tax cut." In cowboy boots, brown slacks, and a beige,
western-style shirt, the president joined his guests for half an hour of
coffee, orange juice, and bloody marys on the Aspen patio and then
walked them to Laurel for hot dogs, hamburgers, potato salad, chili
beans, and fresh corn.[17] A similar delegation of thirty-eight members of
Congress and senior White House aides was invited for lunch and a
tour of the camp in August, 1982, before the pattern of almost purely
private use took over. Commenting on such lobbying techniques as bar-
becues at Camp David, one alumnus of the Reagan White House was to
say, "This is powerful stuff; we didn't use them enough."[18]

At Camp David in July, 1981, Reagan made a decision that would
help to stamp him as a strong president and at the same time raise
doubts about his judgment. Secretary of Transportation Drew Lewis
came up into the Catoctins that day to to tell the president that the
union representing air traffic controllers was threatening to strike. Reagan's response was swift: "no president could tolerate an illegal strike
by federal employees." They struck; he fired them. An influential Briton

in Washington said later that the action, more than anything, stimulated the flood of European investment in the United States. Domestically, however, some thought that the president jeopardized air safety.[19]

As 1982 opened, Reagan, like other presidents before him, went to Camp David to work on his State of the Union speech.[20]

Meese, Deaver, and other senior White House aides held a day-long meeting on political and legislative strategy at the camp on February 5, 1982. But unlike other presidents who had been in the thick of such meetings, Reagan stayed at the White House and got a report later.[21] Among matters discussed was the "Nancy problem" — the bad press the first lady had been receiving for her lavish parties, borrowed designer dresses, and traveling hairdressers.[22] Less than two months later, Mrs. Reagan wowed the Washington press corps at the annual Gridiron Club dinner by poking fun at herself with a song about "second-hand clothes." The skilled hand of Michael Deaver was at work.

On the second weekend in June, Reagan was resting in Aspen Lodge when a telephone call came through that would spell the beginning of the end for Secretary of State Alexander Haig. Haig, anxious to give new instructions to traveling Middle East envoy Philip Habib over the weekend, asked Reagan if the instructions had his approval. To Haig, Reagan seemed puzzled by the query. Haig assumed that the instructions had not been sent to Camp David. They had been (by now, there was a fax in Shangri-La), but the president had not read them. Haig sent them to Habib himself. On Monday in the Oval Office, brought up to date on what had happened, Reagan sternly cautioned his secretary of state against taking such actions on his own. Haig's days were numbered. Two weekends later, the President watched on television in Aspen as the secretary of state read his letter of resignation, saying that there was a disagreement on foreign policy. "Actually, the only disagreement was over whether I made policy or the secretary of state did," Haig's boss said.[23]

When George Shultz arrived at Andrews Air Force Base from California as Reagan's choice to succeed Haig, a helicopter was waiting to whisk him to the presidential retreat. Within minutes he was back at Camp David, where he had wrestled with the "gold window" in the Nixon administration. Joining Reagan and top White House aides for lunch under the trees outside Aspen, he found the president "easy and affable." What a contrast, he thought, to his meeting with an "uneasy, defensive" Nixon, who had asked him to be secretary of labor.

By August, struggling with plans for a new Middle East initiative, Shultz took top State Department experts on the region to Camp David to "role play" for the president how U.S. officials would present the plan to Begin and Arab leaders and how they would react. After the drama, described by Shultz as tense, the president gave his secretary of state the go-ahead.[24] Peace in the Middle East would, however, elude Reagan as it had eluded Carter.

On October 2, 1982, the first lady joined Reagan for the first time in one of his radio addresses. Speaking from the patio of Laurel, they discussed the campaign against drug abuse that Mrs. Reagan had made her principal White House project. A year later, on Columbus Day, 1983, Reagan was "greatly depressed" after sitting in Aspen and watching a television enactment of an imagined nuclear attack upon the United States.

No wonder the emphasis was on retreat. Reagan spelled out his feelings during a visit to a California school on June 30, 1983, when a student asked him how he liked living at the White House. He said he liked it fine, but added,

> At the same time, there is a little feeling of being a bird in a gilded cage. You're rather restricted and limited in what you can do. Once you get upstairs there, that's about where you are until it's time to go to work again. And that's why . . . so many presidents, including myself now, on weekends go to Camp David, where you can get back to a normal house and open a front door and walk out in the yard if you want to, take a hike and do things of that kind. You are restricted there in the heart of the city.[25]

There, in the heart of the city, Reagan noticed in his first year as president that the White House grounds abounded in squirrels but had few oak trees. From then on, after an autumn weekend at Camp David, he would bring back acorns in a plastic sack and scatter them outside the Oval Office each morning.[26]

Nancy Reagan invited her favorite interior decorator, Ted Graber, from Los Angeles to consult with her on redecoration of Aspen and the guest cabins. Over the years, a startling variety of bright colors had been added. With Navy Commander Jim Broaddus overseeing the work, the interiors were redone in earthy colors designed to be more in keeping with the surroundings. Broaddus' wife also played a role. "They didn't teach interior decorating in engineer school, and she has been my eyes and ears on a lot of these issues," the Seabee commander said. In one of the most far-reaching changes, the windows in Aspen were lowered, to give the president and his guests full advantage of the view while seated. Mrs. Reagan also enlarged the kitchen and had some of the furniture slipcovered and painted. At Laurel, she added new tablecloths in the dining room, painted the walls white, and hung Army, Navy, and Marine posters on the walls. "For me, one of the best parts about Camp David was that there wasn't a whisper of controversy about the renovations I made there," she wrote in her memoirs. "Because the entire place is off-limits to the press, nobody ever knew what I did."[27]

The maintenance and operation budget request for Camp David had grown to $1.6 million by 1986. "That's primarily for keeping the lights on, keeping the grass cut, paying any civilians who are up there," said a Senate Appropriations Committee aide. It did not include military pay.

Meanwhile Kenneth Plummer, the building contractor, who had first known the Camp David area on Boy Scout camping trips, was at work on his old idea of a permanent house of worship. Semiretired and serving as president of the National Lay Leaders Association of the United Methodist Church, Plummer formed a nonprofit corporation in 1987 to raise funds to build a stone-and-wood chapel on the grounds. Reagan approved the plan and made the first contribution, writing the fund a $1,000 check. He and Mrs. Reagan selected a site west of Linden Cottage. The Navy contributed a ship's bell from the USS *Endicott,* a destroyer that served in World War II, to hang in a combined bell tower and entry way. The Reagans took part in ground breaking ceremonies for the chapel on July 2, 1988. The $1 million building, which looks from the outside like the other green-painted structures at Camp David but has stained glass windows, was dedicated on April 21, 1991. The Reagans, Carter, and Ford agreed to be honorary members of an interdenominational board for the project. Mrs. Reagan said she had "often wished that Camp David had a chapel, because after the shooting, the increased security measures made it virtually impossible for us to go to church." On Sunday mornings, the Reagans watched television talk shows—one of Nancy's favorites was *This Week with David Brinkley*—before returning to Washington.[28]

On July 13, the ruggedly healthy Reagan, already the oldest president ever to serve in office, underwent surgery for colon cancer. At Bethesda Naval Hospital, Nancy had pictures of the camp hung in his room. "They really help," Reagan wrote. Paraphrasing a famous W. C. Fields line, he thought to himself, "All in all, I'd rather be at Camp David." Doctors said the malignancy was fully removed and chances of recurrence were slight. The presidential physician, Dr. John Hutton, vetoed Reagan's proposal to go horseback riding at the camp a week

40. Kenneth Plummer, Sr., a builder and active Methodist layman, led a crusade to build a chapel at Camp David. It was dedicated in 1991. *Courtesy Kenneth H. Plummer, Sr.*

after his operation. "But I feel fine," the president protested. Hutton did tell Reagan on his July 26 visit that he could walk in the shallow end of the pool to help his muscle tone, but unfortunately it rained.[29]

Reporters, sensitive to anything affecting the president's health, peppered Press Secretary Larry Speakes with questions after they noticed a scar on the president's nose as he addressed a group at the White House on August 1. Speakes, under pressure from a first lady who believed details of her husband's health were a private matter, was evasive but finally conceded that a biopsy would be performed—something the president did not learn until his wife told him the next day at Camp David. After returning from the Catoctins, Reagan invited six reporters into the Oval Office and told them he had basal cell carcinoma, the most common and easily cured form of skin cancer.[30]

As he flew to the camp on the last weekend in October 1987, the president took with him a red-bound folder with names of more than a dozen suggested nominees for a vacancy on the Supreme Court. The Senate had rejected his first choice, Robert H. Bork. Among the names were those of Douglas H. Ginsburg, a federal appeals court judge in Washington, and Anthony M. Kennedy of the Ninth United States Circuit Court in San Francisco. Reagan chose Ginsburg, who withdrew after admitting that he had smoked marijuana as a law school student and professor. The president's third choice, Kennedy, was confirmed.[31]

Reagan routinely took a briefing book with him to the presidential retreat on the weekend before a press conference and studied the questions his staff expected and their suggestions for answers.[32] But much of the time was spent relaxing — going for walks on the nature trail, riding, bowling, getting in a little golf, reading before the fireplace. In good weather, he and the first lady swam. Often, on summer days, they dined on the patio. The Reagans also liked to watch the deer come to the salt lick placed below Aspen, which the Seabees replenished just before the president and his wife arrived.

As always, tremors half a world away were felt at Camp David. On Sunday, June 7, 1981, a few months after he took office, Reagan had just boarded the helicopter for the return flight to Washington when a call came from his national security adviser, Richard Allen. Israeli warplanes had carried out a surprise attack against the Osirak nuclear reactor near Baghdad in Iraq.[33] On a cold, gray Saturday late in 1983, Reagan took calls to Aspen saying that Syria had launched a missile at a U.S. reconnaissance plane. He ordered an air strike against the Syrian batteries.[34]

The president was also at Camp David on Sunday, February, 23, 1986, when Shultz and other government foreign policy officials gathered around a fireplace at the secretary of state's suburban Washington home to discuss the crisis in the Philippines. Reagan's old friend President Ferdinand Marcos had amassed a force of tanks and troops to attack units of the Philippine army. Their crime was that they supported Corazon Aquino's claim, endorsed by United States observers, that she had defeated the corrupt Marcos in a fair election. The president returned early from his weekend in the Catoctins and presided in his western shirt and boots as the group assembled by Shultz reconvened in the White House Situation Room. Reagan reluctantly decided that Marcos must leave the Philippines and take refuge in Hawaii.[35]

Shortly after taking office, Reagan got out his yellow pad at the camp and drafted a letter to Soviet leader Leonid Brezhnev outlining his persistent and hard-to-realize dream of a world without nuclear weapons. Haig thought the letter naïve and dissuaded the president from sending it. Haig still objected when Reagan wrote a similar letter weeks later, while recuperating at the White House from his bullet wound.

Reagan sent it anyway, signaling the beginning of the thaw in United States-Soviet relations.[36]

The biggest foreign policy crisis of Reagan's administration was reflected in a bizarre conversation about Camp David in a room in the Sheraton Hotel at the Frankfurt, West Germany, Airport on October 6, 1986, at the height of the Iran-Iraq War in the Persian Gulf. Lt. Col. Oliver North, a midlevel aide to the National Security Council, offering to sell arms to Iran while seeking release of American hostages held in Lebanon, told Iranian negotiators that he had carried their demands to Reagan at the Catoctin retreat. As North told it, Reagan pounded the table and roared, "Stop coming in here like a gun merchant! I want to end the war!"

The story was inherently improbable. The president was not in the habit of meeting privately with officials at North's level, and there was no record of North ever having been at Camp David. Reagan told the Special Review Board, which he appointed to investigate the Iran arms sales, that North's account was "absolute fiction."[37] North had made it up, like much else in the saga that would lead to his conviction, later overturned, on charges including conspiracy to mislead Congress.

Camp David also figured in one of the central mysteries of the Iranian arms deal—whether Reagan ever expressly approved it. Former National Security Adviser Robert C. McFarlane testified that Reagan did so in a telephone call from the camp to him at his home "a day or two after" an August 6, 1986, meeting at which the plan was hotly opposed by Shultz and Secretary of Defense Caspar Weinberger. As McFarlane told it, Reagan said that despite the opposition of Shultz and Weinberger "we've got to try to find out if there are any people in Iran who are ready to change. And we've got to get the hostages back." Reagan said he did not recall this telephone call, the White House did not have a record of it, and he was in Washington, rather than Camp David, from August 6 to August 10, when he flew to California for a vacation that lasted until after Labor Day. The Special Review Board and congressional investigators concluded that, one way or another, it appeared Reagan had given his approval to the sales.[38]

After news of the arms dealings broke a few weeks later, Dan Rather of CBS television mistakenly called Reagan "Nixon" in one of his reports. White House Chief of Staff Donald Regan insisted on a correction, telling Speakes, "There are a couple of people up at Camp David tonight who are quite interested in what Dan is going to say." Rather said he feared that correcting his error would just call attention to the inadvertent comparison, but Regan did not think the Reagans would be satisfied. "Dan," said Speakes, "you're playing to an audience of two." Rather corrected the error.[39]

Regan, meanwhile, was having his own troubles with the first lady. On January 24, by Regan's account, she called him from Camp David to lobby for the removal of CIA Director William Casey, who was mortally ill with a brain tumor. Regan said the president would probably tactfully ask Casey to step aside soon. "Do it Monday," he quoted her as saying. That same weekend, with speechwriter Ken Khachigian on hand to write the coming State of the Union speech, Mrs. Reagan urged that language against abortion be stricken, telling Regan, "I don't give a damn about the right-to-lifers." Regan pointed out that her husband felt strongly on the issue.[40] In her diary for February 13, Mrs. Reagan wrote, "Today, at Camp David, I talked with Ronnie about Don Regan. For the first time I think he listened. . . . In bed that night, we talked a little more." Two weeks later, Regan was fired.[41]

In March, 1988, as Reagan's term neared its end, he and Mrs. Reagan spent one of their Camp David weekends reading a book, *On the Outside Looking In,* written by Michael Reagan, the adopted son of the president and his first wife, actress Jane Wyman. The book told of a troubled childhood and family problems, and Michael, 43, had given an interview to *People* magazine saying, "I've spent my life trying to figure out how to make Ronald Reagan my friend." The Reagans said they called Michael that Sunday evening to compliment him on the book.

A few weeks later came Regan's book, *On the Record.* In his most attention-getting passages, the fired chief of staff revealed that the first lady often consulted an astrologer and relied on her advice on such matters as the president's schedule. The astrologer, Joan Quigley of San Francisco, said Mrs. Reagan called her from both the White House and Camp David. "If she had to call me back," said Mrs. Reagan, "the White House and Camp David operators knew her as a friend of mine, and put the calls through."[42]

The scene that might most appropriately have marked the Reagans' passage from the Catoctins apparently never took place. Despite their fondness for old movies, there is no record that they ever watched *Lost Horizon.* It would have been a fitting moment — the fortieth president of the United States, a Mr. Smith come to Washington, sitting in the darkness of what had been Roosevelt's Bear's Den as Ronald Colman stumbled into Shangri-La.

For their last flight to Camp David, the Reagans flew in a new helicopter, a specially equipped VH-60 designed primarily for overseas use. But when they returned on Sunday, they were aboard the familiar VH3-D that had been Marine One for them for eight years. At the camp, Reagan said his farewells to the sailors and marines. Outside the White House, a reporter asked the president if he would miss the Catoctin retreat. "Yes, very much," he said. The only souvenirs they took were the jackets, inscribed with the words "Camp David," that are given to all guests.[43]

Epilogue

It was Friday afternoon. The big green helicopter, flown from Anacostia Naval Station, just a few minutes away on a branch of the Potomac, waited with its rotors idling on the temporary landing pad protecting the meticulously kept South Lawn of the White House. The president and first lady stepped out from the Diplomatic Entrance and walked to the helicopter steps. From a roped-off area to the right of the entrance, a few reporters shouted questions. The president waved to them, but did not answer. Sometimes he would, but not this day. The president and his wife climbed into the aircraft. An aide climbed another set of steps to the rear carrying the "football," the suitcase containing codes with which the man up front could signal a nuclear retaliation. The stairs were withdrawn. The rotors roared. Reporters and guests behind the ropes turned their heads for shelter from the blast, and the helicopter rose.

Like Franklin Roosevelt rolling out of the Southwest Gate on a Friday afternoon in 1942 for the ride to Shangri-La, George Bush was on his way to Camp David. The president sat by a window to the left of the aisle, looking forward, with Barbara Bush seated facing him. The presidential pooch, Millie, was at their feet. Aides sat on benches, upholstered like the rest of the interior in gray and light blue. Presidential photographs adorned the walls.

Because it was carrying the president, the helicopter was called Marine One. The Secret Service called it Nighthawk One. A second helicopter, called Nighthawk Two, had Secret Service agents aboard. It took off from Anacostia and joined Nighthawk One in flight. The presidential helicopter flew past the Washington Monument — so close, Betty Ford said, that "you'd feel as though you could reach out and touch it" — and crossed to the Potomac River. Following the river, it flew at five hundred feet altitude to avoid traffic from National Airport. If the air traffic had been exceptionally heavy, the pilot would have taken an alternate route over the Naval Observatory. At the Cabin John Bridge, which carries the Capital Beltway across the Potomac, the helicopter rose to two thousand feet. The pilot, using visual flight rules, followed the route of the Beltway and Interstate 70 as he headed north.

High-rise office buildings and suburban neighborhoods with swimming pools gave way to ploughed fields crisscrossed by two-lane highways. Approaching the timbered slopes of the Catoctins, the aircraft did not rise. It was already at the elevation of the camp. Suddenly it arrived, passing over a security fence and hovering over a green field ringed with trees and a hangar. Off to one side the passengers saw a backstop for softball.

A White House limousine was on hand to meet the president and his wife. As the weather was good, they chose to walk to Aspen Lodge. At other times, they would ride. Even though they were walking, the presidential limousine went by their side. At Camp David as elsewhere, rigid security rules applied. They walked up a sun-dappled walkway, past the chapel site and the tennis courts, past the camp office, past Poplar, past Hickory with its two-lane bowling alley and its bar and dance floor. At intervals there were orange-topped fire hydrants. Signs said the speed limit was fifteen miles an hour. They turned and walked down a slope, past old Laurel, now Holly, where FDR and Churchill talked on the front porch. Sometimes they had seen deer on the well-tended grass, sitting so still that visitors might mistake them for lawn ornaments. They crossed the narrow, one-way road to a larger lodge. The sign over the door, between the two ship's lanterns, read "Aspen."[1]

As the presidency passed from Reagan to his vice president, Camp David had again become more of a working vacation spot and less of a purely private retreat.

Dick Cheney, who had first come to Camp David as Gerald Ford's chief of staff, returned as George Bush's defense secretary on a cloudy Saturday morning, August 4, 1990. The president, Cheney, and other top military and civilian brass sat around the twenty-five-foot-long conference table in Laurel. Five small model airplanes were arranged down the middle. Two days earlier, Iraq had crossed the border into Kuwait. The talks at Camp David led within days to the dispatch of land, naval, and air forces to Saudi Arabia. The United Nations passed a series of tough resolutions and, in November, set a deadline of January 15, 1991, for Iraqi withdrawal.

Bush met with the Joint Chiefs of Staff at Camp David on December 1, receiving his first detailed outline of the prospects and the probable cost in lives of U.S. military action. On Sunday, December 16, returning to Washington from the camp by helicopter for a taped public television interview, he scanned a seventy-nine-page report from Amnesty International on torture and murder by the Iraqi regime of Saddam Hussein. He told interviewer David Frost that Mrs. Bush read two pages and said she could read no more because it was so terrible.

On January 6, 1991, the president took a leaf from Reagan's book and taped a five-minute radio talk at Laurel. He called the United Nations ultimatum "a deadline for Saddam Hussein to choose, to choose peace over war." The message was broadcast to allied nations the following Monday by the United States Information Agency. The next weekend, Cheney and the others were back again for last-minute talks on the launching of U.S. air strikes on Baghdad.[2]

On Saturday, January 17, Bush called Israeli Prime Minister Yitshak Shamir from Camp David to thank him for refraining from retaliation against Iraqi Scud missile attacks on Israel. On Friday, February 22, Bush flew to the Catoctins as usual, but this time it was a device to divert the news media. On Saturday morning, he flew back. The ground war that would be known as Desert Storm had begun.[3]

Although the war ended in a quick U.S. victory, its aftermath lingered. Returning from the camp on his last weekend in office, Bush was peppered by reporters' questions about Iraq as he crossed the South Lawn in his familiar tan raincoat. Saddam Hussein was again defying United Nations commands, and U.S. pilots were in the skies.[4]

When Mikhail Gorbachev came to the United States in the spring of 1990, Bush invited him to the Catoctins as a second choice after the Soviet leader turned down an offer to visit the president's family home at Kennebunkport, Maine. Like Khrushchev in 1959, Gorbachev rode to the presidential hideaway by helicopter, with the American president pointing out sights. The ship's bell from the *Endicott,* which had been part of the convoy that took Roosevelt to Yalta, was rung for their arrival. The visitor drove a golf cart, chatted with Marines, and tried his hand at horseshoes, a favorite Bush pastime. His host, ever polite, said he "literally threw a ringer the first time."[5]

41. President Bush and Mikhail Gorbachev joined in a golf cart ride during the Soviet leader's 1990 visit. Unlike Reagan, Bush entertained many foreign visitors at Camp David. *Courtesy AP/Wide World.*

Bush's relationship with Margaret Thatcher was not as cordial as Reagan's. The British prime minister felt that he distanced himself from her as a way of declaring independence from his predecessor, although outward forms were preserved. When Mrs. Thatcher sent Bush a message expressing her apprehensions about German reunification, the American president telephoned 10 Downing Street to say he looked forward to the two of them "putting our feet up at Camp David for a really good talk." Mrs. Thatcher did meet with Bush at the camp, on November 24, 1989, but not "with my feet up." She found Bush friendly, but "distracted and uneasy" and reported that "the atmosphere did not improve as a result of our discussions."[6]

Almost exactly a year later, Britain's "iron lady" resigned, in the face of revolt within her own party, and was succeeded by John Major. On June 6, 1992, the forty-eighth anniversary of the Normandy landing that Roosevelt and Churchill had pondered at Shangri-La, Bush met with Major at Camp David to discuss new problems in Yugoslavia and elsewhere that confronted the old allies.[7]

On the domestic scene, when the president's abrasive chief of staff, John Sununu, got into political hot water for abuse of air travel and other White House perquisites, he was summoned to Camp David as H. R. Haldeman had been before him. This time the chief of staff was unwilling to bow to the pressure. "I can survive this thing," he told Bush. "I can work it through." Bush, unlike Nixon, could not bring himself to lower the ax at his Catoctin retreat. He suggested they meet again back at the White House. Two days later, Sununu submitted his resignation.[8]

Bush used the place to unwind. He took the grandchildren with him and sometimes invited Vice President Dan Quayle's children along. Even before the helicopter landed he might be talking up a jog on the perimeter trail. Once he had pro Pam Shriver up for a weekend of tennis. He visited the camp on approximately 130 weekends in his four years in office. He invited Cabinet members, White House aides and their spouses. He pitched horseshoes. He played "wally ball," a kind of volleyball played on a squash court. He took along a family cook, Mexican-born Paula Rondoon, who made fajitas and tamales. The movies were newer: *Sea of Love* and *Shirley Valentine* instead of John Wayne and Fred Astaire favorites. And there was now a Nintendo game at Camp David. At Christmastime there were sleigh rides for the children. "This place is being used the way it should be," said one of the Marines.[9]

This was not to last, however. The gregarious Bill Clinton, the first president to be born after the establishment of Shangri-La, had less use than his predecessors for FDR's retreat in the woods.

The first visit was on his second weekend in office. With his administration off to a rocky start, Clinton summoned advisers to a corporate-style retreat, a new thing for the Catoctins. To help his aides share personal experiences, he used a professional facilitator whom Vice President Albert Gore, Jr. had hired to guide a similar exercise for his Senate staff. Clinton talked about being taunted as a fat youngster at school. Secretary of Education Richard W. Riley told of his youthful struggle with spinal disease. Such intimate revelations were not the kind of talk Dwight Eisenhower and Ezra Taft Benson exchanged at Laurel Lodge — or, for that matter, that the reserved Bush would have been comfortable with either.[10]

He visited the camp four more times in his first year in office and had been there only eighteen times after nearly two-and-a-half years in the White House. Most times, he and Hillary Clinton had guests. In June, 1994, he went to Camp David on three weekends in a row, and Press Secretary Dee Dee Myers said he spent much of the time reading.[11]

Now it is Sunday afternoon. The helicopter and its security backup lift off from the pad by the softball backstop. A lone photographer stands in the press area, taking no pictures. The Clintons make the return trip without incident, as ten presidents before have done so many times by motorcade and helicopter. As always, it is a spectacular vista. Raymond Price, flying with Nixon, said, "Day or night, in any season of the year, the helicopter ride from Camp David to the White House is beautiful." Even John Ehrlichman, on his way to the retreat to be fired, found himself soothed by the "bright spring green" of the landscape unfolding before him. For Bill and Hillary Clinton, the Lincoln Memorial comes into view, with the Capitol dome in the distance. As they swing past the Washington Monument, the Secret Service helicopter peels off and heads for Anacostia. The White House balconies loom through the window.[12] Once more, the president is home from the hills.

Notes
Bibliography
Index

Notes

Prologue

1. William M. Rigdon, with James Derieux, *White House Sailor* (Garden City, N.Y.: Doubleday, 1962), 11.

2. Samuel I. Rosenman, ed., *The Public Papers and Addresses of Franklin D. Roosevelt, 1942 Volume* (New York: Harper, 1950), 213–16.

3. Harold L. Ickes, *Summary of the Catoctin Lodge Development* (Washington, D.C.: U.S. Dept. of the Interior, 1943).

1. The Shangri-La of Franklin D. Roosevelt

1. *Brief History of Camp Hoover,* with reservation list for 1986 and 1987 (Washington D.C.: U.S. Dept. of the Interior, 1987).

2. Robert E. Sherwood, *Roosevelt and Hopkins: An Intimate History* (New York: Harper, 1950), 498.

3. Rigdon, 213.

4. James Rowley, interview with author, Washington, D.C., Sept. 23, 1988.

5. A. Merriman Smith, *Thank You, Mr. President: A White House Notebook* (New York: Harper, 1946), 123.

6. Conrad Wirth, *Parks, Politics and the People* (Norman: Univ. of Oklahoma Press, 1980), 200.

7. *Roosevelt Presidential Press and Radio Conferences* (New York: De Capo Press, 1972), 23:142–43.

8. Tom Horton, *Bay Country* (Baltimore: Johns Hopkins Univ. Press, 1987), 190–91.

9. Jean Golightly, *Circuit Hikes in Virginia, West Virginia, Maryland and Pennsylvania* (Washington D.C.: Potomac Appalachian Trail Club, 1981), 61; Chris Lampton, "One Man and His Mountain," *Maryland,* Autumn 1980, 2–5.

10. Wirth, 201–2, and Ickes.

11. *Conferences,* 23:142–43.

12. Grace Tully, *F. D. R. My Boss* (Chicago: People's Book Club, 1949), 55.

13. Wirth, 201; memo, Michael F. Reilly to Frank J. Wilson, Apr. 22, 1942, Secret Service records, FDR Library; Charles McC. Mathias Jr. to President Carter, Dec. 8, 1977, Jimmy Carter Library, Atlanta.

14. Barbara M. Kirkconnell, *Catoctin Mountain Park: An Administrative History* (Washington D.C.: National Park Service, 1988), 75.

15. Ickes.

16. Rigdon, 215.

17. William D. Hassett, *Off the Record with F. D. R. 1942–1945* (New Brunswick, N.J.: Rutgers Univ. Press, 1958), 115.

18. Wirth, 202; Rowley, interview.

19. Smith, *Thank You, Mr. President,* 124.

20. Rigdon, 214; Michael F. Reilly, as told to William J. Slocum, *Reilly of the White House* (New York: Simon and Schuster, 1947), 15.

21. Ickes.

22. Reilly, 239.

23. Secret Service Records, FDR Library; Hassett, 113.

24. Ickes.

25. Franklin D. Roosevelt, *U.S.S. Shangri-La,* logbook in FDR Library.

26. Secret Service Records, FDR Library.

27. Kirkconnell, 88; David C. Martin, *Wilderness of Mirrors* (New York: Harper and Row, 1980), 12.

28. Logbook; James F. Byrnes, *All in One Lifetime* (New York: Harper, 1958), 195.

29. Kirkconnell, 84, 210; Samuel I. Rosenman, *Working with Roosevelt* (Harper, 1952), 351–55; Rowley, interview; Brig. Gen. S. U. Marietta to President Roosevelt, 1942, FDR Library; Tully, 7–8.

30. Logbook.

31. Elliott Roosevelt and James Brough, *A Rendezvous with Destiny* (New York: Putnam, 1975), 321; James Roosevelt, with Bill Libby, *My Parents: A Differing View* (New York: Playboy Press, 1976), 218.

32. Joseph P. Lash, *Love, Eleanor: Eleanor Roosevelt and her Friends* (Garden City, N.Y.: Doubleday, 1982), 414; logbook; Joseph P. Lash, *A World of Love: Eleanor Roosevelt and her Friends, 1943–1962* (Garden City, N.Y.: Doubleday, 1984), 10, 50, 93.

33. William O. Douglas, *Go East, Young Man: The Early Years* (New York: Random House, 1974), 334–35.

34. Smith, *Thank You, Mr. President,* 125.

35. Hugh D. McClendon, *A History of Camp David* (Thurmont, Md.: Department of the Navy, 1985), 4

36. Smith, *Thank You, Mr. President,* 125.

37. Sherwood, 626–27.

38. Tully, 263–64.

39. Winston S. Churchill, *The Hinge of Fate* (Boston: Houghton Mifflin, 1950), 795–97.

40. McClendon, 12.

41. Rowley, interview.

42. Warren F. Kimball, ed., *Churchill and Roosevelt: The Complete Correspondence* (Princeton: Princeton Univ. Press, 1984–1988), 2:297.

43. Rigdon, 215

44. Tully, 115; Elliott Roosevelt, 321.

45. McClendon, 7.

46. Rowley, interview.

47. Army Information Digest, Aug. 1947, 27.

48. Rigdon, 214–16; Rosenman, *Working with Roosevelt,* 349; Smith, *Thank You, Mr. President,* 124–25; Jerrold M. Packard, *American Monarchy: A Social Guide to the Presidency* (New York: Delacorte, 1983), 105; Tully, 20–21.

49. Rosenman, *Working with Roosevelt,* 349–50.

50. Ickes; Hassett, 115; James U. Cross to John A. Roosevelt, Sept. 2, 1965, Lyndon Baines Johnson Library, Austin; Smith, *Thank You, Mr. President,* 126.

51. McClendon, 7; Secret Service records, FDR Library.

52. Hassett, 112.

53. Reilly, interoffice communication, Oct. 18, 1943, FDR Library.

54. Rowley, interview.

55. Secret Service records, FDR Library.

56. President's Secretary's Files, FDR Library.

57. *Conferences,* 2:142–45.

58. Edward D. MacMahon, M.D. and Leonard Curry, *Medical Cover-ups in the White House* (Washington, D.C.: Farragut, 1987), 93–100.

59. Sherwood, 8.

60. Jim Bishop, *FDR's Last Year* (New York: William Morrow, 1974), 39; Frank Freidel, *Franklin D. Roosevelt: A Rendezvous with Destiny* (Boston: Little, Brown, 1990), 526 in uncorrected proof; logbook.

61. Hassett, 260; John Keegan, *Six Armies in Normandy* (New York: Viking, 1982), 297; Secret Service records, FDR library.

2. Harry Truman Comes to Shangri-La

1. Wilson Brown to commanding officer, U.S.S. *Potomac,* William M. Rigdon papers, cross reference and miscellaneous file, box no. 2, Harry S. Truman Library, Independence, Mo.

2. George W. Wireman, *Gateway to the Mountains* (Hagerstown, Md.: Hagerstown Bookbinding and Printing, 1959), 191.

3. William M. Rigdon, interview by Jerry N. Hess, Jan. 1972, Truman Library, Independence, Mo.

4. William M. Rigdon, interview with author, Bethesda, Md., Sept. 25, 1987.

5. Memo in Shangri-La file, Truman Library.

6. Smith, *Thank You, Mr. President,* 126.

7. Margaret Truman, *Harry S. Truman* (New York: William Morrow, 1973), 334.

8. Margaret Truman, *Bess W. Truman* (New York: Macmillan, 1976), 287; William M. Rigdon, interview on "Camp David" (Maryland Public Television, 1987); Rigdon, author's interview.

9. F. W. Besley, *The Forests of Frederick County* (Baltimore: Maryland State Board of Forestry, 1922), 8–10, 15–19.

10. Edward C. Papenfuse et al., eds., *Maryland: A New Guide to the Old Line State* (Baltimore: Johns Hopkins Univ. Press, 1976), 64; *Washington Herald,* Oct. 17, 1935.

11. *Cozy News,* Thurmont, Md., Winter, 1985–86; McClendon, 2.

12. "Camp David . . . an etching in history," prepared for Richard Moore by Frank

Leonard, Feb. 16, 1973, 53, National Archives Nixon Presidential Materials Project, College Park, Md.; President Truman to Herbert O'Connor, Truman Library.

13. Oscar Chapman to President Truman, cited in undated memo in William M. Rigdon papers, Truman Library.

14. Kirkconnell, 91; Clinton Anderson, letter to Matthew J. Connelly, Apr. 20, 1946, William M. Rigdon papers, Truman Library; Julius A. Krug, memo to Matthew J. Connelly, May 15, 1946, William M. Rigdon papers, Truman Library; Maryland League for Crippled Children, letter to President Truman, Aug. 1, 1947, Truman Library.

15. Rigdon, 222.

16. *Sunday Sun Magazine,* Baltimore, Sept. 16, 1945; Rigdon, 223.

17. Note in unknown hand, Dec. 1947, papers of Eben A. Ayers, Truman Library; James H. Grove, letter to William D. Hassett, Aug. 1, 1949, folder Grove-J, General File, White House Central Files, Truman Library.

18. Rigdon, author's interview.

19. Margaret Truman, *Bess W. Truman,* 287; McClendon, 15; Rigdon, author's interview; Rowley, interview.

20. Rigdon, 222.

21. William D. Hassett papers, FDR Library; Rigdon, author's interview; Clark M. Clifford, with Richard Holbrooke, *Counsel to the President* (New York: Random House, 1991), 45–49, 60–66; David McCullough, *Truman* (New York: Simon & Schuster, 1992), 745.

22. Memo from Clark Clifford, Apr. 5, 1946, William M. Rigdon papers, Truman Library.

23. McClendon, 14–15.

24. Rigdon, author's interview; Rigdon papers, Truman Library; Rigdon, 222.

25. Hassett papers, FDR Library; Roger W. Tubby, diary, cited by McCullough, 862.

3. Dwight D. Eisenhower: Camp David Comes into Being

1. Rigdon, author's interview; Merriman Smith, *Meet Mister Eisenhower* (New York: Harper, 1955), 195.

2. Edward L. Beach, interview with author, Washington, Aug. 8, 1988, and Kirkconnell, 85.

3. J. Glenn Beall, letter to the president, Mar. 14, 1953, in Official File, Dwight D. Eisenhower Library, Abilene, Kan.

4. James D. McCully to James C. Hagerty, Feb. 16, 1953, and reply, Feb. 21, 1953, Thomas E. Stephens to Neil C. Fraley, Mar. 14, 1953, and other correspondence, General File, Eisenhower Library.

5. Daily Log, White House Office file, Office of the Staff Secretary, Eisenhower Library; Robert Griffith, ed., *Ike's Letters to a Friend, 1941–1958* (Lawrence, Kan.: Univ. Press of Kansas, 1984), 111.

6. J. B. West, *Upstairs at the White House: My Life with the First Ladies* (New York: Coward, McCann and Geoghegan, 1973), 160.

7. Smith, *Meet Mister Eisenhower,* 196; "Camp David," an unsigned memo in the files of the Washington bureau of the Associated Press; E. P. Aurand, memo to the author, 1989; Douglas B. Cornell, Associated Press wire story, Mar. 18, 1959, Washington files.

8. *Public Papers of the Presidents of the United States: Dwight D. Eisenhower, 1953* (Washington, D.C.: GPO), 126.

9. Griffith, 61.

10. Beach, interview; Dwight D. Eisenhower to Robert Trent Jones and Mark Sullivan Jr., April 7, 1954, Eisenhower Library; Homer H. Gruenther to Ann Whitman, undated, Official File, Eisenhower Library.

11. Richard B. Cheney, interview with author, 1985.

12. Michael R. Beschloss, *Mayday: Eisenhower, Khrushchev and the U-2 Affair* (New York: Harper and Row, 1986), 33.

13. Aurand, memo to author, Apr. 17, 1989; Edward L. Beach, memo for the president, April 23, 1953, Official File, Eisenhower Library; Beach, memo to James C. Hagerty, May 2, 1956, papers of Edward Beach and Evan P. Aurand, Eisenhower Library; E. P. Aurand, memo to president, March 10, 1958, Ann Whitman File, Eisenhower Library.

14. Edward L. Beach, memo to the president, June 11, 1954, Official File, Box 395, Eisenhower Library.

15. Stephen E. Ambrose, *Eisenhower, Volume Two: The President* (New York: Simon and Schuster, 1984), 198.

16. West, 160, 167.

17. Beach, interview.

18. Ambrose, *Eisenhower: The President,* 279.

19. Sherman Adams, *Firsthand Report: The Story of the Eisenhower Administration* (New York: Harper, 1961), 191.

20. Dwight D. Eisenhower, *The White House Years: Mandate for Change, 1953–1956* (Garden City, N.Y.: Doubleday, 1963), 545.

21. Richard M. Nixon, *Six Crises* (Garden City, N.Y.: Doubleday, 1962), 152.

22. Townsend Hoopes, *The Devil and John Foster Dulles* (Boston: Atlantic Monthly Press, 1973), 331–32; President's Schedule, Ann Whitman File, Eisenhower Library.

23. Aurand, memo to the president, and Eisenhower, memo to Aurand, Nov. 8, 1957, Ann Whitman File, Eisenhower Library; Helicopter log, Beach and Aurand File, Eisenhower Library.

24. Beach, interview; Aurand, memo to the president, March 10, 1958, Eisenhower Library.

25. Associated Press memo; Beach, interview.

26. Press conference transcript, March 12, 1959, Beach and Aurand papers, Eisenhower Library.

27. Harold Macmillan, *Riding the Storm, 1956–1959* (New York: Harper and Row, 1971), 644–49; Dwight D. Eisenhower, *The White House Years: Waging Peace, 1956–1961* (Garden City, N.Y.: Doubleday, 1965), 352–55; John S. D. Eisenhower, *Strictly Personal* (Garden City, N.Y.: Doubleday, 1974), 229–31; Nigel Fisher, *Harold Macmillan: A Biography* (New York: St. Martin's, 1982), 214–15; Harold Macmillan, unpublished diary, August 11, 1958, Harold Macmillan Archives, quoted in Alistair Horne, *Harold Macmillan: Volume II, 1957–1968* (New York: Viking, 1989), 131; and Aurand memo to author.

28. James C. Hagerty, oral history interview, 1967–68, Eisenhower Library.

29. Whitman Diary, March 21, 1959, Ann Whitman File, Eisenhower Library.

30. Associated Press memo.

31. Andrew J. Goodpaster, "Memorandum of Conference with the President,

March 20, 1959, 7 p.m.," Mar. 23, 1959, Ann Whitman File, Eisenhower Library; State Department, memorandum of conference, Ann Whitman File, Eisenhower Library.

32. Ambrose, *Eisenhower: The President*, 547–48.

33. Dwight Eisenhower, *Waging Peace*, 405–7, 433.

34. Strobe Talbott, ed., *Khrushchev Remembers* (Boston: Little, Brown, 1970), 371–72; H. R. Haldeman, *The Haldeman Diaries: Inside the Nixon White House* (New York: G. P. Putnam's Sons, 1994), 511; Jonathan Aitken, *Nixon: A Life* (Washington, D.C.: Regnery; 1994), 496–97.

35. Beschloss, 204.

36. C. Douglas Dillon, memo to the president, Sept. 8, 1959, Ann Whitman File, Eisenhower Library.

37. Dwight Eisenhower, *Waging Peace*, 235.

38. Evan P. Aurand, oral history interview by John T. Mason, May 1, 1967, Columbia Univ. Oral History Project, 40–41.

39. Whitman Diary, Sept. 25, 1959, Ann Whitman File, Eisenhower Library.

40. State Department, memorandum of conference, Sept. 15, 1959, Ann Whitman File, Eisenhower Library.

41. Don Shannon, "President Starts Talks with Mr. K," *Los Angeles Times*, Sept. 26, 1959.

42. Shannon; Edward T. Folliard, "Big 2 Leaders Fly in Helicopter to Maryland Camp," *Washington Post*, Sept. 26, 1959.

43. Harrison E. Salisbury, "Eisenhower, Khrushchev Begin Camp David Talks After Helicopter Flight," *New York Times*, Sept. 26, 1959.

44. Beschloss, 205–6; State Department, memorandum of conference, Jan. 16, 1960, Ann Whitman File; movie list, Beach and Aurand Papers, Eisenhower Library.

45. John Eisenhower, 260; A. J. Goodpaster, memo for the record, Nov. 13, 1959, Ann Whitman File, Eisenhower Library.

46. George B. Kistiakowski, *A Scientist at the White House* (Cambridge, Mass.: Harvard Univ. Press, 1976), 89; James C. Hagerty, news conference transcript, Sept. 26, 1959, 1:47 P.M., Hagerty Papers, Eisenhower Library.

47. Kistiakowski, 92; "Sailor Blandly Bowls 218 for President, Khrushchev," *Sunday Star*, Washington, Sept. 27, 1959; Hagerty, news conference.

48. Kistiakowski, 90–91; Hagerty Papers, Eisenhower Library; Whitman, memo to the president, and Dwight D. Eisenhower, handwritten reply, Sept. 16, 1959, Ann Whitman File, Eisenhower Library; Hagerty, oral history interview, Eisenhower Library.

49. Salisbury.

50. Kistiakowski, 92; Salisbury.

51. Andrew Goodpaster, interview with author, Washington, Aug. 9, 1988; Talbott, 411; Dwight Eisenhower, *Waging Peace*, 444.

52. Salisbury; Adams, 454–55; Peter Michelmore, "Camp David: Hideaway for Presidents," *Reader's Digest*, Nov. 1975, 111–14.

53. Beach and Aurand Papers, Eisenhower Library.

54. Rowley, memo to U. E. Baughman, Sept. 29, 1959, Ann Whitman File, Eisenhower Library.

55. Talbott, 409.

56. Dwight Eisenhower, *Waging Peace*, 447.

57. Joseph Alsop, "Matter of Fact," *Washington Post*, Sept. 30, 1959.

58. *Public Papers of the Presidents of the United States: Dwight D. Eisenhower, 1959* (Washington, D.C.: GPO), 277.

59. Beschloss, 232.

60. Aurand, memo to author; Harold Macmillan, *Pointing the Way, 1959–1961,* (New York: Harper and Row, 1972), 190.

61. Beschloss, 10, 33.

62. Goodpaster, author's interview and interview on "The American Experience: Eisenhower," Public Broadcasting Service, Nov. 10, 1993.

4. John F. Kennedy: Camelot in the Catoctins

1. Dwight Eisenhower, *Waging Peace,* 714; West, 236; Harold W. Chase and Allen H. Lerman, eds., *Kennedy and the Press: The News Conferences* (New York: Thomas Y. Crowell, 1965), 21.

2. Herbert S. Parmet, *JFK: The Presidency of John F. Kennedy* (New York: Dial, 1983), 175–76; Ambrose, *Eisenhower: The President,* 638–39; Robert H. Ferrel, ed., *The Eisenhower Diaries* (New York: W.W. Norton, 1981), 386–88; Richard Reeves, *President Kennedy: Profile of Power* (New York: Simon and Schuster, 1993), 102; card index to presidential diaries, John Fitzgerald Kennedy Library, Boston; David F. Powers, "Camp David" interview, Maryland Public Television.

3. Associated Press wire story, Apr. 24, 1961, Washington bureau files.

4. Card index, Kennedy Library.

5. West, 237; Clifford, 362.

6. Kenneth P. O'Donnell and David F. Powers, with Joe McCarthy, *Johnny, We Hardly Knew Ye* (Boston: Little, Brown, 1970), 356; Reeves, 533; Navy film, Kennedy Library.

7. Charles Bartlett, interview by Fred Holborn, Jan. 6, 1966, Kennedy Library.

8. David F. Powers, author's interview, 1985.

9. Still and moving pictures, Kennedy Library; Theodore C. Sorensen, *Kennedy* (New York: Harper and Row, 1965), 378.

10. Kenneth Plummer Sr., interview, Chambersburg, Pa., Apr. 8, 1988.

5. Lyndon B. Johnson: Camp David and Vietnam

1. Ferrel, 38; Jack Valenti, "July 21–27, 1965 Meetings on Vietnam," Meeting Notes File, Lyndon Baines Johnson Library, Austin, Tex.; Clark Clifford, interview with author, Aug. 21, 1989.

2. Lyndon Baines Johnson, *The Vantage Point: Perspectives of the Presidency, 1963–1969* (New York: Holt, Rinehart and Winston, 1971), 148.

3. Lyndon Johnson, 500–501; McClendon, 22; "Notes of the President's Meeting at Camp David," Meeting Notes File, Johnson Library.

4. W. Averell Harriman and Elie Abel, *Special Envoy to Churchill and Stalin, 1941–1945* (New York: Random House, 1975), 168–71; Rudy Abramson, *Spanning the Century: The Life of W. Averell Harriman, 1891–1986* (New York: William Morrow, 1992), photograph following 576, 659.

5. William S. White, *The Professional: Lyndon B. Johnson* (Boston: Houghton Mifflin, 1964), 250; President's Daily Diary for July 25, 1965, Daily Diary Collection, Johnson Library.

6. Nicholas Lemann, "The Unfinished War," *The Atlantic Monthly,* Dec. 1988, 53.

7. Lynda Robb, "Camp David" interview, Maryland Public Television; author's telephone interview, Mar. 30, 1989.

8. Richard Nixon, *RN: The Memoirs of Richard Nixon* (New York: Grosset and Dunlap, 1978), 501.

9. Lady Bird Johnson, *A White House Diary* (New York: Holt, Rinehart and Winston, 1975), 41–42; Keith Snider, "Harriet Chapel has hosted presidents," *Herald-Mail,* Hagerstown, Md., Jan. 28, 1990; White, 249–50.

10. McGeorge Bundy, memo for the president, July 8, 1964, Johnson Library.

11. Lyndon B. Johnson, letter to Dwight D. Eisenhower, July 20, 1965, Johnson Library.

12. Memo to Marvin Watson, May 31, 1966, Johnson Library; Mike Manatos, letter to Roy Elson, May 28, 1968, Johnson Library.

13. Mike Manatos, memos for the president, July 5 and Nov. 8, 1967, Johnson Library.

14. Traphes Bryant, with Frances Spatz Leighton, *Dog Days at the White House* (New York: Macmillan, 1975), 118–30, 164–67.

15. Lyndon Johnson, 187–90.

16. Lady Bird Johnson, 302–303; Elaine Steinbeck and Robert Wallsten, eds., *Steinbeck: A Life in Letters* (New York: Viking, 1975), 828.

17. Associated Press wire story, July 23, 1965, Washington bureau files.

18. Bryant, 138.

19. Lady Bird Johnson, 42.

20. McClendon, 21.

21. Lady Bird Johnson, 302.

22. Lyndon Johnson, 478–79, and W. W. Rostow, *The Diffusion of Power: An Essay in Recent History* (New York: Macmillan, 1972), 378.

23. McClendon, 21; Clark Clifford, "Camp David" interview, Maryland Public Television.

24. *Public Papers of the Presidents of the United States: Lyndon B. Johnson, 1965* (Washington, D.C.: GPO), 378–79; *Toronto Star,* Apr. 20, 1965.

25. Lady Bird Johnson, 724.

26. Clifford, 546.

6. Richard Nixon: Refuge from Watergate

1. Julie Eisenhower, *Pat Nixon: The Untold Story* (New York: Simon and Schuster, 1986), 188, 318; Nixon, *Six Crises,* 312.

2. Raymond Price, *With Nixon* (New York: Viking, 1977), 60–61; Haldeman, *Diaries,* 44–45.

3. Jeb Stuart Magruder, *An American Life* (New York: Atheneum, 1974), 71.

4. Bill Gulley, interview with author, Washington D.C., 1987.

5. H. R. Haldeman File, National Archives Nixon Presidential Materials Project, College Park, Md.

6. Bill Gulley, with Mary Ellen Reese, *Breaking Cover* (New York: Simon and Schuster, 1980), 149.

7. Plummer, interview.

8. Gulley, 42; Haldeman, memo to Don Hughes, in Bruce Oudes, ed., *From: The President: Richard Nixon's Secret Files* (New York: Harper and Row, 1989), 156; Haldeman, *Diaries,* 61.

9. Nixon, *RN,* 401–14; Haldeman, *Diaries,* 103.

10. Nixon, *RN,* 445–59; Henry Kissinger, *Years of Upheaval* (Boston: Little, Brown, 1982), 3.

11. John Ehrlichman, *Witness to Power: The Nixon Years* (New York: Simon and Schuster, 1982), 312–15.

12. Charles W. Colson, *Born Again* (Tarrytown, N.Y.: Chosen Rooks, 1976), 79.

13. Archie Roosevelt, *For Lust of Knowing: Memoirs of an Intelligence Officer* (Boston: Little, Brown, 1988), 471.

14. Ehrlichman, 235.

15. Helen Thomas, *Dateline: White House* (New York: Macmillan, 1975), 179.

16. William Safire, *Before the Fall: An Inside View of the Pre-Watergate White House* (Garden City, N.Y.: Doubleday, 1975), 509–28; Tad Szulc, *The Illusion of Peace: Foreign Policy in the Nixon Years* (New York: Viking, 1978), 454–55; Ehrlichman, 255–56.

17. Haldeman File, Nixon Project.

18. Ehrlichman File, Nixon Project.

19. Nixon, *RN,* 677; Haldeman, *Diaries,* 496, 555, 558.

20. Safire, 620–21.

21. Richard Nixon, *In the Arena: A Memoir of Victory, Defeat and Renewal* (New York: Simon and Schuster, 1990), 159–62.

22. Ehrlichman, 364.

23. Ehrlichman File, Nixon Project.

24. John Osborne, *The Fourth Year of the Nixon Watch* (New York: Liveright, 1973), 191.

25. Charles Colson, interview by Frederick J. Graboske, June 15, 1988, Nixon Project.

26. Ehrlichman File, Nixon Project; George Bush, with Victor Gold, *Looking Forward* (Garden City, N.Y.: Doubleday, 1987), 120–22; Haldeman, *Diaries,* 545, 552–53.

27. Al Kamen and Fred Barbash, excerpts from interviews, *Washington Post,* July 5, 1987.

28. Ehrlichman, 141; Ehrlichman File, Nixon Project.

29. Spiro T. Agnew, *Go Quietly . . . or else* (New York: William Morrow, 1980), 102–3.

30. Elizabeth Drew, *Washington Journal: The Events of 1973–1974* (New York: Random House, 1975), 39–40; Robert T. Hartmann, *Palace Politics: An Inside Account of the Ford Years* (New York: McGraw Hill, 1980), 21.

31. McClendon, 24.

32. Talbott, 406.

33. Julie Eisenhower, *Special People* (New York: Simon and Schuster, 1977), 97–98.

34. Kissinger, 142; Nixon, *RN,* 786–87.

35. Nixon, *RN,* 872.

36. Kissinger, 289–90.

37. Nixon, *RN,* 880.

38. Richard Nixon, *Leaders* (New York: Warner, 1982), 203.

39. Gulley, 215.

40. Committee on Government Operations, *Hearings Before a Subcommittee, Oct. 10, 11, 12 and 15, 1973,* 93d Cong., 1st sess. (Washington, D.C.: GPO, 1973), 463.

41. Gulley, 148.

42. Haldeman File, Nixon Project; Haldeman, *Diaries,* 429.

43. Gulley, 42–43, 148–49.

44. House Committee, *Hearings Before a Subcommittee,* 459.

45. Oudes, 496.

46. Rigdon, author's interview.

47. Haldeman File, Nixon Project.

48. Nancy Reagan, "Camp David" television interview, Maryland Public Television.

49. Ron Reagan, interview with author, Aug. 25, 1989.

50. Safire, 292, 618.

51. Maureen Dean, with Hays Gorey, *"Mo": A Woman's View of Watergate* (New York: Simon and Schuster, 1975), 195–99.

52. Packard, 104.

53. Gulley, 149.

54. Julie Eisenhower, *Pat Nixon,* 319.

55. Price, 99.

56. Simon Winchester, "Camp David Now a Fortress," *Washington Post,* June 26, 1973.

57. McClendon, 25; Haldeman File, Nixon Project; Gulley, interview.

58. Larry Higby, memo to Hughes, Haldeman File, Nixon Project.

59. Winchester.

60. Ehrlichman, 95–96.

61. Senate Select Committee on Presidential Campaign Activities, *Hearings, July 11, 12, 13, 16 and 17, 1973* (Washington, D.C.: GPO, 1973), 2077; Oudes, 638–39.

62. Hughes, memo to Haldeman, Haldeman File, Nixon Project.

63. House Committee, *Hearings Before a Subcommittee,* 462.

64. Lester David, *The Lonely Lady of San Clemente: The Story of Pat Nixon* (New York: Thomas Y. Crowell, 1978), 4, 10, 188; Haldeman, *Diaries,* 334, 346, 356.

65. Maurice H. Stans, *The Terrors of Justice: The Untold Side of Watergate* (New York: Everest House, 1978), 141.

66. Hughes memo, Haldeman File, Nixon Project; Haldeman, *Diaries,* 404, 424.

67. Ehrlichman, 108.

68. Alexander Butterfield to Brent Scowcroft, Haldeman File, Nixon Project.

69. McClendon, 25; Higby to Butterfield and Haldeman, Haldeman File, Nixon Project.

70. Winchester.

71. Joint Committee on Internal Revenue Taxation, *Examination of President Nixon's Tax Returns for 1969 through 1972,* 93d Cong., 2d sess. (Washington, D.C.: GPO, 1974), 141–44.

72. Oudes, 34; Sheila Rabb Weidenfeld, *First Lady's Lady: With the Fords at the White House* (New York: G. P. Putnam's Sons, 1979), 338.

73. Bill McCloskey, "Nixon Papers—Sports." Associated Press, Dec. 2, 1985.

74. John W. Dean III, *Blind Ambition: The White House Years* (New York: Simon and Schuster, 1976), 155–58.

75. New York Times, *The White House Transcripts* (New York: Bantam Books, 1974), 203–15.

76. John Dean, 213–22; Maureen Dean, 194–95.

77. Senate Select Committee on Presidential Campaign Activities, *Watergate and Related Activities, Phase I, Book 3* (Washington, D.C.: GPO, 1973), 1258; Ehrlichman, 385.

78. Nixon, *RN,* 845–46.

79. Haldeman, 287–95; Ehrlichman, 389–91; John Ehrlichman, interview, Nov. 15, 1990, "Nixon," Public Broadcasting Service.

80. Price, 100–102; Nixon, *RN,* 849.

81. John C. Bennett, testimony, Nov. 6, 1973, in re Grand Jury, Misc., 611; Rose Mary Woods, testimony, Nov. 8, 1973, in re Grand Jury, 625–61, in House Committee on the Judiciary, *Statement of Information* 93d Cong., 2d Sess. (Washington, D.C.: GPO, 1974).

82. President Nixon Daily Diary, Sept. 29, 1973, Exhibit 115, in re Grand Jury.

83. Alexander Haig, testimony, Dec. 5, 1973, in re Grand Jury (Indistinct Document Retyped by House Judiciary Committee staff), 621.

84. Stephen Bull, testimony, Nov. 6, 1973, in re Grand Jury, 682.

85. J. Anthony Lukas, *Nightmare: The Underside of the Nixon Years* (New York: Viking, 1975), 550–51.

86. Price, 264.

87. Nixon, *RN,* 1007, 1057, 1061.

88. John Osborne, *The Last Nixon Watch* (New York: Liveright, 1975), 188–89.

89. William M. Welch, "Nixon Papers," Associated Press, May 29, 1987.

7. Gerald R. Ford: Camp David Meets the Press

1. McClendon, 27.

2. Gerald R. Ford, *A Time to Heal: The Autobiography of Gerald R. Ford* (New York: Harper and Row, 1979), 127.

3. Smith, *Thank You, Mr. President,* 127.

4. Chalmers Roberts, interview with author, 1985.

5. Mary Freeze, interview with author, 1985.

6. Charles Ross, letter to A. Vernon Davis, July 31, 1949, "The President's Camp," Truman Library.

7. George Reedy, letter to Arnold Miller, Apr. 8, 1965, Johnson Library.

8. Associated Press memo.

9. Whitman Diary, Mar. 21, 1959, Ann Whitman File, Eisenhower Library.

10. George Dixon, "Washington Scene," *Washington Post,* Sept. 30, 1959.

11. James C. Hagerty, news conference, Sept. 25, 1959, 7:35 P.M., Hagerty papers, Eisenhower Library; James Rowley, memo to U. E. Baughman, Sept. 29, 1959, Whitman File, D. E. Diary Series, Eisenhower Library.

12. E. P. Aurand, memo to Goodpaster, Hagerty and Secret Service, Sept. 12, 1959, Beach and Aurand papers, Eisenhower Library.

13. Hugh Sidey, *John F. Kennedy, President* (New York: Atheneum, 1963), 143–44.

14. Haldeman, *Diaries,* 523; Frank Cormier, interview with author, Apr. 22, 1988.

15. Ron Nessen, memo to Warren Rustand, Oct. 13, 1974, Press Release File, Gerald R. Ford Library, Ann Arbor, Mich.

16. "ABC Delays Ford Visit, Cites Election," *New York Times,* undated clipping, Ford Library.

17. "A Conversation at Camp David: The Reasoner Report," tape and transcript, Nov. 16, 1974, Ford Library.

18. "ABC Delays Ford Visit."

19. John W. Hushen, memo to Ron Nessen, Oct. 26, 1974, Press Release File, Ford Library.

20. Memos, May 22, 1975, Richard B. Cheney File, Ford Library.

21. Marvin L. Beaman Jr., letter to Charles MacC. Mathias Jr., Dec. 22, 1977; Beaman, memo to Hugh Carter, Dec. 28, 1977, Jimmy Carter Library Atlanta, Ga.

22. Donnie Radcliffe, "Washington Ways," *Washington Post*, Sept. 29, 1987.

23. *Public Papers of the Presidents of the United States: Gerald R. Ford, 1975* (Washington, D.C.: GPO), 1279–85; Howard Benedict, interview with author, Apr. 1, 1988.

24. Transcript, Aug. 7, 1976, Ford Library; Dick Barnes, "Ford Interview," Associated Press, Aug. 9, 1976; Richard H. Growald, "President," United Press International, Aug. 9, 1976; Benedict, interview.

25. Robert Hartmann File, Ford Library; Michelmore, 111–14.

26. Kollmorgen to Warren Silver, Buildings and Grounds File, Aug. 9, 1974–Dec. 31, 1974, Ford Library.

27. Betty Ford, with Chris Chase, *The Times of My Life* (New York: Harper and Row, 1978), 168.

28. Gerald Ford, letter to Homer Gruenther, Buildings and Grounds File, Ford Library.

29. Betty Ford, 194.

30. Ron Nessen, *It Sure Looks Different from the Inside* (New York: Playboy Press, 1978), 78.

31. Press Release File, Ford Library.

32. Memos, Cheney File, Ford Library.

33. William E. Timmons, memo to Warren Rustand, Aug. 30, 1974, Buildings and Grounds File, Ford Library; Nessen, 143.

34. Rustand, memo to Cheney, Buildings and Grounds File, Box 1, Ford Library.

35. Memos, James E. Connor File, Ford Library; Weidenfeld, 338.

36. Russell A. Rourke, letter to Thomas K. Latimer, Buildings and Grounds File, Ford Library.

37. "Sa" to "Eleanor," undated, Connor File, Ford Library.

38. Hartmann, 390.

39. Philip W. Buchen, letter to John Ashbrook, Jan. 7, 1977, with attachments, Clemency Review File, Ford Library.

40. Frances Spatz Leighton, "New Job at the White House: Betty Ford's Best Friend," *Family Weekly*, Mar. 2, 1975, 29; Weidenfeld, 97–99.

41. Nessen, 174–75.

42. Elizabeth Toland, "How the President Came to Harriet Chapel on Easter," *Maryland Church News*, June 1976, 8–9; Rev. Charles O. Shaffer, quoted in the *Herald-Mail*, Hagerstown, Md., Jan. 28, 1990; Jim Cavanaugh to Terry O'Donnell, memo, Ford Library.

43. Weidenfeld, 314–15, 336–40, 397–98.

44. George Rush, "Confessions of a Secret Service Agent," *The Washingtonian*, August, 1988, excerpted from *Confessions of an Ex-Secret Service Agent* (New York: Donald I. Fine, 1988).

45. Buildings Management File, Ford Library.

8. Jimmy Carter: Arab and Jew at Camp David

1. Zbigniew Brzezinski, *Power and Principle: Memoirs of the National Security Adviser, 1977–1981* (New York: Farrar, Straus and Giroux, 1983), 240–41, 250–51.

2. Jehan Sadat, *A Woman of Egypt* (New York: Pocket Books, 1989), 465.

3. Jody Powell, *The Other Side of the Story* (New York: William Morrow, 1984), 60; Jimmy Carter, interview with author, 1985.

4. Eddie Adams, Aug. 8, 1978, and David Hume Kennerly, Aug. 11, 1978, letters to Gerald Rafshoon; Jim Purks, memo to Rex Granum, Aug. 10, 1978; Billie Shaddix, memo to Rafhshoon, Aug. 11, 1978; Rafshoon, memo to the president, Aug. 25, 1978, Carter Library.

5. Powell, 65–66.

6. Anne Edwards, reference slip with attachment, Sept. 6, 1978, Carter Library.

7. R. Lee Fisher to Edwards, Sept. 28, 1978, Carter Library.

8. Edwards, memos, Aug. 30, 1978, Carter Library.

9. Moshe Dayan, *Breakthrough: A Personal Account of the Egypt-Israeli Peace Negotiations* (New York: Knopf, 1981), 154; Rosalynn Carter, *First Lady from Plains* (Boston: Houghton Mifflin, 1984), 235–37; Brzezinski, 254.

10. Rosalynn Carter, 236.

11. Jimmy Carter, *Keeping Faith: Memoirs of a President* (New York: Bantam, 1982), 331–32; Dayan, 154–55.

12. William B. Quandt, *Camp David: Peacemaking and Politics* (Washington: The Brookings Institution, 1986), 231; Eric Silver, *Begin: The Haunted Prophet* (New York: Random House, 1984), 191–92.

13. Rosalynn Carter, 237.

14. Dayan, 157–58; Martin Schram and Jim Klurfeld, "Inside Camp David," *Newsday*, Sept. 24, 1968; Brzezinski, 259; Silver, 192.

15. Quandt, 216, 218, 220.

16. Silver, 192.

17. Brzezinski, 230.

18. Brzezinski, 254; Powell, 62.

19. Jimmy Carter, *Keeping Faith,* 333.

20. Jimmy Carter, handwritten notes, Sept. 7, 1978, Carter Library.

21. Brzezinski, 255–56.

22. Quandt, 224.

23. Sadat, 389.

24. Cyrus Vance, *Hard Choices: Critical Years in America's Foreign Policy* (New York: Simon and Schuster, 1983), 220; Quandt, 229.

25. Dayan, 156–57.

26. Powell, 76–77; Schram and Klurfeld.

27. Rush, 230.

28. Jimmy Carter, *Keeping Faith,* 333; Quandt, 224.

29. Quandt, 230–31.

30. Brzezinski, 258, 262–63.

31. Finlay Lewis, *Mondale: Portrait of an American Politician* (New York: Perennial Library, 1984), 228.

32. Powell, 65.

33. Quandt, 234–35.

34. Brzezinski, 264–65.

35. Brzezinski, 271–72.

36. Sadat, 391.

37. Quandt, 239.

38. Vance, 224.

39. Brzezinski, 268.

40. Powell, 85; Vance, 226; Quandt, 254.

41. Brzezinski, 270–71.

42. Speech text, Associated Press, July 18, 1988, Washington bureau files.

43. Jimmy Carter, *Keeping Faith,* 114–21; Jack W. Germond and Jules Witcover, *Blue Smoke and Mirrors: How Reagan Won and Why Carter Lost the Election of 1980* (New York: Viking, 1981), 32–35.

44. Clifford, 634; "Newfangled Bike Throws Clifford," *Washington Post,* July 10, 1979.

45. Steele Hays, "Clinton Talks with Carter," *Arkansas Gazette,* July 12, 1979; Bill Dawson, "Clinton Emphasizes Conservation," *Arkansas Democrat,* July 12, 1979.

46. Undated handwritten memo to the president, apparently by Hamilton Jordan, Carter Library.

47. Haynes Johnson, "Crisis," *Washington Post,* July 9, 1979; Meg Greenfield, "Report from Camp David," *Washington Post,* July 16, 1979; Germond and Witcover, 35.

48. Hamilton Jordan, *Crisis: The Last Year of the Carter Presidency* (New York: G.P. Putnam's Sons, 1982), 32.

49. Pierre Salinger, *America Held Hostage: The Secret Negotiations* (Garden City, N.Y.: Doubleday, 1981), 30.

50. Jordan, 72.

51. McClendon, 30.

52. Brzezinski, 487; Jimmy Carter, *Keeping Faith,* 501.

53. Rosalynn Carter, 3.

54. Gulley, 271–72.

55. Stephen Hess, *Organizing the Presidency* (Washington: The Brookings Institution, 1989), 251–52; Hess, interview with author, Aug. 22, 1989.

56. Nixon, *In the Arena,* 159–62.

57. Carter, interview; Greg Schneiders, interview with author, Aug. 28, 1989.

58. Carter, handwritten note to Bert Lance, Feb. 27, 1977, Carter Library; Carter, interview.

59. Lt. Comdr. Long, memo to Marvin L. Beaman Jr., Oct. 25, 1978; Hugh Carter, memo to the president, Dec. 21, 1978, with president's handwritten note; J. Fliakis, memo, Apr. 25, 1977, Carter Library.

60. Beaman, memo, Apr. 1, 1980, Carter Library.

61. Woodburning Project File, Carter Library.

62. "Listing of President Carter's Trips to Camp David, Maryland," Carter Library.

63. Rick Hutcheson, memo to Susan Clough, Aug. 3, 1979, Carter Library.

64. Al McDonald, memo to the president, Jan. 29, 1980, with Carter's handwritten note, Carter Library.

65. McDonald, memo to Hugh Carter, Feb. 4, 1980, Carter Library.

66. Hugh Carter and Beaman, memos for file, Aug. 29, 1980, Carter Library.

67. Jordan, memo to Hugh Carter, June 23, 1977, Carter Library.

68. Clough, undated memo to the president; Hugh Carter, memo to the president, Nov. 11, 1977, Carter Library.

69. Frank Cormier, "Jimmy's White House," Associated Press, July 27, 1977.

70. Hugh Carter, memo to the president, Nov. 11, 1977, with note by Rosalynn Carter, Carter Library.

71. G. A. Zimmerman, memo to Gulley, Apr. 13, 1977, Carter Library.

72. Beaman, memo to Hugh Carter, with attachment, Dec. 13, 1978, Carter Library.

73. Brzezinski, 41–42.

74. Frederick J. Bower, letter to the president, Apr. 18, 1977; Gulley, memo to the president, May 13, 1977, Carter Library; Lorraine Voles, interview with author, Oct. 1993.

75. Rush, 230; Jordan, 70–72; Jimmy Carter, *An Outdoor Journal: Adventures and Reflections* (New York: Bantam, 1988), 7–8.

76. Roger D. Counts, memo to SAIC Parr, Sept. 27, 1979, Carter Library; *Daily Mail*, (Hagerstown, Md.), Sept. 17, 1979.

77. McClendon, 31.

78. Carter, author's interview.

79. Jimmy Carter, *Outdoor Journal*, 76.

9. Ronald Reagan: Horseback in Shangri-La

1. Susanne M. Schafer, "Reagan Does Radio Because He Likes It," Associated Press, Sept. 5, 1986; *Public Papers of the Presidents of the United States: Administration of Ronald Reagan* (Washington, D.C.: GPO, 1983, 487–88); Nancy Reagan, with William Novak, *My Turn: The Memoirs of Nancy Reagan* (New York: Random House, 1989), 31, 256.

2. Former President Reagan's office, Los Angeles.

3. Maureen Reagan, *First Father, First Daughter: A Memoir* (Boston: Little, Brown, 1989), 309; Ronald Reagan, *An American Life: The Autobiography* (New York: Simon and Schuster, 1990), 378; Nancy Reagan, 253.

4. Edwin Meese III, *With Reagan: The Inside Story* (Washington, D.C.: Regnery Gateway, 1992), 25.

5. Ronald Reagan, 396.

6. George Plimpton, "A Sportsman Born and Bred," *Sports Illustrated,* Dec. 26, 1988; Nancy Reagan, 257.

7. Kirkconnell, 201–2; Park Service official, author's informal interview; Nancy Reagan, 255.

8. Christopher Sullivan, "Dying Dogwoods," Associated Press, Apr. 15, 1991.

9. Ronald Reagan, 397; George Stevens Jr., speech, Washington, D.C., May 21, 1988; Lou Cannon, "President Goes to the Movies," *Washington Post,* June 13, 1983.

10. Amanda Deaver, as told to Danna L. Walker, "Growing Up Fast: It was Never Easy Being Mike Deaver's Daughter," *Washington Post Magazine,* Nov. 27, 1988; Michael K. Deaver, with Mickey Herskowitz, *Behind the Scenes: In Which the Author Talks About Ronald and Nancy Reagan . . . and Himself* (New York: William Morrow, 1987), 36.

11. Michael Deaver, 101.

12. Maureen Reagan, 276–77.

13. Mark Weinberg, interview with author, Aug. 25, 1989; Nancy Reagan, 256–57.

14. George P. Shultz, *Turmoil and Triumph: My Years as Secretary of State* (New York: Charles Scribner's Sons, 1993), 999.

15. David Dimbleby and David Reynolds, *An Ocean Apart: The Relationship Between Britain and America in the Twentieth Century* (New York: Random House, 1988), 342–43; Ronald Reagan, 609; John Newhouse, "The Diplomatic Round," *The New Yorker,* July 22, 1985, 44; Geoffrey Smith, *Reagan and Thatcher* (London: The Bodley Head, 1990), 153–58; Margaret Thatcher, *The Downing Street Years* (New York: HarperCollins, 1993), 466–68, 472–73.

16. Selwa "Lucky" Roosevelt, *Keeper of the Gate* (New York: Simon and Schuster, 1990), 280.

17. Hedrick Smith, "Taking Charge of Congress," *New York Times Magazine,* Aug. 8, 1981, 12.

18. Bradley H. Patterson, Jr., *The Ring of Power: The White House Staff and its Expanding Role in Government* (New York: Basic Books, 1988), 211.

19. Ronald Reagan, 282; Haynes Johnson, *Sleepwalking Through History: America in the Reagan Years* (New York: W.W. Norton, 1991), 153–54 in uncorrected proof copy.

20. Ronald Reagan, 315.

21. James Gerstenzang, "Top Reagan Aides Confer at Camp David," Associated Press, Feb. 5, 1982.

22. Frances Spatz Leighton, *The Search for the Real Nancy Reagan* (New York: Macmillan, 1987), 274.

23. Ronald Reagan, 362; Lou Cannon, *President Reagan: The Role of a Lifetime* (New York: Simon and Schuster, 1991), 202; Shultz, 7–9.

24. Shultz, 90.

25. *Public Papers of the Presidents of the United States: Administration of Ronald Reagan, 1983* (Washington, D.C.: GPO, 1984), 955.

26. Maureen Reagan, 325–26; personal observation.

27. Ted Graber, interview with author, Washington, D.C., July 25, 1988; Cmdr. J. A. Broaddus, remarks at Change of Command Ceremony, Camp David, July 25, 1988; Nancy Reagan, 258–59.

28. Kenneth Plummer Sr., interview with author, Chambersburg, Pa., Apr. 8, 1988, and by telephone, Aug. 9, 1989; White House news release, July 2, 1988; Donnie Radcliffe, "The Bells of Camp David," *Washington Post,* Jan. 26, 1988; Ted Haas, "Chapel called gift from 'people of faith,'" *Public Opinion,* Chambersburg, Pa., Dec. 7, 1987; Nancy Reagan, 258.

29. Ronald Reagan, 500–501; Warren King, "Reagan regarded AIDS 'like it was measles,'" *Seattle Times,* Aug. 31, 1989; Nancy Reagan, 281.

30. Larry Speakes, with Robert Pack, *Speaking Out: The Reagan Presidency from Inside the White House* (New York: Charles Scribner's Sons, 1988), 196–99.

31. Personal observation; Ruth Marcus and David Hoffman, "Reagan Reviews List of Court Candidates," *Washington Post,* Oct. 25, 1987.

32. Speakes, 236.

33. Richard Allen, interview with author, Dec. 17, 1990.

34. Ronald Reagan, 464.

35. Speakes, 206–7; Ronald Reagan, 363–64; Shultz, 632–35.

36. Cannon, 298–301.

37. President's Special Review Board, *Report of the President's Special Review Board* (Washington, D.C.: GPO, 1987), 3:18; Jane Mayer and Doyle McManus, *Land-*

slide: The Unmaking of the President, 1984–1988 (Boston: Houghton Mifflin, 1988), 276–77.

38. Mayer and McManus, 128–29.

39. Speakes, 223.

40. Donald T. Regan, *For the Record: From Wall Street to Washington* (New York: Harcourt Brace Jovanovich, 1988), 74–77.

41. Nancy Reagan, 327.

42. Nancy Reagan, 47.

43. Author's notes; undated White House news release.

Epilogue

1. Personal observation; J. C. McKinney, interview with author, Washington, D.C., July 25, 1988; Betty Ford, 279.

2. Bob Woodward, *The Commanders* (New York: Simon and Schuster, 1991), 247–55; *Public Papers of the Presidents of the United States: Administration of George Bush, 1991* (Washington, D.C.: GPO), 12–13.

3. Dan Quayle, *Standing Firm: A Vice-Presidential Memoir* (New York: Harper-Collins, 1994), 230, 238.

4. Michael Duffy and Dan Goodgame, *Marching in Place: The Status Quo Presidency of George Bush* (New York: Simon and Schuster, 1992), 168.

5. Joan Mower, "Summit — Mr. President," Associated Press, June 2, 1990.

6. Thatcher, 783, 793–94.

7. *Washington Post,* June 7, 1992.

8. Duffy and Goodgame, 128.

9. W. Dale Nelson, "Bush's Camp," *The Repository* (Canton, Ohio), Oct. 8, 1989; George Bush, interview on C-Span, Dec. 22, 1991; Quayle, 96; Ary Moleon, Associated Press, "La Ayudante de los Bush, feliz y mexicanisima en la Casa Blanca," Nov. 23, 1990; Anna Perez, interview with author, Aug. 9, 1989; Marine's conversation with author.

10. Ann Devroy, "Bonding at Camp David," *Washington Post,* Feb. 5, 1993; Katherine Boo, "The Drama of the Gifted Vice President," *Washington Post Magazine,* Nov. 28, 1993, 24, 26.

11. The White House, Office of the Press Secretary, *Press Briefing by Dee Dee Myers,* June 27, 1994.

12. White House film PPP:26, Kennedy Library; Price, 103; Ehrlichman, 390.

Bibliography

Archives

Dwight D. Eisenhower Library, Abilene, Kan.
Franklin D. Roosevelt Library, Hyde Park, N.Y.
Gerald R. Ford Library, Ann Arbor, Mich.
Harry S. Truman Library, Independence, Mo.
Jimmy Carter Library, Atlanta, Ga.
John Fitzgerald Kennedy Library, Boston, Mass.
Lyndon Baines Johnson Library, Austin, Tex.
National Archives Nixon Presidential Materials Project, College Park, Md.
National Archives — Los Angeles Branch, Laguna Niguel, Calif.

Interviews

Allen, Richard. By telephone, Dec. 17, 1990.
Beach, Edward L. Washington, D.C., Aug. 8, 1988.
Benedict, Howard. By telephone, Apr. 1, 1988.
Carter, Jimmy. By telephone, 1985.
Cheney, Richard B. By telephone, 1985.
Clark, Bob. Washington, D.C., May 4, 1988.
Clifford, Clark M. By telephone, Aug. 21, 1989.
Cormier, Frank. By telephone, Apr. 22, 1988.
Freeze, Mary. By telephone, 1985.
Goodpaster, Andrew. Washington, D.C., Aug. 9, 1988.
Graber, Ted. Washington, D.C., July 25, 1988.
Gulley, Bill. Washington, D.C., 1987.
Hess, Stephen. By telephone, Aug. 22, 1989.
McKinney, J.C. Washington, D.C., July 25, 1988.
Perez, Anna. By telephone, Aug. 9, 1989.
Plummer, Kenneth Sr. Chambersburg, Pa., Apr. 8, 1988; by telephone, Aug. 9, 1989.
Powers, David F. By telephone, 1985.
Reagan, Ron. By telephone, Aug. 25, 1989.

Rigdon, William M. Bethesda, Md., Sept. 25, 1987.
Robb, Lynda. By telephone, Mar. 30, 1989.
Roberts, Chalmers M. By telephone, 1985.
Rowley, James. Washington, D.C., Sept. 23, 1988.
Schneiders, Greg. By telephone, Aug. 28, 1989.
Voles, Lorraine. By telephone, Oct., 1993.
Weinberg, Mark. By telephone, Aug. 25, 1989.

Government Publications

Brief History of Camp Hoover. Washington, D.C.: Dept. of the Interior, 1987.
Ickes, Harold L., *Summary of the Catoctin Lodge Development.* Washington, D.C.: U.S. Dept. of the Interior, 1943.
Joint Committee of Internal Revenue Taxation. *Examination of President Nixon's Tax Returns for 1969 Through 1972.* 93d Cong., 2d sess. Washington, D.C.: GPO, 1974.
President's Special Review Board. *Report of the President's Special Review Board.* Washington, D.C.: GPO, 1987.
Public Papers of the Presidents of the United States. Washington, D.C.: GPO.
U.S. House Committee on Government Operations. *Hearings Before a Subcommittee, Oct. 10, 11, 12 and 15, 1973.* 93d Cong., 1st sess. Washington, D.C.: GPO, 1973.
U.S. House Committee on the Judiciary. *Statement of Information.* 93d Cong., 2d sess. Washington, D.C.: GPO, 1974.
U.S. Senate Select Committee on Presidential Campaign Activities. *Hearings, July 11, 12, 13, 16 and 17, 1973.* Washington, D.C.: GPO, 1973.

Books

Abramson, Rudy. *Spanning the Century: The Life of Averell Harriman, 1891–1986.* New York: William Morrow, 1992.
Adams, Henry H. *Harry Hopkins: A Biography.* New York: G.P. Putnam's Sons, 1977.
Adams, Sherman. *Firsthand Report: The Story of the Eisenhower Administration.* New York: Harper, 1961.
Agnew, Spiro T. *Go Quietly . . . or else.* New York: William Morrow, 1980.
Aitken, Jonathan. *Nixon: A Life.* Washington, D.C.: Regnery, 1994.
Ambrose, Stephen E. *Eisenhower, Volume Two: The President.* New York: Simon and Schuster, 1984.
———. *Nixon: The Education of a Politician, 1913–1962.* New York: Simon and Schuster, 1987.
———. *Nixon: The Triumph of a Politician, 1962–1972.* New York: Simon and Schuster, 1990.

Ben-Veniste, Richard, and George Frampton, Jr. *Stonewall: The Real Story of the Watergate Prosecution.* New York: Simon and Schuster, 1977.

Beschloss, Michael R. *Mayday: Eisenhower, Khrushchev and the U-2 Affair.* New York: Harper and Row, 1986.

Besley, F. W. *The Forests of Frederick County.* Baltimore: Maryland State Board of Forestry, 1922.

Biddle, Francis. *In Brief Authority.* Garden City, N.Y.: Doubleday, 1962.

Bishop, Jim. *FDR's Last Year.* New York: William Morrow, 1974.

Bryant, Traphes, with Frances Spatz Leighton. *Dog Days at the White House.* New York: Macmillan, 1975.

Brzezinski, Zbigniew. *Power and Principle: Memoirs of the National Security Adviser, 1977–1981.* New York: Farrar, Straus and Giroux, 1983.

Burner, David. *Herbert Hoover: A Public Life.* New York: Knopf, 1979.

Burns, George MacGregor. *Roosevelt: The Soldier of Freedom.* New York: Harcourt Brace Jovanovich, 1956.

Bush, George, with Victor Gold. *Looking Forward.* New York: Doubleday, 1987.

Byrnes, James F. *All in One Lifetime.* New York: Harper, 1958.

Cannon, Lou. *President Reagan: The Role of a Lifetime.* New York: Simon and Schuster, 1991.

Carter, Jimmy. *Keeping Faith: Memoirs of a President.* New York: Bantam, 1982.

————. *An Outdoor Journal: Adventures and Reflections.* New York, Bantam, 1988.

Carter, Rosalynn. *First Lady from Plains.* Boston: Houghton Mifflin, 1984.

Chase, Harold W. and Allen H. Lerman, eds. *Kennedy and the Press: The News Conferences.* New York: Thomas Y. Crowell, 1965.

Churchill, Winston S. *The Hinge of Fate.* Boston: Houghton Mifflin, 1950.

Clifford, Clark M., with Richard Holbrooke. *Counsel to the President.* New York: Random House, 1991.

Colson, Charles W. *Born Again.* Tarrytown, N.Y.: Chosen Books, 1976.

David, Lester. *The Lonely Lady of San Clemente: The Story of Pat Nixon.* New York: Thomas Y. Crowell, 1978.

Dayan, Moshe. *Breakthrough: A Personal Account of the Egypt-Israeli Peace Negotiations.* New York: Knopf, 1981.

Dean, John W., III. *Blind Ambition: The White House Years.* New York: Simon and Schuster, 1976.

Dean, Maureen, with Hays Gorey. *"Mo": A Woman's View of Watergate.* New York: Simon and Schuster, 1975.

Deaver, Michael K., with Mickey Herskowitz. *Behind the Scenes: In Which the Author Talks About Ronald and Nancy Reagan . . . and Himself.* New York: William Morrow, 1987.

Dimbleby, David, and David Reynolds. *An Ocean Apart: The Relationship Between Britain and America in the Twentieth Century.* New York: Random House, 1988.

Douglas, William O. *Go East, Young Man: The Early Years.* New York: Random House, 1974.

Drew, Elizabeth. *Washington Journal: The Events of 1973–1974.* New York: Random House, 1975.

Duffy, Michael, and Dan Goodgame. *Marching in Place: The Status Quo Presidency of George Bush.* New York: Simon and Schuster, 1992.

Ehrlichman, John. *Witness to Power: The Nixon Years.* New York: Simon and Schuster, 1982.

Eisenhower, Dwight D. *The White House Years: Mandate for Change, 1953–1956.* Garden City, N. Y.: Doubleday, 1963.

———. *The White House Years: Waging Peace, 1956–1961.* Garden City, N.Y.: Doubleday, 1965.

Eisenhower, John S. D. *Strictly Personal.* Garden City, N.Y.: Doubleday, 1974.

Eisenhower, Julie. *Pat Nixon: The Untold Story.* New York: Simon and Schuster, 1986.

———. *Special People.* New York: Simon and Schuster, 1977.

Ferrel, Robert H., ed. *The Eisenhower Diaries.* New York: W. W. Norton, 1981.

Fisher, Nigel. *Harold Macmillan: A Biography.* New York: St. Martin's, 1982.

Ford, Betty, with Chris Chase. *The Times of My Life.* New York: Harper and Row, 1978.

Ford, Gerald R. *A Time to Heal: The Autobiography of Gerald R. Ford.* New York: Harper and Row, 1979.

Freidel, Frank. *Franklin D. Roosevelt: A Rendezvous with Destiny.* Boston: Little, Brown, 1990.

Gallagher, Hugh Gregory. *FDR's Splendid Deception.* New York: Dodd, Mead, 1985.

Gentry, Curt. *J. Edgar Hoover: The Man and the Secrets.* New York: W. W. Norton, 1991.

Germond, Jack W., and Jules Witcover. *Blue Smoke and Mirrors: How Reagan Won and Why Carter Lost the Election of 1980.* New York: Viking, 1981.

Golightly, Jean. *Circuit Hikes in Virginia, West Virginia, Maryland and Pennsylvania.* Washington, D.C.: Potomac Appalachian Trail Club, 1981.

Griffith, Robert, ed. *Ike's Letters to a Friend, 1941–1958.* Lawrence, Kan.: Univ. Press of Kansas, 1984.

Gulley, Bill, with Mary Ellen Reese. *Breaking Cover.* New York: Simon and Schuster, 1980.

Halberstam, David. *The Best and the Brightest.* New York: Random House, 1972.

———. *The Haldeman Diaries: Inside the Nixon White House.* New York: G.P. Putnam's Sons, 1994.

Haldeman, H. R., with Joseph DiMona. *The Ends of Power.* New York: Times Books, 1978.

Harriman, W. Averell, and Elie Abel. *Special Envoy to Churchill and Stalin, 1941–1945.* New York: Random House, 1975.

Hartmann, Robert T. *Palace Politics: An Inside Account of the Ford Years.* New York: McGraw Hill, 1980.

Hassett, William D. *Off the Record with F. D. R. 1942–1945.* New Brunswick, N.J.: Rutgers Univ. Press, 1958.

Hersch, Seymour M. *The Price of Power: Kissinger in the Nixon White House.* New York: Summit, 1983.

Hess, Stephen. *Organizing the Presidency.* Washington: The Brookings Institution, 1989.

Higgins, George V. *The Friends of Richard Nixon.* Boston: Little, Brown, 1975.

Hilton, James. *Lost Horizon. School Edition.* Boston: Houghton Mifflin, 1962.

Hoopes, Townsend. *The Devil and John Foster Dulles.* Boston: Atlantic Monthly Press, 1973.

Horne, Alistair. *Harold Macmillan, Volume II, 1957–1968.* New York: Viking, 1989.

Horton, Tom. *Bay Country.* Baltimore: Johns Hopkins Univ. Press, 1987.

Johnson, Haynes. *Sleepwalking Through History: America in the Reagan Years.* New York: W. W. Norton, 1991.

Johnson, Lady Bird. *A White House Diary.* New York: Holt, Rinehart and Winston, 1975.

Johnson, Lyndon Baines. *The Vantage Point: Perspectives of the Presidency, 1963–1969.* New York: Holt, Rinehart and Winston, 1971.

Jordan, Hamilton. *Crisis: The Last Year of the Carter Presidency.* New York: G. P. Putnam's Sons, 1982.

Keegan, John. *Six Armies in Normandy.* New York: Viking, 1982.

Kimball, Warren F., ed. *Churchill and Roosevelt: The Complete Correspondence.* Vol. 2. Princeton: Princeton Univ. Press, 1984–88.

Kirkconnell, Barbara M. *Catoctin Mountain Park: An Administrative History.* Washington, D.C.: National Park Service, 1988.

Kissinger, Henry. *Years of Upheaval.* Boston: Little, Brown, 1982.

Kistiakowski, George B. *A Scientist at the White House.* Cambridge, Mass.: Harvard Univ. Press, 1976.

Klein, Herbert G. *Making it Perfectly Clear.* Garden City, N.Y.: Doubleday, 1980.

Kramer, Michael, and Sam Roberts. *"I Never Wanted to Be Vice President of Anything!": An Investigative Biography of Nelson Rockefeller.* New York: Basic Books, 1976.

Lash, Joseph P. *Love, Eleanor: Eleanor Roosevelt and her Friends.* Garden City, N. Y.: Doubleday, 1982.

―――. *A World of Love: Eleanor Roosevelt and her Friends, 1943–1962,* Garden City, N.Y.: Doubleday, 1984.

Leighton, Frances Spatz. *The Search for the Real Nancy Reagan.* New York: Macmillan, 1987.

Lewis, Finlay. *Mondale: Portrait of an American Politician.* New York: Perennial Press, 1984.

Lukas, J. Anthony. *Nightmare: The Underside of the Nixon Years.* New York: Viking, 1975.

MacMahon, Edward D., M.D. and Leonard Curry. *Medical Cover-ups in the White House.* Washington, D.C.: Farragut, 1987.

Macmillan, Harold. *Pointing the Way, 1959–1961.* New York: Harper and Row, 1972.

———. *Riding the Storm, 1956–1959.* New York: Harper and Row, 1971.

Magruder, Jeb Stuart. *An American Life.* New York: Atheneum, 1974.

Martin, David C. *Wilderness of Mirrors.* New York: Harper and Row, 1980.

Mayer, Jane, and Doyle McManus. *Landslide: The Unmaking of the President, 1984–1988.* Boston: Houghton Mifflin, 1988.

McCarthy, Dennis V. N., with Philip W. Smith. *Protecting the President: The Inside Story of a Secret Service Agent.* New York: William Morrow, 1985.

McClendon, Hugh D. *A History of Camp David.* Thurmont, Md.: Department of the Navy, 1985.

McCullough, David. *Truman.* New York: Simon and Schuster, 1992.

Meese, Edwin, III. *With Reagan: The Inside Story.* Washington, D.C.: Regnery, 1992.

Nessen, Ron. *It Sure Looks Different from the Inside.* New York: Playboy Press, 1978.

New York Times. *The White House Transcripts.* New York: Bantam, 1974.

Nixon, Richard. *In the Arena: A Memoir of Victory, Defeat and Renewal.* New York: Simon and Schuster, 1990.

———. *Leaders.* New York: Warner, 1982.

———. *RN: The Memoirs of Richard Nixon.* New York: Grosset and Dunlap, 1978.

———. *Six Crises.* Garden City, N.Y.: Doubleday, 1962.

O'Donnell, Kenneth P., and David F. Powers, with Joe McCarthy. *Johnny, We Hardly Knew Ye.* Boston: Little, Brown, 1970.

Osborne, John. *The Fifth Year of the Nixon Watch.* New York: Liveright, 1974.

———. *The Fourth Year of the Nixon Watch.* New York: Liveright, 1973.

———. *The Last Nixon Watch.* New York: Liveright, 1975.

Oudes, Bruce, ed. *From: The President: Richard Nixon's Secret Files.* New York: Harper and Row, 1989.

Packard, Jerrold M. *American Monarchy: A Social Guide to the Presidency.* New York: Delacorte, 1983.

Papenfuse, Edward C. et al., eds. *Maryland: A New Guide to the Old Line State.* Baltimore: Johns Hopkins Univ. Press, 1976.

Parmet, Herbert S. *JFK: The Presidency of John F. Kennedy.* New York: Dial, 1983.

Patterson, Bradley H., Jr. *The Ring of Power: The White House Staff and Its Expanding Role in Government.* New York: Basic Books, 1988.

Powell, Jody. *The Other Side of the Story.* New York: William Morrow, 1984.

Price, Raymond. *With Nixon.* New York: Viking, 1977.

Quandt, William B. *Camp David: Peacemaking and Politics.* Washington, D.C.: The Brookings Institution, 1986.

Quayle, Dan. *Standing Firm: A Vice-Presidential Memoir.* New York: Harper-Collins, 1994.

Reagan, Maureen. *First Father, First Daughter: A Memoir.* Boston: Little, Brown, 1989.

Reagan, Nancy, with William Novak. *My Turn: The Memoirs of Nancy Reagan.* New York: Random House, 1989.

Reagan, Ronald. *An American Life: The Autobiography.* New York: Simon and Schuster, 1990.

Reeves, Richard. *President Kennedy: Profile of Power.* New York: Simon and Schuster, 1993.

Regan, Donald T. *For the Record: From Wall Street to Washington.* New York: Harcourt Brace Jovanovich, 1988.

Reilly, Michael F., as told to William J. Slocum. *Reilly of the White House.* New York: Simon and Schuster, 1947.

Rigdon, William M., with James Derieux. *White House Sailor.* Garden City, N.Y.: Doubleday, 1962.

Roosevelt, Archie. *For Lust of Knowing: Memoirs of an Intelligence Officer.* Boston: Little, Brown, 1988.

Roosevelt, Elliott, and James Brough. *A Rendevous with Destiny.* New York: G.P. Putnam's Sons, 1975.

Roosevelt, Franklin D. *Roosevelt Presidential Press and Radio Conferences.* New York: De Capo Press, 1972.

Roosevelt, James, with Bill Libby. *My Parents: A Differing View.* New York: Playboy Press, 1976.

Roosevelt, Selwa "Lucky." *Keeper of the Gate.* New York: Simon and Schuster, 1990.

Rosenman, Samuel I. *Working with Roosevelt.* New York: Harper, 1952.

————, ed. *The Public Papers and Addresses of Franklin D. Roosevelt, 1942 Volume.* New York: Harper, 1950.

Rostow, W. W. *The Diffusion of Power: An Essay in Recent History.* New York: Macmillan, 1972.

Sadat, Jehan. *A Woman of Egypt.* New York: Pocket Books, 1989.

Safire, William. *Before the Fall: An Inside View of the Pre-Watergate White House.* Garden City, N.Y.: Doubleday, 1975.

Salinger, Pierre. *America Held Hostage: The Secret Negotiations.* Garden City, N.Y.: Doubleday, 1981.

Schlesinger, Arthur M., Jr. *The Imperial Presidency.* Boston: Houghton Mifflin, 1973.

Sherwood, Robert E. *Roosevelt and Hopkins: An Intimate History.* New York: Harper, 1950.

Shultz, George P. *Turmoil and Triumph: My Years as Secretary of State.* New York: Charles Scribner's Sons, 1993.

Sidey, Hugh. *John F. Kennedy, President.* New York: Atheneum, 1963.

Silver, Eric. *Begin: The Haunted Prophet.* New York: Random House, 1984.

Smith, A. Merriman. *Thank You, Mr. President: A White House Notebook.* New York: Harper, 1946.

———. *Meet Mister Eisenhower.* New York: Harper, 1955.

Smith, Geoffrey. *Reagan and Thatcher.* London: The Bodley Head, 1990.

Sorensen, Theodore C. *Kennedy.* New York: Harper and Row, 1965.

Speakes, Larry, with Robert Pack. *Speaking Out: The Reagan Presidency from Inside the White House.* New York: Charles Scribner's Sons, 1988.

Stans, Maurice H. *The Terrors of Justice: The Untold Side of Watergate.* New York: Everest House, 1978.

Stein, Kenneth W., and Samuel W. Lewis, with Sheryl J. Brown. *Making Peace Among Arabs and Israelis: Lessons from Fifty Years of Negotiating Experience.* Washington, D.C.: U.S. Institute of Peace, 1991.

Steinbeck, Elaine, and Robert Wallsten, eds. *Steinbeck: A Life in Letters.* New York: Viking, 1975.

Sullivan, William C., with Bill Brown. *The Bureau: My Thirty Years in Hoover's FBI.* New York: W.W. Norton, 1979.

Szulc, Tad. *The Illusion of Peace: Foreign Policy in the Nixon Years.* New York: Viking, 1978.

Talbott, Strobe, ed. *Khrushchev Remembers.* Boston: Little, Brown, 1970.

Thatcher, Margaret. *The Downing Street Years.* New York: HarperCollins, 1993.

Thomas, Helen. *Dateline: White House.* New York: Macmillan, 1975.

Truman, Harry S. *Memoirs by Harry S. Truman, Volume One: Year of Decisions.* Garden City, N.Y.: Doubleday, 1955.

Truman, Margaret. *Bess W. Truman.* New York: Macmillan, 1976.

———. *Harry S. Truman.* New York: William Morrow, 1973.

Tully, Grace. *F. D. R. My Boss.* Chicago: People's Book Club, 1949.

Valenti, Jack. *A Very Human President.* New York: W.W. Norton, 1975.

Vance, Cyrus. *Hard Choices: Critical Years in America's Foreign Policy.* New York: Simon and Schuster, 1983.

Weidenfeld, Sheila Rabb. *First Lady's Lady: With the Fords at the White House.* New York: G. P. Putnam's Sons, 1979.

West, J. B. *Upstairs at the White House: My Life with the First Ladies.* New York: Coward, McCann and Geoghegan, 1973.

White, William S. *The Professional: Lyndon B. Johnson.* Boston: Houghton Mifflin, 1964.

Wireman, George W. *Gateway to the Mountains.* Hagerstown, Md.: Hagerstown Bookbinding and Printing, 1959.

Wirth, Conrad. *Parks, Politics and the People.* Norman: Univ. of Oklahoma Press, 1980.

Woodward, Bob. *The Commanders.* New York: Simon and Schuster, 1991.

Young, Hugo. *The Iron Lady: A Biography of Margaret Thatcher.* New York: Farrar, Straus and Giroux, 1989.

Articles

Alsop, Joseph. "Matter of Fact." *Washington Post,* Sept. 30, 1959.

Barnes, Dick. "Ford Interview." Associated Press, Aug. 9, 1976.

Benac, Nancy. "Clinton-Camp David." Associated Press, Apr. 24, 1993.

Boo, Katherine. "The Drama of the Gifted Vice President." *Washington Post Magazine,* Nov. 28, 1993.

Brown, Les. "ABC Delays Ford Visit, Cites Election." *New York Times,* undated clipping in Gerald R. Ford Library.

Cannon, Lou. "President Goes to the Movies." *Washington Post,* June 13, 1983.

Cormier, Frank. "Jimmy's White House." Associated Press, July 27, 1977.

Cornell, Douglas B. Associated Press, Mar. 18, 1959.

Dawson, Bill. "Clinton Emphasizes Conservation." *Arkansas Democrat,* July 12, 1979.

Deaver, Amanda, as told to Danna L. Walker. "Growing Up Fast: It was Never Easy Being Mike Deaver's Daughter," *Washington Post Magazine,* Nov. 27, 1988.

Devroy, Ann. "Bonding at Camp David." *Washington Post,* Feb. 5, 1993.

Dixon, George. "Washington Scene." *Washington Post,* Sept. 30, 1959.

Folliard, Edward T. "Big 2 Leaders Fly in Helicopter to Maryland Camp." *Washington Post,* Sept. 26, 1959.

Gerstenzang, James. "Top Reagan Aides Confer at Camp David." Associated Press, Feb. 5, 1982.

Greenfield, Meg. "Report from Camp David." *Washington Post,* July 16, 1979.

Growald, Richard H. "President." United Press International, Aug. 9, 1976.

Haas, Ted. "Chapel called gift from 'people of faith,'" *Public Opinion* (Chambersburg, Pa.), Dec. 7, 1987.

Hays, Steele. "Clinton Talks with Carter." *Arkansas Gazette,* July 12, 1979.

Johnson, Haynes. "Crisis." *Washington Post,* July 9, 1979.

Kamen, Al, and Fred Barbash. Excerpts from interviews. *Washington Post,* July 5, 1987.

King, Warren. "Reagan regarded AIDS 'like it was measles.'" *Seattle Times,* Aug. 31, 1989.

Lampton, Chris. "One Man and His Mountain." *Maryland,* Autumn 1980.

Leighton, Frances Spatz. "New Job at the White House: Betty Ford's Best Friend." *Family Weekly,* Mar. 2, 1975.

Lemann, Nicholas. "The Unfinished War." *Atlantic Monthly,* Dec. 1988.

McCloskey, Bill. "Nixon Papers—Sports." Associated Press, Dec. 2, 1985.

Marcus, Ruth, and David Hoffman. "Reagan Reviews List of Court Candidates." *Washington Post,* Oct. 25, 1987.

Michelmore, Peter. "Camp David: Hideaway for Presidents." *Reader's Digest,* Nov. 1975.

Moleon, Ary. "La Ayudante de los Bush, feliz y mexicanisima en la Casa Blanca." Associated Press, Nov. 23, 1990.

Nelson, W. Dale. "Presidents thrive on serenity of mountain retreat." *New Haven Register,* Feb. 9, 1986.

———. "Bush's Camp." *The Repository* (Canton, Ohio), Oct. 8, 1989.

Newhouse, John. "The Diplomatic Round." *The New Yorker,* July 22, 1985.

Plimpton, George. "A Sportsman Born and Bred." *Sports Illustrated,* Dec. 26, 1988.

Radcliffe, Donnie. "Washington Ways." *Washington Post,* Sept. 29, 1987.

———. "The Bells of Camp David." *Washington Post,* Jan. 26, 1988.

Rush, George. "Confessions of a Secret Service Agent." *The Washingtonian,* August 1988. Excerpted from *Confessions of an Ex-Secret Service Agent* (New York: Donald I. Fine, 1988).

Salisbury, Harrison E. "Eisenhower, Khrushchev Begin Camp David Talks After Helicopter Flight." *New York Times,* Sept. 26, 1959.

Schafer, Susanne M. "Reagan Does Radio Because He Likes It." Associated Press, Sept. 5, 1986.

Schram, Martin, and Jim Klurfeld. "Inside Camp David." *Newsday,* Sept. 24, 1968.

Shannon, Don. "President Starts Talks with Mr. K." *Los Angeles Times,* Sept. 26, 1959.

Smith, Hedrick. "Taking Charge of Congress." *New York Times Magazine,* Aug. 8, 1981.

Snider, Keith. "Harriet Chapel has hosted presidents." *Herald-Mail* (Hagerstown, Md.), Jan. 28, 1990.

Sullivan, Christopher. "Dying Dogwoods." Associated Press, Apr. 15, 1991.

Toland, Elizabeth. "How the President came to Harriet Chapel on Easter." *Maryland Church News,* June, 1976.

Welch, William M. "Nixon Papers." Associated Press, May 29, 1987.

Winchester, Simon. "Camp David Now a Fortress." *Washington Post,* June 26, 1973.

Oral Histories, Audio-Visual Sources, and Other Sources

The American Experience: Eisenhower. Public Broadcasting Service, Nov. 10, 1993.

Associated Press. Unsigned memo to Washington bureau files. Mar. 19, 1959. News stories variously dated.

Aurand, Vice-Admiral, Evan P., USN, ret. Interviewed by John T. Mason, May 1, 1967. Columbia Univ. Oral History Project.

———. Memo to the author, 1989.

Bartlett, Charles W. Interviewed by Fred Holborn, Jan. 6, 1966. John Fitzgerald Kennedy Library, Boston.

Broaddus, Cmdr. J. A. Remarks at Change of Command Ceremony. Camp David, July 25, 1988.

Bush, George. Interview on C-Span, Dec. 22, 1991.

"Camp David." Maryland Public Television, 1987.

Colson, Charles W. Interviewed by Frederick J. Graboske, June 15, 1988. National Archives Nixon Presidential Materials Project, College Park, Md.

————. Interviewed by Frederick J. Graboske and Paul A. Schmidt, Sept. 21, 1988. Nixon Project.

Hagerty, James C. Oral history interview, 1967–68. Dwight D. Eisenhower Library, Abilene, Kan.

"Nixon." Public Broadcasting Service, Nov. 15, 1990.

Rigdon, William M. Interviewed by Jerry N. Hess, Jan. 1972. Harry S. Truman Library.

Roosevelt, Franklin D. *U.S.S. Shangri-La.* Handwritten logbook in Franklin D. Roosevelt Library, Hyde Park, N.Y., 1942–44.

Secret Service Records. Franklin D. Roosevelt Library, Hyde Park, N.Y.

Stevens, George J. Speech. Washington, D.C., May 21, 1988.

Still and moving pictures in Kennedy Library.

Index